Piles of Slain, Heaps of Corpses

Piles of Slain, Heaps of Corpses

Reading Prophetic Poetry and Violence in African Context

JACOB ONYUMBE WENYI

With a foreword by ELLEN F. DAVIS

CASCADE Books · Eugene, Oregon

PILES OF SLAIN, HEAPS OF CORPSES
Reading Prophetic Poetry and Violence in African Context

Copyright © 2021 Jacob Onyumbe Wenyi. All rights reserved. Except for brief quotations in critical publications or reviews, no part of this book may be reproduced in any manner without prior written permission from the publisher. Write: Permissions, Wipf and Stock Publishers, 199 W. 8th Ave., Suite 3, Eugene, OR 97401.

Cascade Books
An Imprint of Wipf and Stock Publishers
199 W. 8th Ave., Suite 3
Eugene, OR 97401

www.wipfandstock.com

PAPERBACK ISBN: 978-1-7252-6831-9
HARDCOVER ISBN: 978-1-7252-6830-2
EBOOK ISBN: 978-1-7252-6832-6

Cataloguing-in-Publication data:

Names: Onyumbe Wenyi, Jacob, author. | Davis, Ellen F., foreword writer.

Title: Piles of slain, heaps of corpses : reading prophetic poetry and violence in African context / Jacob Onyumbe Wenyi ; foreword by Ellen F. Davis.

Description: Eugene, OR: Cascade Books, 2021 | Includes bibliographical references and index.

Identifiers: ISBN 978-1-7252-6831-9 (paperback) | ISBN 978-1-7252-6830-2 (hardcover) | ISBN 978-1-7252-6832-6 (ebook)

Subjects: LCSH: Bible.—Nahum—Criticism, interpretation, etc. | Political violence—Congo (Democratic Republic) | Violence—Africa—Religious aspects | Violence in the Bible

Classification: BS1625.52 O59 2021 (print) | BS1625.52 (ebook)

Nihil Obstat: Raphaël Okitafumba Lokola, STL, PhD, Censor Librorum
Imprimatur: + Nicolas Djomo Lola, Bishop of Tshumbe (DRC)

To the memory of my brother,
Dr Jean Odimola Okitawonya (1988–2020).
Requiescas In Pace.

Table of Contents

Foreword by Ellen F. Davis ix
Acknowledgements xiii
Abbreviations xv
Introduction xvii

1   Tripolar Contextual Biblical Hermeneutics of Reconciliation 1
2   War, Traumatic Violence, and Congolese Collective Memory 26
3   On the Genre, the Form, and the Poetics of the Book of Nahum 49
4   The Historical Context of the Vision of Nahum:
    Assyrian Invasions and Judah's Collective Memory 81
5   Imaging God amid Chaos 105
6   The Destruction of Nineveh and Judah's Memories of War 133
7   Reflections on the Way to Appropriation of Nahum in the DRC:
    Context, Form, and Reconciliation 167

Bibliography 181
Scripture Index 189
Name/Subject Index 196

Foreword

"Everyone I knew at that time was writing poetry," Jacob Onyumbe Wenyi said to me, describing his own intellectual formation as a student in the Democratic Republic of Congo during the deadly wars around the turn of the twentieth-first century. His point was that for those living in trauma-inducing situations, and especially where traditional village-based culture has not been long erased, poetry is something much more than a special interest of the few and a bewilderment or annoyance to everyone else, as many North Americans tend to judge it. Rather, poetry is a lifeline. It is a way of making sense out of chaos, of circumscribing the unthinkable with carefully crafted words. For Jacob Onyumbe and his peers, all of them in the early stages of preparing for the Roman Catholic priesthood, writing poetry was also an attempt to make some sense of the ways of God as they experienced them in their own lives.

That intuition of young poets and nascent theologians has come to scholarly maturity in this study of the book of Nahum. Jacob Onyumbe departs from the (European and North American) scholarly consensus, expressed largely through neglect, that this book of vengeful prophetic poetry has no positive value for modern readers, let alone for people of faith. In a time of prolonged international conflict in the region once ruled by Assyria, this prophet seems to strike exactly the wrong note. Nonetheless, Onyumbe explores how Nahum, composing his poems in the wake of the Assyrian devastation of Judah, lives up to his name ("Comfort") through an innovative use of lyric poetry. Being himself a survivor of the violent destruction of his homeland, Jacob Onyumbe writes out of the hard-won insight that portraying God as the terrible Avenger who overwhelms Nineveh and the Great Empire, doing to them blow-for-blow just what they did to Judah, is not simply a primitive and unmodulated expression of the rage of the wounded. Nahum's poetry of vengeance is better seen as the obverse of the more acceptable prophetic proclamation—acceptable, that is, to those whose historical location we might deem more fortunate—that God is Judah's Comforter and Restorer.

Here Jacob Onyumbe offers an innovative exploration of how a dramatic, unprecedented work of the prophetic imagination may contribute to the healing of a people's collective memory. His methodology is appropriately eclectic, undertaken with both discipline and risk, as he carves out a path that has not been clearly marked by either African or Western biblical scholars, although it integrates insights and methods from both.

Jacob Onyumbe's most distinctive exegetical contribution, offered in the historically and linguistically informed style favored by Western scholars, proceeds from his observation that the verbal imagery in Nahum's poetry revolves around themes that are central also to the Assyrian iconography of power. He ventures the entirely plausible suggestion—which, like most fruitful ideas, cannot be proven beyond the shadow of a doubt—that the historical Nahum endured the Assyrian campaign in the last years of the eighth century. Therefore, as a prophet living in the wake of that event, he speaks to and for people burdened with vivid memories of unspeakable suffering, loss, and brutality. In an imaginative move, Onyumbe examines the magnificent propaganda art that the Assyrian rulers Sennacherib (reigned 705–681 BCE) and Ashurbanipal (reigned 668–627 BCE) commissioned for their palaces at Nineveh: two series of exquisite bas reliefs, one depicting the royal lion hunt, the other the siege and destruction of Lachish, Judah's second city, with the subsequent enslavement and exile of its survivors. Like the quotidian icons of power that were generously distributed throughout the vast empire, intended to be seen by every Judean, those incomparable works of art proclaimed to anyone privileged to visit the palace that the Great King was sovereign over both humans and beasts. Attempts to counter or evade his power would be futile.

Nahum appropriates the symbols of Assyrian iconography, including the fierce lion, to depict the fall of the capital city of Nineveh. Thus he answers imperial art with prophetic poetry—that is, with the humble, portable, and ultimately more enduring art of the poor, the justly outraged, the displaced and dispossessed. Reading the book of Nahum as Jacob Onyumbe does, we perceive an acute historical irony. Those grand stone reliefs that once decorated the palace walls were lost for eons, until Nineveh was excavated and they were reinstalled at the British Museum less than two centuries ago. Physically imperishable, they originated as the art of the powerful and were first placed on view for an elite "public": those admitted to an audience with the king. Three millennia later, that public is wider but still comprised mostly of the relatively privileged, who have the economic resources to spend a day in central London and the educational background to know what they are looking at. But the case is somewhat different with Nahum's poems, which were composed for (potentially) every suffering Judean of the seventh century. Underutilized though they may be as a theological resource, they have never been buried in the ground or housed in a rarified and guarded setting. On the contrary, they have been hiding in plain sight within the most widely distributed book on the planet, available to anyone in desperate need of God's action against the overbearing enemy.

It is notable, though not genuinely surprising, that an African scholar from a war-torn land should have been the one to rediscover in a twenty-first-century context the theological, pastoral, and indeed the political value of this book of Nahum. Jacob Onyumbe writes with reference to his own context, but his immediate social and cultural perspective is fully informed by long and deep education in biblical and ancient Near Eastern studies; he takes account of the historical and archaeological data and likewise of the book's structure and other literary features. Further, his theoretical framework is shaped by the new scholarly fields of trauma studies and endo-ethnography. Onyumbe spent months listening to the stories of survivors in Eastern Congo, where he functioned as both insider, a Congolese priest, and outsider, a researcher based at an American university.

Yet in the end, it would have been impossible for Jacob Onyumbe to write the present volume had he not possessed and been willing to draw upon a further credential in addition to his formal education, his priestly status and pastoral skills, and his Congolese citizenship. That crucial credential is his personal memory of war trauma in his own country, to which Onyumbe bore witness in his 2010 semi-autobiographical novel, *Kevin the Wild Boy*. Though not autobiographical, this current study is biblical exegesis and contextual appropriation that reflects painful personal experience. It is born out of a long process of growth in self-awareness, a process that included this scholarly project itself. Because Onyumbe reads Nahum as a member of a community that bears a tragic resemblance to the prophet's own, he sees how his poetry may evoke memories of destruction in ways that can potentially lead to healing for individuals and communities.

Evoking long-buried memories of the unspeakable, with the hope of bringing healing—this is delicate work, not without danger, and so it must be done in community. In other words, the work is inherently political. Onyumbe may not use that word here, but it is implied in what he identifies as the ultimate goal of this study, namely to promote reconciliation in Congolese communities that are still riven by bitter memories. Since this book is being published on the North American continent, probably few of its readers will locate their own personal and political hopes in central Africa. Nonetheless there is an important reason for us to heed Onyumbe's work. As an African exegete and theologian, he is culturally disposed to integrate aspects of thought and experience that Westerners often separate into discrete areas: the personal and religious, the academic, the communal and political. Writing with keen attention to both ancient text and his own society in this historical moment, Jacob Onyumbe models the ever-unfinished work of opening up the biblical text for new generations whose circumstances demand an unblinking reckoning with reality and an honest word of hope.

Ellen F. Davis
Amos Ragan Kearns Distinguished Professor of Bible and Practical Theology
(Duke Divinity School)

Acknowledgements

THIS BOOK IS A revision of my 2017 doctoral dissertation submitted to the Divinity School of Duke University. During my studies, my research and the writing of the dissertation, as well as during the transformation of the dissertation into a book, Dr. Ellen F. Davis has been my advisor, my teacher, my mentor, and my friend. She has shown me how to read biblical texts responsibly, how to preach, how to write, and how to teach. Her suggestions, comments, and guidance have been indispensable for the writing of this book. I am very humbled that she wrote the foreword for this book. I am deeply grateful to her. I also thank Dr. Anathea Portier-Young, Dr. Stephen Chapman, and Dr. Gerald West (South Africa), who served as members of my dissertation committee and made important and instructive suggestions on how my dissertation could become a good book. Their observations made this book a much better product.

I am thankful to Bishops Nicolas Djomo of Tshumbe, William Murphy, and Richard Henning of Rockville Centre (New York, USA) for their interest in my scholarly work and for their ongoing support.

As I was writing this book, I depended on the support of many friends to whom I am very thankful: Fr. Raphael Okitafumba (who read the draft of this book), Fr. Laurent Okitakatshi, Fr. André Olongo, Fr. Valentin Kasende, Fr. Tharcisse Onema Yohe, Fr. Daniel Onawembo, Fr. Lambert Matondo, Fr. Joseph Lomendja, Fr. Lambert Konga, Sr. Catherine Takotshe, Fr. Richard Ongendangenda, Msgr. Crispin Otshudiema, Sr. Rosalie Akenda, Fr. Mike Shosongo, Sr. Marie-Faustine Beloko, Fr. Albert Shuyaka, Sr. Christine Amena, Bob Dougherty, The Zahner family (especially Kathy, Mary Ann, and Herb), Msgr. Joseph DeGrocco and the parish of Our Lady of Perpetual Help (Lindehurst, NY), Sr. Jolanta Varhatyuk, Sr. Justyna and the Missionary Sisters of Saint Benedict in Huntington (New York), Fr. John Sureau, Msgr. Jim Vlaun, Corine Addis,

Lana, Linda Matera, Ann Marie Wagner, Elyse Hayes and the library of the Seminary of the Immaculate Conception, and Britt Evans.

I am very thankful to my family: My dad Michel Okitawonya and my mother Marie Konge, my siblings Mathilde, Nicolas, Sophie, Michel, Jean, Jules, Raphael, Jadot, and Pierre. They are my first cheerleaders and my first support team. Sincere thanks!

I also thank Caritas Goma, Caritas Bukavu (especially Maria Masson), and Justice et Paix Bukavu (especially Fr. Justin Nzuzi and Thérèse Mema Mapenzi) for assisting and protecting me during my field research in eastern DRC.

I am thankful to Duke Divinity School for providing me with a fellowship that allowed me to study for a doctorate and write the dissertation that led to this book. I am also thankful to Rev. Dr. Anthony Petrotta and Saint Francis Episcopal Church in Wilsonville (OR) for supporting me financially during my studies at Duke and for funding my field research (twice) in Africa.

Sincere thanks to Michael Thomson, Matthew Wimer, and Revd. Dr. Robin Parry at Wipf and Stock for their wise advice and guidance during the process of writing this book. I am grateful to all the survivors of violence who shared their stories with me.

Abbreviations

DRC	Democratic Republic of the Congo
FDLR	Forces Démocratiques pour la Libération du Rwanda
FM	Falker Mike
JTSA	*Journal of Theology for Southern Africa*
JBL	*Journal of Biblical Literature*
JOAS	*Journal of the American Oriental Society*
LXX	The Septuagint
MT	Masoretic Text
NICOT	New International Commentary on the Old Testament
OTE	Old Testament Essays
SAK	*Studien zur Altägyptischen Kultur*
ZAW	*Zeitschrift für die Alttestamentliche Wissenschaf*

Introduction

THE BOOK OF NAHUM depicts a world of desolation, devastation, and destruction: a world of "piles of slain, heaps of corpses" (3:3). With its description of God as wrathful and vengeful and its graphic depiction of war and violence, Nahum has often been treated as a dangerous book, both in church settings and in academic circles. Its God is said to be discriminatory, violent and encouraging of violence, misogynistic and patriarchal, a rapist, a "throwback to the God of battles of the early days of the kingdom," and "a militant nationalist [who] infers that Judah is not as other nations, especially Assyria."[1] The prophet Nahum himself has even been called a false prophet and an enthusiastic patriot whose "narrow and shallow prophetism"[2] should have found no place in the canon of Scripture. The highly vivid images of war in the book are viewed as proof that this "nationalistic poet" encourages violence against his enemies and mirthfully indulges in depicting the suffering of those whom he intends to annihilate.

This negative view on Nahum's violent images finds resonance in the liturgical life of the Church, where Nahum is used only sparingly. The Protestant *Revised Common Lectionary* of 1983 contains no readings from the book of Nahum. In the Roman Catholic liturgy, even though Nahum found a place in the two-year cycle of weekday readings,[3] the book is still largely ignored and rarely preached.

The question should be asked: Does this lack of interest in the book of Nahum, or even a policy of avoidance, point the Church in the

---

1. Cleland, "Exposition on Nahum," 957.

2. Smith, *A Critical and Exegetical Commentary on Micah, Zephaniah, Nahum, Habakkuk, Obadiah and Joel*, 281.

3. Nah 2:1, 3; 3:1–3, 6–7 is used once as the first reading of the Friday of Week 18 in Ordinary Time, Year II. Nahum does not even appear in the Protestant *Revised Common Lectionary* (1983).

right direction? The devastating effects of recent and current wars have shown us that we continue to live in a world of "piles of slain and heaps of corpses," and so ignoring a book like Nahum might be a great loss for the Church and society. A few years ago, Anathea Portier-Young sounded the alarm and invited biblical scholars, theologians, and pastors to confront and name the abominations in Scripture and in our daily lives that often maim, batter, and destroy us, rather than avoid them. Portier-Young finds "a direct correlation between our willingness to attend to the shocking violence in our Scriptures and our willingness to attend to violence and its effects in the world we inhabit."[4]

This book is an effort to confront violence, both in my community and in the book of Nahum. It views Nahum through four scholarly lenses: poetic analysis, study of Assyrian iconography related to eighth- and seventh-century Judah (the Lachish Reliefs and Lion Hunt reliefs), ethnographic research among survivors of war in the Democratic Republic of the Congo (hereafter, DRC), and modern studies on the impact of war trauma on communities of survivors.

I argue that Nahum's description of God and its depiction of war scenes were meant to evoke in seventh-century BCE Judahite audiences the memory of war and destruction at the hands of the Assyrians. The vivid images of YHWH's war against Nineveh do not give readers a historical report on the fall of Nineveh, neither do they intend to foreshadow the historical fall of that Neo-Assyrian capital city in 612 BCE. Rather, they more likely reflect the prophet-poet's attempt to depict a world that would have spoken to the painful collective memory of those who survived the destruction of Lachish and other Judahite towns during Sennacherib's invasion of Judah in 701 BCE. The prophet uses lyric poetry to evoke (rather than narrate) Judah's memory of war and reveal the immediate and comforting presence of YHWH within the conditions of war. He presents that revelation by adapting two traditional literary forms, the biblical oracle against foreign nations (OAN) and the ancient Near Eastern (ANE) city lament.

Viewed thus, the book of Nahum cannot be dismissed as irrelevant or merely vindictive. On the contrary, this study shows that this book is essential, especially for traumatized communities. The connection that I make between this prophetic violent text and the possibility of healing is anchored in my theological commitment to reconciliation and my

---

4. Portier-Young, "Drinking the Cup of Horror," 390.

conviction that, even in violent biblical texts, God intends to offer us something transformative.

This book is divided into seven chapters. In the first chapter, I propose a "Tripolar Biblical Hermeneutics of Reconciliation" as the model most suitable for post-conflict DRC. The tripolar biblical hermeneutics, pioneered by South African scholars Gerald O. West and Jonathan A. Draper, draws from both African contextual biblical interpretations and Western scholarly modes of reading Scripture. It begins with analysis of the contemporary context of the reader; next, it analyzes the text within its historical and literary contexts; finally, it brings the results of these two analyses into a conversation that draws further upon the reader's own theological background and ideological orientation. Concerning the analysis of the contemporary context, I show that the biblical interpreter needs to combine reflection on his[5] life history (autobiographical analysis) and an ethnographic study of a sample of the population from the context in which the reader lives. I underscore the importance of reconciliation as the central concern of biblical interpretation in the DRC, because the journey of reconciliation stands out as the remedy for the current trauma and continual divisions among Congolese people.

In the second chapter, "War, Traumatic Violence, and Congolese Collective Memory," I analyze the Congolese context after the wars that have devastated the country since the mid-1990s. I begin by introducing the concept of "collective and personal memory," and then I show how recent wars in the DRC might have shaped the collective and personal memories and identities of Congolese people. I select some personal stories of the subjects whom I interviewed in eastern DRC in January-February 2016 and analyze them to see the impact of war on those interviewees and their communities.

Chapter 3, "On the Genre, the Form, and the Poetics of the Book of Nahum," discusses the poetics of the book of Nahum. In it, I analyze the book's genre and form. I show that the book is an OAN and an indirect city lament written in lyric poetry. As such, the book of Nahum evokes Judah's memory of the Assyrian war. It does not recount the story of that

---

5. Throughout this book, in places where it is necessary to use a gender-neutral term, I will avoid awkward constructions like "he/she", "he or she", "s/he," etc. I will simply choose either "he" and its cognates or "she" and its cognates. The choice between the two will sometimes depend on my experiences with survivors of violence in eastern DRC. Examples: in DRC, most survivors of violence are female and most perpetrators are male; in a place where the gender of the person is not known, I will use "he" for the perpetrators and "she" for the victims/survivors.

war, but presents images that would awaken that memory in a Judahite audience. The book does not overtly express the lament of the Judahites. However, by presenting YHWH's attack on Nineveh—the capital city of the empire that destroyed Judah—it indirectly voices that lament.

In chapter 4, "The Historical Context of the Vision of Nahum: Assyrian Invasions and Judah's Collective Memory," I discuss the historical context of the book of Nahum. Rather than focusing on the destruction of Nineveh in 612 BCE (as has been done by the majority of scholars reflecting on Nahum's historical context), I focus on the Assyrian campaign in Judah in 701 BCE. I show that what Nahum depicts is likely a poetic evocation of the destruction of Lachish and other Judahite towns—an evocation that would have spoken to Judahite collective memory—rather than a report on the historical fall of Nineveh. This study does not seek to establish a direct historical correlation between Lachish and Nahum. Rather, I focus on the *kind of event* that could have led to Nahum's poetry, which is best known to us from the Assyrian bas-reliefs depicting the fall of Lachish. The constellation of features pertaining to siege warfare in Nahum suggests that we can heuristically choose the capture of Lachish in 701 BCE (the best-known siege warfare from Judah in the Assyrian period) as an event against whose background we can read the book of Nahum.

Chapters 5 and 6 are exegetical. I begin them by noting that the book of Nahum centers on two interrelated themes: the description of the presence of YHWH in situations of violence and the evocation of the memory of war through the poetic depiction of YHWH's battle against Nineveh. Chapter 5, "Imaging God amid Chaos," analyzes the poet's description of YHWH and shows that the God of Nahum is not an advocate of violence. Although YHWH certainly appears violent in the book, humans are not encouraged to use violence. Nor is YHWH a nationalistic deity; notably, Judah is not identified as "*his* people." I will demonstrate that the focus of the description of YHWH is more on what that description can do to encourage Judah and comfort the afflicted than on the effects of such description on Nineveh (or any other enemy nation).

In chapter 6, "The Destruction of Nineveh and Judah's Memories of War," I show that the war scenes depicted by Nahum may bring to Judah's collective memory the memory of Assyrian war. These images are not meant to be specific descriptions of the fall of Lachish or any other city. However, they are sufficiently vivid to make a survivor of destruction, be it of Lachish or any other Judean city or town, feel directly addressed by them.

Chapter 7, "Reflections on the Way to the Appropriation of Nahum in the DRC: Context, Form, and Reconciliation," starts a conversation on how what we see about Nahum in chapters 3 through 6 might speak to a contemporary traumatized reader. I cannot presume how other readers might respond to this book; I only suggest possible ways of establishing a dialogue between my context and the book of Nahum. I hope that other readers will find the model that I present informative and useful within their communities of faith, in order to foster reconciliation among members of those communities.

1

Tripolar Contextual Biblical Hermeneutics of Reconciliation

> Interesting readings abound in the New Testament Society of South Africa (e.g., the 1988 Conference Papers collected in Neotestamentica 22), but outside the gate stand the angry youth asking why they should read the Bible at all.[1]

Introduction

IN HIS 2011 POST-SYNODAL Apostolic Exhortation, *Africae Munus*, Pope Benedict XVI, echoing the wishes and the concerns of African Catholic bishops, urged African Christians to reflect on the plagues of war and violence that have destroyed the African continent and to recognize that they are "called, in the name of Jesus, to live reconciliation between individuals and communities and to promote peace and justice in truth for all."[2] In the same document, Benedict XVI warns against "withdrawal or evasion present in a theological and spiritual speculation which could serve as an escape from concrete historical responsibility"[3] and calls "for transforming theology into pastoral care, namely into a very concrete pastoral ministry in which the great perspectives found in sacred

---

1. Draper, "'For the Kingdom Is Inside You and It Is Outside of You,'" 23.
2. Benedict XVI, *Africae Munus*, no. 1.
3. Benedict XVI, *Africae Munus*, no. 17.

Scripture and Tradition find application in the activity of bishops and priests in specific times and places."[4] The African continent then needs to reflect on war, violence, healing, and reconciliation and to imagine a theological methodology that grounds theological reflections and biblical interpretations on the realities of ordinary Africans living in contexts of war and violence. The contribution of African biblical scholars should consist in finding methods of connecting the biblical texts to African contexts in a way that brings healing to deeply divided communities and wounded individuals.

In this chapter, I reflect on the model of biblical interpretation that I find suitable to the context of war trauma in the DRC. What does a survivor of war trauma mean when she says, "I understand this text" or "this text makes sense to me?" Even though I address some general questions about African contextual biblical hermeneutics, I focus on the particular biblical hermeneutics that tries to respond to questions raised by war and its consequences. I propose that the context of violence and deep divisions demands a model of biblical hermeneutics that puts *reconciliation* at the center of biblical interpretation and promises to provide divided Christian communities with a resource to help them come to term with the legacy of wars and violence. This biblical hermeneutics of reconciliation falls under the larger umbrella of African contextual biblical interpretations, which take the living realities of the readers as the starting point of biblical exegesis.[5] This hermeneutics is not a single methodology, but a conversation between a number of methodologies that help me make sense of biblical texts within my context, a context of divisions and war trauma. I follow the recent contextual hermeneutics developed by African scholars, while also making use of European and

---

4. Benedict XVI, *Africae Munus*, no. 10.

5. Note for example the statement by South African biblical scholar Gerald O. West, "My primary accountability as a biblical scholar, then, is to the South African context of struggle. The struggle is not over, it continues, though our struggles have shifted to include, along with race and class, gender, culture, sexual orientation, disability, globalization and HIV/AIDS (to name the most prominent). My primary interlocutors remain the poor, the working class, and the marginalized, both directly as I work with particular communities, and indirectly through the organic intellectuals with whom I work (including especially my colleagues in the Ujamaa Centre for Community Development and Research, as well as the aforementioned Black and African theologians). It is from within this context of accountability that I do my biblical studies." (West, "The Vocation of an African Biblical Scholar," 311).

North American methodologies of literary analysis, historical criticism, and modern trauma studies.

Methodological discussions about biblical interpretation in Sub-Saharan Africa have, for the most part, taken for granted the importance of the context of the reader for the interpretation of biblical texts.[6] Scholars carry out their study of the Bible with the assumption that the way one reads the Bible has repercussions on the life of the community in which the reader lives and also that the life experiences of the reader influence the way one reads and makes sense of biblical texts. Of course, the fact that Sub-Saharan biblical interpreters share this assumption about the importance of the context of the reader for biblical interpretation neither means that they operate with one unified hermeneutical ideology nor does it suggest that they are unanimous about the way one negotiates the relationship between the biblical text and the context of the reader. Readers emphasize different things when it comes to the goal of biblical interpretation and to how one relates the text to the context. Various readers work with "ideo-theological orientations"[7] that focus on enculturating the message of the Bible in African contexts; others focus on the theme of liberation, while still others focus on reconstruction or on the status of women and children.[8] In addition, not every African scholar believes that the Bible is on the side of believers to help them live flourishing lives: some African scholars actually suspect that the Bible might hold views that can impede the flourishing of communities and individuals.[9] Nonetheless, whether they suspect the Bible or believe that it has the power to transform communities, African scholars have not ignored the role of the Bible (for good or for ill) in African societies.

This question of the connection between the biblical text and the context of the reader—both the social and the theological contexts—has been of interest to two South African scholars, Jonathan A. Draper and Gerald O. West. Working within the framework of liberation hermeneutics, they assume that it is important to find a way of relating the

6. West, "Contextual Bible Reading," 131.

7. This expression is used by Gerald West to speak about "Lived Faith," which includes our ideological and theological orientations and commitments facilitating the dialogue between the biblical text and the African context. See West, "Interpreting 'the Exile' in African Biblical Scholarship," 254–55.

8. West, "Biblical Hermeneutics in Africa," 23–29.

9. For a discussion on the dangers that scholars perceive in some biblical texts, see Magessa, "From Privatized to Popular Biblical Hermeneutics in Africa," 26–27.

Bible to the realities of believers. They have lamented the lack of explicit theoretical reflections on the relationship between the biblical text and the context of the reader among African scholars.[10] That has led them to develop the project of "tripolar" biblical hermeneutics. A tripolar biblical hermeneutics engages the pole of the African context, the pole of the biblical text, and the pole of the ideo-theological orientation of the reader.[11] It goes through three phases: the phase of contextualization (analysis of the context of the reader), that of distanciation (analysis of the biblical text in its historical and literary contexts), and that of appropriation (the dialogue between the reader and the text).

I have chosen to follow the tripolar model developed by Draper and West because this model offers the advantage of putting the questions of the reader at the center of biblical interpretation, while also leaving enough independence for the biblical text to confront the reader. However, I differ from them both on the ideological-theological orientation of my study and on the way I undertake each of the three stages of interpretation. In the remainder of this chapter, I review African tripolar hermeneutics as developed by Draper and West; then I will offer autobiographical comments in order to show how my interpretation is grounded in my theo-ideological orientation; I will conclude by showing how the context of war requires a hermeneutics that puts *reconciliation* at the center of biblical interpretation.

African Tripolar Biblical Hermeneutics: Draper and West

The works of Draper and West can be understood as part of the "prophetic theology" called for by the 1985 South African *Kairos Document*. This document emerged from a context in which the Bible functioned more to maintain the status quo of oppression by the apartheid state than as a text of liberation for all South Africans. On the one hand, there was an academic community that engaged in historical and structural studies of the Bible without reflecting on how their studies could become relevant or challenging to the contexts in which they lived. On the other hand, there was a non-academic community that "remained within a pre-critical,

---

10. West, "Interpreting 'the Exile,'" 249.

11. West, "Biblical Hermeneutics in Africa," 21; cf. Draper, "'For the Kingdom Is Inside You,'" 235–57; Draper, "Old Scores and New Notes," 148–68; Draper, "African Contextual Hermeneutics," 3–22.

naïve frame of reference,"[12] but cared about the meaning of the Bible in their lives. Formed in historical and structural studies, "[the] academics and clergy within the churches have remained methodologically silenced or immobilized, while the people have continued to read the Bible without any assistance from the South African academic community."[13] In this context, neither the academic community nor the ordinary readers of the Bible were well equipped to offer a viable alternative to the state theology of the apartheid system. The church contented itself with teaching a form of theology that proved inadequate to challenge the status quo or to deal with issues that had impact on the life of society. This passive "church theology," according to the *Kairos Document*, not only distanced itself from the real life issues facing South Africans, but also supported the theology of the apartheid state, which sponsored discrimination, racism, and murder.[14] It failed to transform society because it lacked social analysis and tended "to make use of absolute principles like reconciliation, negotiation, non-violence and peaceful solutions, and applied them indiscriminately to all the situations. Very little attempt was made to understand what was actually happening in our society and why it was happening."[15] "Church theology" also lacked adequate understanding of politics and political strategy and pushed the church to make "a virtue of neutrality and sitting on sidelines."[16] The Bible then became "the tool of the oppressors in South Africa."[17]

It was thus important for some Christians, in Draper's words, "to develop, out of this perplexing situation, an alternative biblical and theological model that will in turn lead to forms of activity that will make a real difference to the future of our country."[18] The theologians who emerged from that context chose the hermeneutics of liberation and chose to take sides with the poor and the outcast, because, in that society, not taking sides meant that one sided with the oppressive system that reduced the poor to mere commodities. When scholars like West and Draper read every passage of the Bible from the perspective of the poor and the outcast,

12. Draper, "For the Kingdom Is Inside You," 235.
13. Draper, "For the Kingdom Is Inside You," 238.
14. *Kairos Document*, chapter 2.
15. *Kairos Document*, 20.
16. *Kairos Document*, 20.
17. *Kairos Document*, 238.
18. *Kairos Document*, Preface.

they do it not simply because they think the Bible's intrinsic shape and its fundamental message require them to do so but because the times and place in which they live demand such an approach.

Some precision is in order at this point. South African liberation exegetes are not naïve about the *liberative* power of the Bible; they do not claim that the Bible is always a good tool for human flourishing. On the contrary, while believing that the Bible can be a source of liberation from oppressive systems, they are also aware that the Bible can become a "source of oppression and domination."[19] From the experience of the misuse of biblical texts by the apartheid state in order to justify injustice, racism, capitalism, totalitarianism, and the oppression of the poor by the powerful, scholars have become suspicious of certain interpretations of biblical texts. They have also sought to discover, within the Bible itself, elements that could be oppressive to readers, and read them "against the fundamental axis of liberation, love and justice, which characterizes God's dealing with his people."[20] That being the context within which Draper and West have constructed their tripolar hermeneutics, we can now look closely at how they have come to this methodological model.

In his 1991 essay, "For the Kingdom Is Inside You," Draper views biblical hermeneutics as a two-step process. The first step—borrowing concepts developed by Rudolph Bultmann and Paul Ricoeur—consists in *explanation* (Ricoeur) or *re-construction* (Bultmann).[21] In this step, the interpreter analyzes historical, sociological, and textual data, in order to "re-create the text within the real world in which it was written."[22] This first step is an effort of *distantiation,* through which the reader lets the text speak in its own voice and in its own historical and literary contexts, without tinting it with the reader's concerns and questions. The distance between the text and the reader allows the reader to perceive the world that the text proposes and prevents her from invading the text with her own presuppositions and biases. The second step is that of *understanding* (Ricoeur) or *interpretation* (Bultmann). In this stage, the reader discovers the meaning of the text for her, in her context. What the text means for the reader in her context leads the reader to action. Understanding is not simply cognitive; it is actualized as the reader acts upon what the text

---

19. West, "Biblical Hermeneutics in Africa," 27.
20. Draper, "Reading the Bible as Conversation," 18.
21. Draper, "For the Kingdom Is Inside You," 242.
22. Draper, "For the Kingdom Is Inside You," 242.

has revealed to her. At this stage, the reader and the text belong together. Not only has the text shown the reader a new way of being, but also the life experiences of the reader have shed new light on the understanding of the text.

At that time Draper chose to read the Bible within the context of a community of the oppressed, "because the fundamental paradigm of the Bible is God's *liberative* design for humankind."[23] The connection between the text and the context was facilitated by the conviction that the Bible *itself* expects us to choose the option for the poor and participate in the struggle for their liberation.

Ten years later, Jonathan Draper revisited the question of contextual biblical interpretation in South Africa. His 2001 essay draws from the work of Cristina Grenholm and Daniel Patte on "Scriptural Criticism."[24] Grenholm and Patte developed a tripolar model of interpretation that takes into account the three poles of the *scriptural text*, the *believer's life*, and the *believer's religious perception of life*.[25] Draper, for his part, constructs his methodology around the three poles of *contextualization, distantiation, and appropriation*.[26] He does not seem to have changed his understanding of *distantiation* from ten years earlier. What is new is the addition of the concepts of *contextualization* and *appropriation*. By *contextualization*, Draper means the moment of analysis of the situation of the reader/hearer.[27] Here Draper states that it is our context that both guides us in the "questions we bring to the text and decides what counts as an answer."[28] *Appropriation* is the process of "accepting the meaning and *implications* of the text for myself and my community."[29] Draper also adds that, in order for this model to work, we ought to assume that the Bible is the "normative text of a faith community."[30] That is to say, in addition to the everyday life conditions of readers of the Bible, we also need to take into account our beliefs and/or our trust in the Bible as an

23. Draper, "For the Kingdom Is Inside You," 243; emphasis in the original.

24. Grenholm and Patte, "Receptions, Critical Interpretations, and Scriptural Criticism," 1–54.

25. Grenholm and Patte, "Receptions, Critical Interpretations, and Scriptural Criticism," 14.

26. Draper, "Old Scores and New Notes," 152.

27. Draper, "Old Scores and New Notes," 152.

28. Draper, "Old Scores and New Notes," 153.

29. Draper, "Old Scores and New Notes," 152; emphasis added.

30. Draper, "Old Scores and New Notes," 152.

authoritative text (not necessarily a safe text to be used without caution). In this essay, Draper assumes that appropriation is the final moment of interpretation; but he believes that it does not matter whether one begins with distantiation or with contextualization.

Draper goes on to explore his model by reading Matthew 5:23–26:

> So when you are offering your gift at the altar, if you remember that your brother or sister has something against you, leave your gift there before the altar and go; first be reconciled to your brother or sister, and then come and offer your gift. Come to terms quickly with your accuser while you are on the way to court with him, or your accuser may hand you over to the judge, and the judge to the guard, and you will be thrown into prison. Truly I tell you, you will never get out until you have paid the last penny. (NRSV)

He chooses to begin his interpretation with *distantiation,* in order to let the text speak for itself, freeing it from preconceptions and prejudices.[31] Draper begins his explanation of the text (distantiation) by placing Matthew 5:23–26 within the larger literary context of Matthew 5:20—7:28, where Jesus teaches the disciples about the need to have a surplus of righteousness, which goes beyond that of the Scribes and the Pharisees (Matt 5:20). Draper notes that it is difficult to find direct connection between this passage (Matt 5:23–26) and the passage that precedes it (Matt 5:21–22), where Jesus speaks about anger and murder:

> You have heard that it was said to your ancestors, "You shall not kill; and whoever kills will be liable to judgment." But I say to you, whoever is angry with his brother will be liable to judgment, and whoever says to his brother, "Raqa," will be answerable to the Sanhedrin, and whoever says, "You fool," will be liable to fiery Gehenna. (NRSV)

Before Draper, Hans D. Betz had shown that the interdiction to be angry is what connects Matt 5:21–22 and Matt 5:23–26:

> Once the root cause is identified as anger, the ethical demand follows: one must control anger. One achieves this goal by avoiding situations that could lead to anger, or, if the situations already exist, by defusing them through reconciliation and restoration

---

31. Draper, "Old Scores and New Notes," 158–59.

of the peaceful brotherly relationship. This ethical demand was a standing topic in contemporary Jewish and Hellenistic ethics.[32]

Draper, on the contrary, shows that Betz's focus on anger reduces Jesus's teaching "to a platitude with no cutting edge" because it suggests that anger is always bad and that we should preserve peace at all costs.[33] Betz, according to Draper, should have perceived the connection between cultic offering and economic exploitation. Draper supports his arguments by studying various Hebrew Bible texts that speak about economic exploitation and offerings (Deuteronomy, Amos, Ezekiel, and Micah).

Matthew 5:23–26 does not mention economic exploitation, even though Draper finds allusion to that exploitation. It seems that Betz's interpretation is the more logical one because Matt 5:23–26 is connected to Matt 5:22 by the inferential particle οὖν ("therefore, accordingly"), which suggests that we should read Matt 5:23 as a consequence of what comes before, namely the instructions on anger and insults (5:21–22). Here, the focus is not on the act of killing, but on the emotions that can lead to that act. The passage speaks about anger as liable to judgment. Jesus does not think of anger as a merely "spiritual"[34] matter. Anger can be corrosive to the relationship between brothers and can lead to murder.

My focus is not on Draper's exegetical precision. I am more interested on what makes Draper privilege an interpretation that focuses on economic issues over the one that focuses on anger. When Draper analyzes his context, he names indebtedness and economic exploitation as some of the problems facing society.[35] It seems that Draper chooses to focus on economic exploitation, not because the text speaks on its own about economic issues, but because economic exploitation is one of the concerns of the context in which he lives.

Gerald West has critiqued Draper for not overtly owning his ideo-theological orientation as the element that connects text and context.[36] West points out that Draper's model gives the impression that the connection between the text and the context of the reader can happen without the help of the ideo-theological orientation of the reader. He shows to the contrary that it is not so much methodological precision that connects

32. Betz, *The Sermon on the Mount*, 230.
33. Draper, "Old Scores and New Notes," 160.
34. Draper, "Old Scores and New Notes," 162.
35. Draper, "Old Scores and New Notes," 165.
36. West, "Interpreting 'the Exile'," 257.

the text to the context of the reader. Scholarly resources are important in our reading of biblical texts; but the connection between our social location and the biblical text is facilitated by the ideo-theological orientation of our lived faith.[37] For a scholar who cares about the liberation of the outcast and the poor in society, it is likely that the meaning of biblical texts will be determined by the scholar's interest in liberation and solidarity with the poor. West has shown that Draper ought to become more explicit about the role his own ideologies and theological beliefs play in the process of biblical interpretation. In addition, West has shown that the three poles of biblical interpretation (text, context, and ideo-theological orientation) are in a dynamic relationship. Our ideo-theological orientation influences the way we see ourselves, our contexts, and our reading of biblical texts. But the influence is not a one-way influence. Our ideo-theological orientation itself is constructed by both our context and the biblical text.[38] For most scholars who have lived in a context where the Bible and faith have been part of society's life, this relationship is circular: one cannot tell exactly which pole first shapes the two others. A reader would care about the poor, justice, and liberation because the context in which she lives treats those issues as important. Another can also care about those issues because engagement with the biblical text has led her to raise questions about the conditions of life in society.

Following West's critique, Draper has recognized that

> The text and the reader's context do not in themselves have anything to say to each other—they are not naturally in conversation at all. Therefore, the ideal of an equal conversation between text in its context and the context of the reader producing an appropriation in some kind of spontaneous fashion is a naïve one![39]

He then acknowledges that it is his ideo-theological orientation that makes the connection possible. The new tripolar hermeneutics that he develops begins with *contextualization*, then *distantiation,* and ends with *appropriation.*[40] Draper rightly begins with contextualization because it is important for the reader to know who she is and where she lives before she can "let the text speak on its own voice." This analysis of the reader's

---

37. West, "Interpreting 'the Exile,'" 267.
38. West, "Interpreting 'the Exile,'" 257.
39. Draper, "African Contextual Hermeneutics," 13.
40. Draper, "African Contextual Hermeneutics," 14–15.

context and ideologies helps the reader become aware of what she brings into the conversation with the text. Whether it is for West or for Draper, biblical exegesis is not neutral: the reader always has a purpose in reading biblical texts. Biblical exegesis, they would say, is ideological and presupposes a reader who has goals and aspirations.

Insistence on the context and on its effect on the meaning of the text therefore does not undermine the power of the biblical text to confront its readers, to tell them things they may not expect or want to hear. The biblical text itself has the power to expand the reader's horizon in order to reveal to her realities that she cannot envision without engaging the biblical text.[41]

Before I take up the question of what a tri-polar biblical hermeneutics looks like within the context of war trauma, I will make a few autobiographical comments, in order to relate my approach to biblical interpretation to my life experiences.

Autobiographical Comments

I would like to preface the discussion on my approach to biblical interpretation with this autobiographical note in order to show that I take the approach that informs this study because of my formal theological training and of my experience with war, violence, and trauma. I come to this study as one having the awareness of being part of a community that is deeply wounded and divided. I choose to study the book of Nahum because this book takes me back to moments of trauma that have mostly characterized my life. The book of Nahum, imagining the destruction of Nineveh by God, evoked in the survivors of Judahite cities destroyed by the Assyrian army in 701 BCE their experience with war. I see that this book can similarly evoke memories of destruction in Congolese Christians who have suffered the trauma of war. I study this book from the perspective of war trauma and argue for the necessity of practicing biblical interpretation that fosters reconciliation in wounded communities, not only because I think that the Bible gives us incentives to do so, but also because I see that the community in which *I* live is destroyed and is in need of healing and reconciliation. I neither *adopt* this perspective, in the sense of choosing that which is foreign to me, nor do I try to identify with a group (the victims of war violence) to which I do not belong. I

---

41. Draper, "African Contextual Hermeneutics," 15.

read from the perspective of war trauma because I have experienced the trauma of war.[42]

My formal theological education took place in the United States, that is, geographically and culturally away from that context of wars and violence in which I grew up (although the USA too experiences violence in other ways). In the two institutions where I studied theology and biblical interpretation (the Seminary of the Immaculate Conception in Huntington, New York and Duke Divinity School, North Carolina), emphasis was placed on philological, literary, historical, sociological, and theological questions. At both institutions, the Bible was understood as a "divine word that is uniquely powerful to interpret our experience,"[43] that aims to tell us "about the nature and will of God," to instruct us "in the manifold and often hidden ways in which God is present and active in our world," and to give us "a new awareness of our selves and our actions," showing us "that in everything we have to do with God."[44]

My theological formation also emphasized the importance of thinking about the connection between exegesis and preaching. That is, biblical interpretation was viewed as part of the ministry of a church at prayer, and its task to equip the church to "speak with wisdom, imagination and courage to the challenges of our time."[45] My work as a seminary teacher and my ministry as a priest have forced me to face the challenges of finding ways of relating the divine word to the questions and aspirations of the people of our time.

Toward the end of my doctoral studies at Duke, I discovered the field of African biblical hermeneutics and the work of the Great Lakes Initiative (GLI) Leadership Institute.[46] The meetings of the GLI focus on the theme of reconciliation as a way of imagining the life of new creation within a war-torn region. Various members of religious communities

---

42. My novel, *Kevin the Wild Boy* (2010) bears witness to those conditions.

43. Davis, "Reading the Bible Confessionally in the Church," 9; cf. Second Vatican Ecumenical Council, *Dei Verbum*, no. 11–12.

44. Davis, "Reading the Bible Confessionally in the Church", 11; cf. Davis and Hays "Beyond Criticism," 23.

45. Davis and Hays "Beyond Criticism," 23; cf. *Dei Verbum*, no. 23; Benedict XVI, *Verbum Domini*, no. 45.

46. The Great Lakes Initiative (GLI) is a platform that seeks "to mobilize restless Christian leaders from across the Great Lakes region of Africa, create a space for their transformation, and empower them to participate in God's mission of reconciliation in their own communities, organizations, and nations." (https://divinity.duke.edu/initiatives/cfr/gli , accessed on July 7, 2016).

from war-torn African Great Lakes nations, for a whole week (each year), engage in the interpretation of biblical texts and try to make sense of their lives. The GLI begins its reflections and prayers from the concrete realities of broken communities and wounded individuals. It aims at healing those wounds through prayers, scriptural reflections, and conversations among the participants. The meetings of the GLI have highlighted to me the need for biblical scholars to provide Christian communities with models of contextual biblical interpretations that can enlarge the imagination of African Christians and point them to fresh visions and dreams of a healed and reconciled world.

What precedes shows that I conduct this study as a member of a community that has suffered the trauma of war and violence. I also come to this study as a scholar, a pastor, and a Christian. Because I received my formal theological education in the United States, even though I see myself as primarily an African biblical interpreter, my work as both a biblical scholar and as a pastor is influenced by the two intellectual worlds of the USA and Sub-Saharan Africa. In the remainder of this chapter, I will show how my location determines the kinds of methodologies that I use, the questions that I bring to this study and how that location also has a bearing on the meanings that I find in the book of Nahum.

Tripolar Biblical Hermeneutics of Reconciliation

I draw from the works of West and Draper, yet I distance myself from them in the way I approach each step of the process. This section shows how I have modified their model and adapted it to the context of violence and war trauma.

Contextualization

I pointed out above that some readers of biblical texts choose to focus on certain themes because of the context in which they live. I agree with Draper that the reader should start with contextualization, "with the acknowledgement of the pre-understanding she or he brings to the text, the reason for reading it, the questions being addressed. Every reader reads from her or his context."[47]

---

47. Draper, "African Contextual Hermeneutics," 14–15.

Because the reader needs to become aware of her prejudices before the interpretation of a text, it should be emphasized that the interpretation of biblical texts should be prefaced by the interpreter's self-examination and the examination of her context in order to know her concerns, her interests, her worries, and her values. Introspection, reflections on one's biography, and ethnographic study can play an important role in that examination of the self and of one's context. These reflections on the self cannot be relegated either to the appendix or to a footnote, but should be part of the interpretative process itself.

Autobiography, according to novelist and physician Sherif Hetata, has the power to "present the truth of the individual self, how the self relates to the world, to society, to family, to a spouse or a lover, to friends and rivals, to the system and values that govern life. These are the treasures auto-biography can open up for us, the insights it can provide."[48] Through reflection on her biography, the interpreter of biblical texts can discover her self anew and can also give to possible readers of her work a key to understanding her choices in the interpretation of a particular text. Through reflection on her own life, the interpreter of biblical texts can become aware of and own the reasons for the choices that she makes in her study and in her life.

Some biblical scholars have been explicit about how their life experiences affect their exegetical work, even though their autobiographic comments are not always part of what they consider to be scholarly work. John Byron and Joel N. Lohr recently edited a series of essays by leading biblical scholars reflecting on their stories of faith and scholarship.[49] The autobiographies written by those scholars show us that their scholarly interests (and methodologies) are often influenced by their life experiences. An illustration of that is the impact that the illness of his wife, Ann, has had on the work of John Goldingay. That illness, among other things, led Goldingay to think more about the question of suffering.[50] What is most important from those essays is the recognition that biblical interpretation is not neutral and that our choices and methodologies often depend on our life experiences.

As much as autobiography can help scholars become more aware of their presuppositions, personal reflection alone cannot be sufficient.

---

48. Hetata, "The Self and Autobiography," 124.
49. Byron and Lohr, eds., *I (Still) Believe*.
50. Goldingay, "How I Have Drifted through Life," 96.

Scholars need also to interrogate the environment in which they live, in order to hear the voices of other members of the same community. To understand better their context, the interpreters need to listen to the stories of the people with whom they share the same experiences. The stories of others not only give the scholars a different perspective on the events that affect their worldviews but also can bring to memory stories that they may have forgotten. Ethnographic fieldwork needs to become integral part of the work of the biblical interpreter. Ethnography is "a form of social research used by sociologists, anthropologists, historians, and other scholars to study living human beings in their social and cultural contexts."[51] Ethnographic work involves both observation and interviews, through which the researcher comes to know the subjects of his study. While autobiography gives us our selves through personal reflection, ethnography reveals our selves to us through the lives of others, especially the lives of those with whom we share life conditions.

Traditionally, scholars used to assume that in order to do ethnographic work the researcher had to "go away" to a place not familiar to her, in order to learn the lives of *other* people.[52] Doing ethnography was almost synonymous with studying the exotic and the unfamiliar. The assumption that one had to leave one's own location in order to conduct ethnographic work seems to have come from the claim that ethnography had to be an objective science with which the biases and concerns of the researcher did not interfere.[53] Thus, studying a foreign context was considered to give the researcher the necessary distance in order to make unbiased observations.[54] Of course, in every ethnographic study, the researcher needs some distance from her subjects (and often from herself) in order to perceive what she could have missed, had she not stood at a distance from her subject of study. Familiarity with a subject can become an obstacle to observation because, when the object is too familiar to the observer, the observer can miss details that an outsider would have found important, outstanding, or unusual. Nonetheless, is it equally true that, in order to create distance between herself and her subject of study, the researcher needs to move from her geographic location? Recent ethnographers say that physical distance is not always necessary. Even one's

---

51. Moschella, *Ethnography as a Pastoral Practice*, 25.
52. Atikson, *For Ethnography*, 5.
53. Moschella, *Ethnography as a Pastoral Practice*, 26.
54. Van Ginkel, "Writing Culture from Within," 5.

own native location can become a subject of study, and the researcher can still distance herself from her subjects of study. What is important for the researcher is to become attentive to her environment and not assume to know her context before careful analysis. Scholars have become more convinced that no location, no context, is self-evident to the researcher —be she a native or an outsider. Researchers thus conduct research even in their own cultures and contexts. Ethnographers and anthropologists are no longer simply "strangers and friends, marginal natives or professional strangers";[55] they may also be members of the same communities that they study. Endo-ethnography (ethnography done by a native) has now become more accepted as a field of study.

As was said above, being a member of a community does not necessarily mean that the ethnographer has full knowledge of the lives, concerns, and aspirations of all the members of the community in which she lives. There can be aspects of the life of the community that might affect the way the researcher perceives reality, but on which the researcher has never reflected; there can also be aspects of the life of the community that the researcher does not know. Whether at home or abroad, the scholar ought to study the lives of the members of the community with an open mind, while also reflecting on how the stories of other members of the community can affect the way the interpreter thinks, reads, and lives.

One possible obstacle to endo-ethnography is that the researcher's informants might feel the pressure to edit out elements that they assume unnecessary to the researcher whom they expect to know about those details or even to know better about them than the informant. Often the informant has an idea about what every native should know, even if what she believes to be common knowledge is unusual to the researcher. The informant might find it unnecessary to answer questions pertaining to aspects that she assumes every native is supposed to know.[56] I encountered such a case with the subjects of my interviews in the villages of Kaniola and Walungu in South Kivu. Because I am a native of the DRC, all my subjects assumed that I knew about a "General Falker Mike" (FM), whom they all praised for having saved them from assailants. The problem was that I knew nothing about FM. That general, they said, saved many villages from assailants, but his name is known only within those villages.

---

55. Van Ginkel, "Writing Culture from Within," 5.
56. Van Ginkel, "Writing Culture from Within," 9.

Despite those limitations, endo-ethnographers have the advantage of getting an insider's view of the context in which they conduct their research. They are privileged to have "a good understanding of the macro-society and its symbol and value systems, no culture-shock, feelings of empathy, and easy access to the intellectual, emotive, and sensory dimensions of behavior."[57] Having a general understanding of the working of society can help the researcher dive into her research with confidence. Informants can also trust the native researcher and recount stories to her that they would not readily tell an outsider, to whom they might refuse to expose the "dirty laundry" of the community. Another advantage of endo-ethnography is the practical use of the results of the research for the informant community. Traditional ethnographers often conducted their research in "remote societies" to help their own societies. The knowledge of foreign tribes and societies contributed to helping colonial administrations and explorers understand those societies; but the information gathered from those researches benefitted the colonial administrations more than the informant communities. They also helped *their* own communities understand themselves by contrasting themselves to other societies. That is, the questions that often drove the ethnographers to their fields came, not from the context they studied, but from the context in which they lived. It is understandable that traditional ethnographers used the knowledge garnered from ethnographic studies to help their own communities. What needs to be done is to raise local researchers whose work can benefit the informant community.[58]

In this book, I begin the interpretation of Nahum by examining my context through the analysis of my life story and through interpretation of the ethnographic fieldwork I conducted in eastern DRC. My work in eastern DRC is a form of endo-ethnography, even though I am both an insider and an outsider to communities in eastern DRC. I am an insider because I identify with many of the stories, worries, and concerns of the populations in eastern DRC. I am a member of the informant community, because I am a Congolese and my informants and I share the experience of having suffered from war and from the hands of the *same* groups of perpetrators, mostly using the same techniques of oppression: mutilations, maiming, rapes, or murder. When I went to eastern DRC, I had a general idea of what one might hear from stories of Congolese

57. Van Ginkel, "Writing Culture from Within," 10.
58. Van Ginkel, "Writing Culture from Within," 7.

wars. Despite cases of language barriers, I could easily converse with informants and blend into society without being suspected of trying to intrude into the lives of native populations.

At the same time, in eastern DRC, I was an outsider in many respects. First, I grew up in the Sankuru (in the center of the DRC); I do not speak the native languages of eastern DRC (Mwashi, Swahili); the Sankuru did not suffer as much as eastern DRC has suffered from violence. Even though I had an idea of how populations suffered from violence, I was not under the illusion that I fully understood what it meant for the people in eastern DRC to have suffered from violence. Since my informants knew that the Sankuru did not suffer from the same degree of violence as the populations in eastern DRC, they did not assume that I knew everything about the war in eastern DRC. Secondly, I went from the United States "to do research" among the populations in eastern DRC. Therefore, even though the informants did not treat me as a foreigner, they considered me as one who had been detached from the realities of violence in which they live.

My position as an insider-outsider helped me remain open to the unexpected. It also made me both a researcher and an informant. I both hear the stories and bring my memories to the interpretations of the stories of my informants.[59] For me, ethnographic fieldwork was a return to the old memories of violence.

The analysis of the context does more than helping me form a better view of the communities in eastern DRC. It ultimately helps me understand *myself* as a reader of biblical texts. Both ethnographic work and biographical reflections help me distance myself from myself—to see myself more clearly—and bring me closer to myself by showing me aspects of myself that I could have ignored. My interviews with survivors of violence in eastern DRC help me understand myself "through understanding others."[60] Through ethnography and autobiographic reflections, I discern the questions that drive my research and how answering those questions can bring healing and reconciliation to war-torn communities.

It should be noted from the preceding discussion that, for me, context is not only about geography; it is especially about personal experience. While geography matters in the way one views the world, it is not the only factor that affects one's worldview. Within the same geographic

---

59. For a discussion on the interaction between a native researcher and her informant, see Gallinat, "Playing the Native Card," 25–44.

60. Collins and Gallinat, "The Ethnographic Self as Resource," 1.

location one can find multiple contexts, based on the experiences of the people living within that geographic location. And because human experience is not static, context is not always static either. Some people could move from one context to another or find themselves within many of those contexts. In some instances, however, we find contexts that are so opposed that a person cannot belong *at the same* time to both; he will belong either to one or to the other. In DRC, for example, even though a perpetrator can later become a victim or a victim can later become a perpetrator, it is almost impossible for one person to be at the same time victim and perpetrator. This is also the case for contexts in which there is a sharp distinction between the rich and the poor: either one is poor (and thus belongs to *that* context) or one is not poor (and belongs to *that* context). It is important to hear the stories of individual members of the community to take into account their worries, fears, and questions. Context, in short, is not necessarily about where one lives, but about what one has experienced in life.

Contextualization and the study of war trauma

Because of the massive losses suffered by the community with which I identify, in addition to ethnography and autobiography, I make use of trauma studies in my social analysis. The study of trauma emerged largely in response to the great wars of the twentieth century. This term has been used in various fields of study to refer to the impact of overwhelming events on the memory/body or behavior of an individual or a group of people.[61] One of the pioneers in these studies is Judith L. Herman. In her 1992 *Trauma and Recovery*, Herman shows how severe violence and disasters can alter the identity that people have formed of themselves prior to the traumatic event.[62] Traumatic events inspire both helplessness and terror. They affect people in such a way that those people can lose part of who they are: their language is affected; their own bodies and emotions become paralyzed or numbed; they lose faith in people, in any sense of order, and in God.[63]

However, the focus on the impact of the individual trauma gives us only a partial picture of the damage that traumatic events can cause.

---

61. Carr, *Holy Resilience*, 7.
62. Herman, *Trauma and Recovery*, 7.
63. Herman, *Trauma and Recovery*, 7.

A new study by Jeffrey C. Alexander has shown that, in addition to individual traumas, it is important to consider collective traumas, which are the breakdown of collective cultural expectations and communal identity. Collective trauma occurs when the community realizes (as a group) that the violence that has been imposed on them (or on some of them) is unmerited and yet it has affected their sense of who they are.[64] For Alexander, collective trauma is not the sum of various individual traumas. Collective trauma is the suffering that "becomes a matter of collective concern, cultural worry, social panic, gut-wrenching fear, catastrophic anxiety," "when social groups . . . construe events as gravely endangering."[65] Alexander adds that, because collective trauma disrupts the collective "we" of the group, in order for that group to recover from trauma, it is not enough to heal individual wounds; the group has to use stories, characters, and symbolic representations to build a new social identity that can experience and confront the danger.[66]

Trauma studies have also helped us understand how traumatic events affect literary and artistic productions. The work of the literary critic Cathy Caruth has made an important contribution in this regard. In her 1996 *Unclaimed Experience*, Caruth shows how traumatic experiences are experiences that one "cannot simply leave behind."[67] These experiences haunt the survivor and often intrude into her life in a way that she might not comprehend. Although the survivor can remember the story of the traumatic experience with all the details, the survivor does not always own the impact of those stories on her life: the stories are unclaimed by the survivor. The traumatic experiences are unclaimed, not only because they can be forgotten by the survivor, but also because they are part of the life and actions of the survivor without the survivor being aware of it. The production of texts and artistic works, according to Caruth, can become occasions in which traumatic memories intrude into the work of the writer or the artist. While I have treated trauma studies as a way of analyzing my social location, these studies are also important in the analysis of the text of Nahum, because, as we will show it in chapter 4, the context from which the book of Nahum emerged was characterized by traumatic violence.

---

64. Alexander. *Trauma: A Social Theory*, 3.
65. Alexander. *Trauma: A Social Theory*, 3.
66. Alexander. *Trauma: A Social Theory*, 3.
67. Caruth, *Unclaimed Experience*, 2.

Scholars have expressed hesitation about the legitimacy of using studies conducted with subjects in contemporary Western countries to make claims about Asian or African countries or about ancient societies.[68] I am well aware of the disparity of cultures and cultural assumptions between the USA and DRC or the USA and ancient Israel. But whatever that disparity might be, one thing remains evident in all these cultures: violence disrupts the lives of individuals and communities. If trauma studies can be of any value for this study, it is because they give me the language to name experiences about which the subjects of my interviews spoke. Adequately distinguishing modern contexts and ancient contexts requires that we also analyze the historical context and the literary conventions according to which the text was produced.

It should be noted that events are not traumatic in themselves. Each person and community can react to an event in a different way. An event that can be traumatic to one person can be harmless to another. As David Hooker puts it,

> Trauma occurs when circumstances are perceived as life threatening or overwhelming to an individual's or a community's capacity to respond. The circumstance or event itself is not the trauma. Trauma is the complex set of physical, emotional, cognitive, spiritual, and relational responses to an experience of utter helplessness.[69]

Distantiation

In a recent essay, Geert van Oyen speaks of an engaged reading of the Bible in which the reader avoids confusing the present with the past and does not replace the text she is reading with her own experience. There should be a *dialogue* between the text and personal experience, not mere *replacement* of one by the other.[70] We have also seen above what Draper writes about distantiation and the need that the text "be allowed to be other, different, over against ourselves and our concerns and our questions. It is rooted in a specific historical, social, cultural and economic

---

68. See, for example, the book by journalist Ethan Watters, *Crazy Like Us: The Globalization of the American Psyche*, in which he warns the world about the exportation of American psychological terms and diagnostic processes.

69. Hooker, *The Little Book of Transformative Community Conferencing*, Kindle loc 277–79.

70. Van Oyen, "'A Bon Lecteur,'" 30–31.

context."[71] In this book, I also acknowledge that it is important to take into account elements of the texts that are independent of the reader: the historical context, the structure, and the literary conventions according to which the text was written. Distantiation certainly will not completely separate the reader from the process of reading; often our prejudices and biases will try to intrude into the reading of the text. But the reader ought to be intentional in suspending his judgment in order to listen to the text in its historical context and according to its structure and literary conventions.

I follow Draper in arguing for that "moment of the text."[72] After acknowledging the context within which I interpret the book of Nahum, I explain the text of Nahum by entering its world through analysis of historical information pertaining to the period in which I believe the book of Nahum to have been written/redacted; I also analyze the text of Nahum following its poetic structures. Distantiation gives me the possibility of hearing from the text a variety of stories, injunctions, and messages that are not part of our contexts and yet can transform our contexts and communities.

In chapter 4, I shall return to the importance of historical information for the interpretation of Nahum; but for now, it will suffice to say that, just as the context of the reader matters in how the reader understands a text, so would Nahum's context have mattered in his interpretation of events that occurred in his community. Knowing that context can prepare us well to listen to the text of Nahum.

The text, according to Paul Ricoeur, is already a closed system of signs, symbols, and structures that discloses a world of its own.[73] In order to have access to the world projected by the text, the reader needs to understand the logic of operations that hold the text together. Explanation consists in showing, through structural analysis, how that logic works.[74] When done with humility and discipline,[75] explanation makes appropriation possible in a way that leaves the text free to say things that the reader might not be willing or prepared to hear. It offers the reader a worldview with which he can wrestle in and for the life of his community. What the

---

71. Draper, "Old Scores and New Notes," 155.
72. Draper, "African Contextual Hermeneutics," 15.
73. Ricoeur, *Interpretation Theory*, 81.
74. Ricoeur, *Interpretation Theory*, 84.
75. Draper, "African Contextual Hermeneutics," 15.

reader appropriates is not the surface meaning of the text, but the deep meaning unveiled by structural analysis.[76]

I will show in chapter 3 how the fact that Nahum is a modified lament written in lyric poetry has a bearing on the way the book conveys its meaning. Unlike narratives that tell us stories with well-defined plots, lyric poetry presents us with images that *evoke* events, rather than recount them.

Appropriation

Explanation of a text makes the world of the text available to the reader. The text that the reader has explained is not simply a copy of past events or of the physical world. The text is revelatory, for it points beyond that which already exists.[77] Having become aware of his own concerns, questions, aspirations, and fears, the reader enters into conversation with that new world proposed by the text. For the reader, the meaning of the text is neither simply the echo of his concerns and questions nor identification with the concerns of the author/redactor of the text. The meaning of the text is the new vision that emerges from the conversation between the world of the reader and the world of the text. For Draper, appropriating the meaning of a text means relating the meaning that one has discovered with lived faith.[78] The meaning of the text therefore is neither in the text itself nor in the reader, rather is revealed through dialogue between the world proposed by the text and the reader. What the reader of the text understands as the meaning of the text is somehow the result of the combination of the perception of what already exists and the imagination of that which does not yet exist. Meaning-making then is not an act of reproduction or a copy of anything in the world; it is more than mere explanation of biblical texts. It means letting our conversation with Scripture expand and transform our imagination, in order to make "us into a new people."[79]

For Paul Ricoeur, through appropriation the reader is "enlarged in his capacity for self-projection by receiving a new mode of being from

---

76. Ricoeur, *Interpretation Theory*, 87.
77. Ricoeur, *Interpretation Theory*, 87.
78. Draper, "Reading the Bible as Conversation," 18.
79. Davis and Hays, "Beyond Criticism," 24.

the text itself."[80] The person that the reader becomes after dialogue with the world of the text is a new self that is not only enlarged by the world of the text, but has also given up some of its own "egoistic and narcissistic ego."[81] Interpretation in that sense consists in losing our old selves in order to find a new self, an enlarged self. The enlarged self that results from the conversation between a text and the reader should be able to wrestle with the problems or the issues that keep the self or the community from reaching the potentials suggested by the text. Often appropriating a text means going through a process of self-critique and *metanoia*.[82]

It is because interpretation can offer new possibilities to readers that a reading of Nahum within the context of war trauma can promise healing and transformation to a war-torn community. Since trauma breaks individuals and communities, interpreting the Bible in this context will need to find a way of mending the wounds that cripple the communities. Reading Scripture is not simply about finding what the Bible says. The book of Nahum, for example, on the surface, suggests retaliation for Nineveh, because Nineveh has destroyed all the nations (3:19). A reader will need to ask, based on her context, what kind of world does this text point us to, and what should we do within our context to heal the wounds that paralyze our communities? Does revenge heal the wounds, or is the journey of reconciliation the best path to choose? The biblical text then will help the reader imagine, out of the unimaginable, the possibility of a new and more peaceful world.

This imagination is at the same time conditioned by historical information, our context, and structural analysis, but it looks beyond all these three poles. Distantiation controls imagination so that we do not give in to careless (and often harmful) assertions that might simply reflect our own egos. It purifies the ego, while also giving it more identity. But we also need to own the world suggested by this text to act within the context in which we live.

Both the analysis of my context and the explanation of the book of Nahum make it clear that healing the wounds that maim communities is vital for the flourishing of those communities. Even though YHWH threatens Nineveh with destruction, YHWH still does not say that what happens to Nineveh is a good thing. Nineveh is disfigured, abused, raped

---

80. Ricoeur, *Interpretation Theory*, 94.
81. Ricoeur, *Interpretation Theory*, 94.
82. Ricoeur, *Hermeneutics and the Human Sciences*, 144.

(3:5–6). These acts of violence, we will see, intend to speak powerfully to a traumatized reader who knows too well the experience of suffering such violence. We know that our communities do not thrive on rape, disfigurement, and abuses. Nahum takes the reader back to the place where she was wounded, and invites her to decide. It reminds the reader that violence can destroy communities, no matter where it comes from. What kind of person or community does this text invite us to be?

Conclusion

In this chapter, I have sketched my approach to biblical interpretation. I have called the hermeneutical model that I follow "a tri-polar contextual biblical hermeneutics of reconciliation." I am oriented toward reconciliation in my biblical interpretation because my context—a context of war trauma and conflicts—compels me to put reconciliation at the center of biblical interpretation. It is only the journey of reconciliation that can respond to the deep questions that my community faces and heal the wounds that cripple that community.

Following the work of West and Draper, my approach proceeds from the analysis of my context, goes to the analysis of the biblical text, and then culminates in engaging the world revealed by text in conversation to imagine ways of responding to the problems that my community faces. The following chapter will describe those problems.

2

War, Traumatic Violence, and Congolese Collective Memory

Introduction

IN CHAPTER 1, I presented the hermeneutical approach that I take in this book. This second chapter analyzes the Congolese context and reflects on how war and violence might have had a bearing on the collective and personal memories and identities of Congolese communities. The chapter will consist mainly in analyzing interviews I conducted with war survivors in North Kivu and in South Kivu (DRC) between January and February 2016. Psychiatrist Judith Hermann says that "only the fortunate" find traumatic experiences unusual in today's world.[1] The interviews that I analyze here will show us that such a statement is particularly true of the citizens of the DRC, who have endured more than twenty years of wars and unspeakable atrocities. These wars that have decimated millions of Congolese have also left indelible scars on both individual survivors and communities. Because war and violence affect communities to their core, before delving into the description of the Congolese context and the analysis of the interviews, I will preface this chapter with a succinct discussion on the concept of "personal and collective memory" and how traumatic events or circumstances can alter the collective "we" of a people.

---

1. Herman, *Trauma and Recovery*, 33.

Personal and Collective Memories

The concepts of "collective memory" and "personal memory" as used here are associated with the works of Maurice Halbwachs and Paul Ricoeur. Halbwachs studies the role played by the social environment in the way individuals remember events. For him, remembering depends on some social framework that defines the group to which the remembering subject belongs.[2] Whether it is the family, the religious group, or the social group in which the person belongs, those contexts often define what the person remembers and how the individual views herself as a member of the group. Individuals remember so-called personal stories and shape their identities around those memories, but what one remembers is often influenced by where and with whom one lives. Even when the individual remembers her own past, sometimes that memory of the past can be but the reflection of what the group makes available to the person's consciousness. The individual can then, to a certain extent, echo the memory of the collectivity.[3] That is, what we think to come from our personal memory can often be the expression of the image that the group wants to make of itself.

The formation of a collective memory may rely on the prominent experience of some individuals, but it transcends the experiences of any individual. Collective memory is created by giving meaning to events, and the meaning that the collectivity gives to an event does not have to coincide with the direct personal experiences of individual members who lived through that event. However, those who conceive the image of the collective "we" also make the effort to persuade all the members of the group that the official narrative presented as the story of the group is *their* story.[4] In other words, members who tell a different story than the one officially held by the collectivity can be perceived as lacking ties to the group to which they are supposed to belong.

When a group intends to (re)define itself in relation to a traumatic event (such as September 11, 2001 in the USA) or in relation to a victorious past (such as the Liberation of France from German occupation in 1945), it can use events (e.g., memorial services), verbal accounts (e.g., national histories), or physical constructions (e.g., historical landmarks) to engrave the memory of the event. This history, landmark, or artistic

---

2. Halbwachs, *Les Cadres Sociaux de la Mémoire*, v.
3. Halbwachs, *La Mémoire Collective*, 28.
4. Halbwachs, *La Mémoire Collective*, 28.

representation becomes the locus where an individual *is supposed* to find her identity as a member of the group. By presenting individuals as belonging to a common story, collective memory creates communal bonding between individuals.

This communal bonding, however, almost always comes at a price for personal memories. Paul Ricoeur builds upon Halbwachs's notion of collective memory to speak about the formation of what he calls "authorized history."[5] Authorized history is the history that every member of the group is supposed to appropriate as her own. It is the story that the group tells about itself, and it is the *only* story that counts as true (hi)story. However, by creating a collective story, by determining what individuals *should* remember about the past, the collectivity at the same time forces individual members to sacrifice their own stories for the sake of the official story,[6] unless somehow they can find a way of making their stories *fit* into the collective story. Similarly, in a study of the function of war memorials and historical landmarks, Laurie Johnson of the "Public Memory Research Centre" at the University of Southern Queensland shows that such memorials and landmarks give the impression of engraving past events in a permanent way. They provide a "seemingly permanent reference point to the stories that we [Australians] tell ourselves about nationhood."[7] However, by becoming the reference point of national identity, they also obliterate personal stories.[8] The memorials apparently connect the community to its past, but this past is devoid of connection to personal experiences. The community remembers what it went through *as community*, but at the same time forgets the stories of individuals who lived through the events engraved in the memorials. Thus, Ricoeur and Johnson warn us against the danger of focusing exclusively on official accounts and commemorations of past events, for such accounts sometimes depend on forgetting or muting personal wounds and experiences of individuals. The nation or the group can claim to commemorate its wounds, but such wounds are not necessarily the reflection of the *real* wounds of individuals who lived through the events.

It appears then that events experienced by communities affect the way each community views itself. However, while paying attention to

---

5. Ricoeur, *La Mémoire*, 580.
6. Ricoeur, *La Mémoire*, 580.
7. Johnson, "Unremembered," 74.
8. Johnson, "Unremembered," 75; cf. Ricoeur, *La Mémoire*, 99.

how the group/community remembers the event and incorporates that event into her collective story, we also need to pay attention to the personal stories of each individual member of the community. In this book, I pay attention both to official stories about the wars in the DRC and to personal stories of individual survivors. In chapter 4, I will also see how Nahum's poem bears witness to Judahite collective memory, while Assyrian bas reliefs give the dominant Neo-Assyrian empire's view on the fall of Judahite towns in 701 BCE.

Congolese Wars: Historical Overview

This section does not intend to give a full account of the complex story of recent wars and violence in the DRC (1996–present). Detailed and well-documented accounts of those wars have already been written.[9] Here, I will only offer a brief overview of that story, so readers may understand the origin of the violence that has destroyed the communities that I interviewed in North Kivu and South Kivu.

Historians of Congolese wars identify three factors that contributed to the implosion of Congolese society: the Rwandan migrations into the DRC since the nineteenth century, the collapse of the state under the totalitarian regime of Joseph-Désiré Mobutu Sese Seko (1965–97), and the 1994 Rwandan genocide.

Since 1881, Rwandan populations have been migrating into the DRC. Some came to the DRC as political refugees, others as workers in Belgian colonial plantations, and others still as immigrants by choice. No matter the reasons for which Rwandans crossed the border to the DRC, their presence alongside Congolese local populations has been the cause of tensions for many decades. Even though the descendants of those migrants (the Banyamulenge[10] of South Kivu and the other Rwandophones

---

9. Stearns, *Dancing in the Glory of Monsters*; Prunier, *Africa's World War*; Turner, *Congo Wars*; Namujimbo, *Je reviens de l'Enfer*.

10. "Banyamulenge" refers to a social group of Congolese Tutsis whose ancestors are believed to have migrated from Rwanda to eastern DRC in the nineteenth century. The name "Banyamulenge" does not refer to their ethnicity, but refers to the village of Mulenge with which they were historically identified. Banyamulenge (or the singular "Munyamulenge") means, "one/people from Mulenge." For more information on the Banyamulenge, see Turner, *Congo Wars*, 78–82.

of North Kivu)[11] have since become Congolese citizens, they are still viewed by the original dwellers of Eastern DRC as foreigners and traitors.

During the years of Mobutu's dictatorship, the political class of the DRC (then called "Zaire") worsened the tensions between populations in Eastern DRC. Mobutu's corrupt regime favored divisions among social groups to prevent possible coalition of those groups for revolt against a centralized government. To please the local populations, Mobutu revoked the citizenship of many Rwandophones, whom he treated as Rwandan citizens residing on Congolese soil.[12] This politics of "*divide ut imperes*" certainly prevented coalition between the local populations and the Rwandophones against the central government; but it also sowed the seeds of the revolutions that would not only end Mobutu's long reign, but also would inaugurate the collapse of Congolese society. The Rwandophones of Eastern DRC, abused by both their neighbors and the central government, felt pushed to revolt and waited for any opportunity to claim their rights as Congolese citizens worthy of respect and dignity.

That much-sought opportunity came in 1993 when a group of Rwandan Tutsis (who had been abused by their own Hutu-led government in Rwanda) started a civil war in Rwanda to overthrow the Hutu government of Juvénal Habyarimana (Mobutu's close friend) in order to reclaim their rights as Rwandan citizens. The Rwandophones of Eastern DRC saw in this Rwandan civil war an opportunity for them to participate in a movement that would put an end to the exclusion of Tutsis in Rwanda and the exclusion of Rwandophones in the DRC. As is well known, that Rwandan civil war lead to the genocide that killed more than 500,000 Rwandan Tutsis and Hutus.[13]

This genocide created a refugee crisis in Eastern DRC because many of the former perpetrators of the Rwandan genocide fled to the DRC. Most of those refugees crossed the borders with their weapons. These refugees formed the militia group FDLR (Forces Démocratiques de Libération du Rwanda). For the new government formed by Paul Kagame, the presence of those Hutu refugees in Eastern DRC represented a threat to the security of Tutsi populations in Rwanda. It also resented the fact that Mobutu had supported Juvénal Habyarimana in the war against Kagame's armed insurrection. Mobutu then had two kinds of enemies from the

---

11. Both groups are often called "Rwandophones," in reference to their language, the Kinyarwanda.

12. Stearns, *Dancing in the Glory of Monsters*, 73.

13. Turner, *Congo Wars*, 3–4.

east: the Congolese Rwandophones and the new Rwandan government. The Congolese Rwandophones wanted a response to their grievances and the Rwandan government wanted to make sure the DRC was not protecting/hiding the *genocidaires* who could later return to commit a second genocide in Rwanda. At the same time, the Congolese (then Zairian) government, composed of Mobutu's friends and relatives, had no organized army to face any external or internal attacks. Also, after thirty-two years of Mobutu's dictatorship, the DRC was at such a level of poverty and insecurity that the majority of Congolese people wanted the end of Mobutu's reign.

These factors led to the wars that have shaken the DRC since 1996. The analysis of the interviews that I conducted with survivors of violence in Eastern DRC sheds light on the conditions of many communities that have suffered from the atrocities of those wars. We can now turn to those interviews.

Into the "Whirlwind of Violence":[14] Listening to the Stories of Survivors in North Kivu and South Kivu

During the more than twenty years of war in the DRC, violence and atrocities have been ubiquitous, but North Kivu and South Kivu have paid a higher price than any other part of the country. I chose this region as a sample for understanding the context from which I read the book of Nahum, because listening to the stories of people living in this region offers me the possibility of better understanding the impact of violence on Congolese individuals and communities.

I had planned to interview between 30 and 100 subjects in two locations: Goma (North Kivu) and Bukavu (South Kivu).[15] I conducted

---

14. The expression "whirlwind of violence" was used by Mathilde Muhindo, a member of the Archdiocese of Bukavu who has worked for more than forty years for the promotion of human rights and human dignity. It is by that expression that she defined the region where she lives, because she feels like everyone in her community is engulfed inside a powerful and destructive force. By that phrase, Muhindo also means the chaotic situation in which the community find themselves: no reliable justice system, no trust in political leaders, and violence seems to have become the only thing ruling the region. Muhindo has worked with many women in order to help them "live a life worth living." The center which she directed for many years, OLAME ("Live!" in Mashi, the local language), has helped many women process the ordeal of sexual abuses and traumatizing violence.

15. Since I planned to work with the Catholic Diocese of Goma and the Archdiocese

interviews with 45 subjects in both locations. The subjects of my interviews were either survivors of war violence, or their counselors, ministers, caretakers, and doctors and nurses. In Goma, I went to the "bureaux d'écoute" (small counseling facilities on diocesan grounds) of Caritas Goma (a network of Catholic charities of the Catholic diocese of Goma) and recruited subjects who agreed to participate in the interviews. All these subjects had been receiving help from the diocese of Goma in the forms of medical assistance, psychotherapy, or adult literacy training. In Bukavu, I worked with the *Commission Diocésaine Justice et Paix*, CDJP (the diocesan commission on "Justice and Peace" of the Catholic archdiocese of Bukavu) and the *Bureau Diocésain des Oeuvres Médicales*, BDOM-Bukavu (the department of health services of the Catholic archdiocese of Bukavu). In both locations, I conducted interviews in French and relied on a professional translator for the subjects who spoke only Kiswahili or Mashi. To keep personal information confidential, I have identified the subjects by pseudonyms and altered some details in their stories, without betraying the authenticity of each story. The only subjects whose actual names appear in this study are people who, because of their work with the survivors, had otherwise made their identity public.

Common parlance claims that "*ex oriente lux*,"[16] but in the DRC, the east is hardly a source of light. Rather, the east is often seen as the entryway for death and desolation: Congolese wars start from the east. My arrival in Goma on January 18, 2016 brought me to a place that had always filled me with fear. As one of my interviewees would tell me later, I indeed was walking into the "whirlwind of violence."

The city of Goma is the capital of the province of North Kivu. It lies on the border between Rwanda and the DRC. With the small rocks and small pools of unclean water that fill many of Goma's streets, I had the impression of stepping into a heap of rubble that testifies to a terrifying past. Indeed, Goma is a city of ruins and debris. In addition to the wars that have disfigured this city since 1996, Goma still bears the scars of volcanic eruptions that have often traumatized its inhabitants.

---

of Bukavu, many of my interviewees came from villages that are outside Goma or Bukavu, because those dioceses extend beyond the cities of Goma and Bukavu. In this study, the names Goma and Bukavu are used to mean also the surrounding villages. In some cases, I travelled to those surrounding villages to meet the survivors in their own homes/villages.

16. "Light comes from the east."

To the South of Goma flows Lake Kivu, beyond which one can see the city of Bukavu, the capital city of the province of South Kivu. Bukavu is surrounded by Kahuzi-Bienga National Park and Lake Kivu. Muddy during the rainy season and often paralyzed by monstrous traffic jams, Bukavu does not, at first sight, look like a city that has lost thousands of its inhabitants. The city looks crowded and alive. Even though a big part of its population perished during the wars, Bukavu has been repopulated by thousands of people who survived atrocities in the surrounding villages (e.g., Kaniola, Walungu, Mulamba, Ninja) and have come to find refuge in the city. These villages have become graveyards where only the bravest still live in order to preserve the memory of their fallen relatives.

In short, Goma, Bukavu, and the surrounding villages have become centers of violence. People of all ages and sexes, entire communities, and families have been destroyed by the violence of war.

The Many Faces of Violence

U.N. Special Representative Margot Wallstrom has called eastern DRC the "rape capital of the world."[17] This statement names an important aspect of violence in the DRC, but it also runs the risk of ignoring the other forms of violence that Congolese populations have suffered during the years of war. It is true that rape has been rampant during the wars in the DRC, especially in North Kivu and South Kivu. As we will see below, rape has often been used as a weapon of war. But we cannot speak of the cases of rape that have taken place in the DRC in isolation from other forms of violence. Indeed, local communities do not view rape as an isolated issue.

During these years of war, rape has been the major issue on which NGOs and international agencies have focused. Because Congolese communities rely on financial and professional assistance from those international NGOs and agencies, they seem to experience pressure to focus on what these agencies and NGOs define as problems. It is true that no effort for healing or reconciliation can succeed in the DRC if it ignores the damage that the rape of women does to the communities. However, in addition to raped women, we also have people whose limbs have been cut off, men and women who bear scars of deep physical wounds, displaced people whose villages have been burned down, and survivors whose families have been decimated. These forms of violence too leave

17. http://news.bbc.co.uk/2/hi/8650112.stm (accessed on July 12, 2016).

terrible marks on individuals and communities. Some of those forms of violence might not easily interest international media, but they nonetheless deserve attention. My point here is that, if we follow the model of intervening only in isolated issues, without looking at all the issues and all the forms of violence, we cannot hope to deal effectively with the problem of violence in the DRC. It is no surprise that, after many years of efforts and after having spent many resources, the international community, NGOs, and charitable agencies have not found lasting solutions to the problem of violence in the DRC. I believe that the failure of those efforts can, at least in part, be attributed to the lack of an approach that looks at all the issues more holistically.

Maria Masson, a Belgian woman who has worked for the health department of the Archdiocese of Bukavu for thirty-four years, shares my observation about the need to avoid this kind of reductionist focus on rape at the expense of other forms of violence. Masson is the director of the diocesan bureau for medical assistance (BDOM). I interviewed Masson about her experience during the years of violence in South Kivu. Even though she has been in Bukavu during all the years of wars, Masson did not speak about her own suffering during the war. Rather, she focused on the experiences of the people whom she has helped through the BDOM. The following is part of her story:

> There have been many kinds of atrocities in this area. Most people hear only about raped women. There certainly have been many horrible cases of rapes in Bukavu, Kaniola, Walungu, and in many other villages. You will hear from women whose genital organs have been mutilated, those who were taken captive and became sex slaves, etc. It is horrible. But focusing on sexual violence runs the risk of making us forget the many other forms of violence in South Kivu. I have been many times to the villages that have been destroyed by armed groups. You can find many survivors of rape in those towns; but rape is not the only thing. There are people whose limbs were cut off; others lost everything: families, property, etc. Even if we focused on rape, we cannot approach the situation as if the woman who is raped did not have family, children, husband, friend, or village. When one woman is raped, it is the whole village that is traumatized, and we should attend to the needs of all the members of the community. Also, in many areas where I have been, people would prefer to help the survivors of rapes as members of the community, not isolate them. It is the village that is traumatized. I mean,

they do not want us to isolate the survivors, because we could expose them to many acts of discrimination. Because many international NGOs would only help survivors of sexual violence, they often ignore people and communities where violence has done much damage.

Maria Masson's story highlights two important issues. The first is the one we have already mentioned: the need to see rape as part of the larger problem of violence. The second is the need to understand the victims or survivors of violence as members of communities, not as isolated individuals whom we want to help. The testimonies of my interviewees support both observations. In what follows I will discuss the different forms of violence that have been used in DRC and their impact on Congolese populations.

Rape and sexual violence

Rape and sexual violence have been some of the most common means of domination, humiliation, and destruction during the Congolese wars, as has been also the case in many other countries. Recent years have seen an increase in attention to recognizing rape as a war crime. On 21 March 2016, the International Criminal Court found Jean-Pierre Bemba Gombo of the DRC guilty of wartime sex crimes.[18] The condemnation of Bemba was the first of its kind, but it shows how the work of concerned individuals and communities has led to the recognition of the use of rape as a "weapon of war."[19] Rape is not simply a *consequence* of war; it is part of the *strategy* of war. For Gita Sahgal of Amnesty International,

> It was a mistake to think such assaults were primarily about the age-old "spoils of war," or sexual gratification. Rape is often used in ethnic conflicts as a way for attackers to perpetuate their social control and redraw ethnic boundaries. Women are seen as the reproducers and care-givers of the community. Therefore if one group wants to control another they often do it by impregnating women of the other community because they see it as a way of destroying the opposing community.[20]

---

18. https://www.icc-cpi.int/car/bemba (accessed on July 23, 2016).

19. See the discussion in Card, "Rape as a Weapon of War," 5–18. Cf. Amnesty International, "Sudan, Darfur: Rape as a Weapon of War."

20. Smith-Spark, "How Did Rape Become a Weapon of War?" (http://news.bbc.co.uk/2/hi/4078677.stm, 2004/12/08. Accessed on April 10, 2016).

The Congolese wars are not primarily "ethnic wars." The rebel groups and militia groups that sow desolation in the DRC do not focus on destroying one particular ethnicity. Struggle for political power and economic advantages (illegal use of minerals, occupation of lands, and ransoms) seem to be the principal causes of wars in the DRC. But Sahgal's statement is true of the Congolese wars, even if those wars are not ethnic. The widespread cases of rape in the DRC, especially in North Kivu and South Kivu,[21] show that rape has become a powerful tool through which the rapist shows his superiority over the raped woman and over the community in which the woman lives. The armed groups that engage in those atrocities (especially the *Mai-Mai*[22] and the FDLR) do not engage in ethnic conflicts, and they do not choose their victims based on ethnic identities. Nonetheless, by raping women in villages, the assailants terrorize the villages, create insecurity and feelings of hopelessness in society, and disfigure members of those communities for the sake of dominating them and plundering them. Here is the story of Faida, a Congolese survivor from the village of Walungu (about 30 kms from downtown Bukavu, South Kivu):

> It was in 2005. They (FDLR) came from Kaniola. They attacked our village. They raped me, then they took knives and started introducing them into my parts. Then they took fire and burned me between the legs. I have scars everywhere. They tied my husband on the bed and beat him many times. He was watching; they tied him. They also raped my daughter. My husband was watching. They took everything from our house and forced my husband to carry. They took me to the forest; the village thought I was dead. We were there with many other women. It was terrible. The guard who was watching over us asked me to do it with him so that he could set me free. I had no choice; he did

21. Angèle Diabang's 2015 documentary, *Congo: The Doctor Who Saves Women* (2015) speaks about the work of the 2018 Nobel Prize co-winner Dr. Denis Mukwege, a Congolese gynecologist and founder of the Panzi hospital. This hospital focuses on helping women who have been victims of sexual violence in eastern DRC.

22. The *Mai-Mai* are local fighters opposed to anyone whom they consider to be colluding with foreign powers to usurp Congolese soil and riches. On paper, the *Mai-Mai* are on the side of local populations against foreign invasions. They are often members of communities that feel that the central government has failed in defending the integrity of national territory. The biggest problem is that the *Mai-Mai* lack financial resources to fund a war. As a result, they terrorize local populations (through rapes of women, looting, attacks on villages, etc.) in order for the populations to provide them with needed resources.

it and set me free. I ran away from the forest. They took everything from me: goats, chickens, everything. When we arrived back in the village, many people came to welcome us, but some laughed at us. We were a bit rejected even from our families. Now, it is only the parish that is supporting us. We have suffered too much. We do not even know how to raise our children. My daughter is very traumatized now.[23] We do not know who will console us. I spent four months in the hospital. Wherever you are, speak about our story. My husband can no longer work after being beaten.

Faida's story includes the forcible assault that opens the scene and the fact that it happens in front of her husband and children. Rape has a different purpose than sexual satisfaction. The most obvious purposes of this rape are the creation of terror, humiliation, domination, and the redefinition of shame boundaries. Physical pain and mutilation left scars in Faida's body, and they continue to remind her of that fateful night. The act of rape not only inflicted physical pain but impacted Faida and her family in many other ways. DRC society is mostly patriarchal. The man is expected to be the protector of his household. Protecting their children and their wives, especially exclusively owning the sexuality of their wives and preventing access to it by other men, are part of men's responsibilities. But in the case of Faida, things have fallen apart. The protector is tied to a bed and is forced to watch the desecration of his household. By raping Faida and her daughter in front of Faida's husband, the assailants send a clear message to their victims: the assailants are the sole masters of that household, and both Faida and her daughter have no one to protect them. The repetition of "my husband was watching" in Faida's story tells us that the husband was not doing what he was supposed to do: he was not supposed to be watching the thing he should have been able to stop. Every member of Faida's family is humiliated, tainted, and tamed. They have been shown that resisting the assailants was useless, because the assailants obviously had power to control even the most intimate parts of their lives. But this message is sent also to neighbors and friends who hear the story of Faida and her family.

Rapes are common in DRC since the beginning of the wars. Every time a woman is raped, other women hear about it and believe they

---

23. Most of the survivors knew the term "trauma" and, by that word, they meant anything from simple fear, feeling of helplessness, feeling too shamed to be seen in public, to complete loss of hope and trust in people or in the orderliness of the world.

could be the next targets. The assailants instill this fear in them and communicate to them that, when their turn arrives, they should offer no resistance.[24]

Rapes have also redefined societies and social boundaries. Some survivors of sexual violence, for example, can no longer think about marriage or sexual intercourse without connecting these acts to their experiences of violence and rape. That is the case with Emilia Kasando from Walungu:

> They came to our house and took my husband and my son. The FDLR. They killed them. They stabbed me with a knife. They tied me, and raped me many times, even with pieces of wood. They beat me all over my body. They tortured me. I was brought to Panzi hospital. They removed my womb. I live with my two daughters. I spent six months in the hospital. I do not want to get married again, because I hate men now. I just take care of my children. I can never finish this story. Life goes on. I have no chance. I am just trying to survive.

Mathilde Muhingu laments the fact that rape threatens the future of South Kivu, "because", she asked, "if women no longer want to get married or bear children, who will replace us? Who will live in our villages after we are gone? What are these people thinking? Do they want our society to end?" Muhingu's questions convey the fear of extinction that violence and rape have sown in many communities in eastern DRC.

Other women also spoke of being forced to hold a lamp while the rebels raped their daughters or their daughters-in-law. Some men were also forced to rape their own daughters, their daughters-in-law, or women with sexually transmittable diseases. According to Georges, a local counselor in Kaniola, local Mashi customs consider it a curse for a man to see the nudity of his daughter or daughter-in-law and vice versa. It is also a curse if a woman sees the nakedness of her daughter-in-law or vice versa. By forcing these people to watch the rapes of the people whose nudity they are culturally forbidden to see or to rape the members of their own families, the rebels communicate to the victims that their villages and themselves have been placed under a curse. The world as they used to know it has ended, and a new world, a world of chaos and terror, has been forced upon them.

---

24. Card, "Rape as a Weapon of War," 7–8.

Some of the survivors whom I met have been infected with HIV/AIDS or other sexually transmissible diseases. Others suffer from vaginal fistulas, which also affect their emotional well-being. In addition, many survivors of rape face social stigma; they are rejected by their spouses or the families of their spouses. That was the case with Agnes from Goma:

> It was in 2002; we met some people on the way to our farms. As we were going, six police officers took me. They raped me. When my husband heard about it, he rejected me. His family also insisted that my husband reject me. Caritas helped me have a meeting with my in-laws and my husband. As a result, my husband took me back. When I see other women, I am very ashamed: I do not think I am like other women. I am so humiliated.

Even though churches and NGOs have been helping these victims, especially by convincing their families to accept them, many victims still struggle with the experience of social stigma. Blaming the victim is common in cases of rapes. In many communities in the DRC, almost everyone lives in fear of the military, paramilitary, and rebel groups, who invade villages to kill and to rape. However, when a woman is raped, it is easy for families and neighbors to suggest that somehow the victim consented to being raped. Rape victims are often called "whores," and their husbands, if they do not send their wives away, are considered weak. Women who are raped on their farms and whose experiences have not been made public often choose to keep their experiences to themselves and suffer in silence, because breaking that silence could make their lives more miserable.

These cases of sexual violence have also created a new kind of vulnerable population: the children born of war. Some victims conceive and give birth to children as the result of rapes. Survivors and their caregivers identify three main challenges resulting from conceiving children from rape. First, for the survivors, these children are a reminder of their ordeals. Waleed, a survivor from Goma, told me that she was not even able to breastfeed or look at her twins when they were born. Because she was raped by many men over a long period of time, she did not know who the father of her children was. Even though she did not consent to being raped, the birth of these children has made her believe that she is "mother of bastards." For her, these children are a curse. Studying the plight of children born of rape in Rwanda, Marie Consolée Mukangendo reports that "numerous victims have rejected their babies after giving birth, ashamed of carrying the child of a Rwandan Hutu militiaman.... Some pregnant women committed suicide rather than give birth to a 'child of hate'... and other women committed infanticide."[25] It took Waleed many months and counseling before she could accept the children or take care of them.

The second problem is the lack of a legal father. Arsene Lumpali, a lawyer working for the diocesan commission on Justice and Peace of the Archdiocese of Bukavu reports the following:

> In this society, children belong to the lineage of their father. But since the rapists are the biological fathers of these children, in society, everyone considers those children to be children of the enemy. It is very difficult to reverse that belief; so many children are stigmatized, even by their own mothers. But as a Christian lawyer, I try to speak to family members to convince them to adopt those children as their own. I help them go to court, where we convince an uncle or the grandfather of the child to adopt her. But this is not easy, because many family members do not accept those children.

The third problem is the status of those children when they start growing up. Many of them are ostracized because, as Mukangendo observed about a similar phenomenon in Rwanda, these children are considered "children of bad memories," "children of hate," "devil's children," or "little killers."

Beating, maiming, abductions, summary executions, and massacres

Rape has been one of the most devastating and most publicized features of violence in eastern DRC. But as it is clear from the stories we are analyzing, rape is not the only form of violence committed against populations in DRC. In Faida's story, we heard of beatings, burnings, and of abductions. In many cases, the militiamen would cut off the limbs of the victims or rip open pregnant women, like in this case of one of the abducted victims from Walungu:

> We had a lot of problems during the war. We were taken to the forest by the FDLR. One friend with whom I was abducted was pregnant. The soldiers wanted to see how a child sits inside a woman's womb. They ripped open her belly, and they killed

---

25. Mukangendo, "Caring for Children Born of Rape in Rwanda," 43.

the child she was bearing; they killed her too. They beat us and forced us to sleep with those uncircumcised men. They wanted to hang us on a cross like Jesus. We were obliged to remain without clothes all the time. One woman could sleep with ten men in one day. I think hell is in that forest. There are all the kinds of sufferings there. They killed our husbands. It was in 2008. They took one woman, then they cut off her breasts and burned them in fire. Then they also burned her. When they are tired of you, they kill you and come to get other women.

It is common for armed groups to torture villagers and disable them. Men and women who are beaten are not able to work or to function in society. Almost all the subjects found that the violence inflicted on them was senseless, since they had never been part of the military or of any group that opposed the activities of these terrorist groups. What stories of destroyed bodies tell us is that violence in eastern DRC has left many communities with disabled individuals who can no longer play a full role in the life of the community. Not only their bodies, but also their lives have been torn apart.

Some villages have also experienced cases of large-scale massacres. The village of Kaniola, for example, has become a symbol of violence and rapes in the DRC, because of the repeated massacres that have been carried out in that village. Before I went to South Kivu, I had heard many horrible stories about violence and rapes in Kaniola: public massacres of hundreds of people, public rapes, burned houses, destroyed or burned farms, destroyed churches, etc. In the middle of the village stands a shrine called "*Place des Martyrs*." The villagers of Kaniola, led by the local Catholic priest, built this modest shrine in order to "preserve the memory of the thousands of people who have been murdered in the village of Kaniola and in the villages around Kaniola," as Georges, the diocesan psychological counselor from Kaniola, told me. The "*Place des Martyrs*" catalogues not only the names of the victims of massacres in Kaniola but also the names of the victims from neighboring villages. Between 1996 and 2008, the archdiocese of Bukavu has identified 230 victims of massacres in the small village of Kaniola alone.[26] Survivors of those massacres continue to live with the fear of facing similar executions in the future.

Survivors also spoke of abductions, detentions, and captivity. In many cases, the victims are enslaved for weeks or months in the forests. During all the time of captivity, the victims are under the total control of

---

26. Nzuzi, *La Pastorale Justice et Paix dans l'Archidiocèse de Bukavu*, 70–79.

their assailants. As is noted by Herman, the victims of abductions have deeper wounds than victims of sporadic attacks because they experience violence on a regular basis and for a long period.[27] Through various means (beating, rape, or mutilation) the perpetrator not only breaks the body of the victim, but also instills the fear of further torture, should the victim try to escape. The victims are often shown heaps of corpses or are invited to watch when their companions are being killed or tortured. These techniques instill fear; they also invite the surviving victim to be thankful for not undergoing the same treatment as their companions. Herman has observed that, in situations of captivity, the perpetrator uses various methods to establish control over the victim. Among the most common are physical violence, threats, and small "rewards" that try to convince the victim of the benevolence of the perpetrator.[28]

In eastern DRC, almost every village experiences abductions on a regular basis. These repeated abductions create a feeling of helplessness in the whole village. Since the abductors use no criteria in selecting captives, every member of the community fears that she or a family member might be the next victim. Such spread of fear in communities immobilizes the villagers and makes it difficult for them to think about or plan for the future.

Economic and environmental consequences of violence

In addition to breaking individuals and communities, abductions have also changed people's relationship with the geography of the country, with economic and ecological repercussions. Even though it was in the forests that villagers used to farm, forests no longer represent opportunities for the communities; they have become a threat, "hell," as one survivor called them. Forests and mountainous regions where abductors take their victims have been destroyed by villagers, because they are perceived as sites of torture. The decision to cut down all trees from forests has offered the immediate benefit that communities can now perceive danger even from a long distance and so can escape to other villages. However, that decision also exposes the communities to stronger winds and warmer temperature, makes agriculture difficult, and deprives the community of resources to build houses and huts. This is a dramatic situation for the

---

27. Herman, *Trauma and Recovery*, 74.
28. Herman, *Trauma and Recovery*, 77.

life of communities that mainly depend on agriculture. Most villagers have decided not to go to the farms anymore because farms have become the places in which the victims are tortured. Besides the fact that terrorists have burned many farms, some of the farms are simply abandoned by their owners who fear for their lives and their security. Villages like Kaniola and Walungu now experience situations of famine that can be reversed only if their inhabitants can return to their farms without fear of violence.

In addition, those attacks on the villages have been accompanied with looting, plundering, and destruction of property. The pattern of most attacks on the villages has been quite consistent in many cases: the terrorists would attack the village, rape women, beat men, and take food and everything valuable from the houses of their victims. In many cases, they would keep hostages and require excessive ransoms, without which they would threaten to kill (or would kill) their victims and/or their families. Kafikuri, a man from Kaniola had such an experience:

> It was during the war in 2000; some people came to my house at 10 pm. I have two children. They took me with them to the forest and forced me to carry the things they had stolen. When we arrived in the forest of Tshikundushe, they required that I give a $400 ransom, without which they would kill my wife. I sent a message to the village that they look for money and send it to me. Unfortunately, when that money came, they had already killed my wife. We were five people. After giving them money, they set me free. They beat me, using knives and pieces of wood. We rarely ate. My wife was killed in 2000. Now, I sell firewood.

In the DRC, most people live on less than one US Dollar a day. Requiring a $400 ransom from Kafikuri meant that he had to find more than a year's wages in order to save his life and those of his family members. Numerous survivors recounted stories like that of Kafikuri. They also spoke about people who were burned inside their houses when the rebels realized that their victims could not provide what they required.

Destruction of communities

I have already hinted at the emotional toll of these violent acts upon the members of the communities in eastern DRC. But an important element we have not addressed in this discussion is the anger that still characterizes many survivors. For many, the FDLR and other armed groups are simply monsters who deserve destruction. No matter who does the job of destruction, such a person would be hailed as the God-sent Moses of the community. In South Kivu, for example, almost everyone regards general Falker Mike (FM) as one of the greatest heroes of the region. FM had been a *Mai-Mai* fighter, but he later joined the national army. After integration into the national army, he was sent back to South Kivu to fight the terrorist groups that orchestrated desolation in that region. Because he had been part of the groups operating in the region, FM knew well where to find his former companions. Within a few weeks, he liberated many hostages, disbanded many terrorist groups, and gave some relief to villages like Kaniola, Walungu, Ninja, and Mulamba. Villagers rejoiced and rushed into forests to see where the corpses of terrorists lay without burial.

FM was eventually recalled by his superiors to Kinshasa, and no one in the region has ever heard of him again. After his departure, the demons of desolation that he had provoked came back and have been unleashing their anger on every village that they suspect to have participated in FM's operations.

Some survivors said that they had started finding ways of moving on with their lives, but none of them even alluded to the possibility of forgiving the terrorists who had destroyed their villages. Rather, they wished there had been more people like FM to liberate them and to avenge the lives of their families and relatives. All the survivors whom I interviewed had been involved in post-traumatic healing programs organized by the Catholic Church. All of them praised the Church for offering them psycho-social assistance, or start-up programs for reintegration into society. However, it was not clear how much the Catholic Church has helped these survivors imagine their lives beyond hate and the sentiment of revenge. The survivors think about the perpetrators only as offenders, people to be destroyed. The perpetrators live in unseen forests far away and in the minds of the survivors, where they continue to inspire anger and fear. Abbé Justin Nzuzi, the director of the CDJP-Bukavu, names the formation of a reconciled society as one of the goals of the work of the Church with the survivors. However, he does not specify how the process of reconciliation will work nor does he say how victims and survivors will be involved in that process.[29]

---

29. Nzuzi, *La Pastorale Justice et Paix dans l'Archidiocèse de Bukavu*, 117, 163.

Anger and hatred directed toward the perpetrators also have repercussions in the lives of communities. Individuals have started suspecting one another, and so mutual trust and solidarity have been eroded. Abbé Jean-Baptiste, the pastor of a Catholic parish in Walungu, gives the following testimony:

> In the past, people used to trust one another in this village. But since the beginning of the wars, people suspect one another. Solidarity is vanishing. Even within the same families, people can easily suspect one another. They fear that others might betray them. We have no institutions that we can trust. We are on our own. Many women now think that all the men are rapists. People used to be very hospitable in this village. But now every foreigner is a potential Interahamwe[30] or FDLR or *Mai-Mai*. Before the war, there was respect for one another, especially for the elders. But children have seen rebels torture the elders; they have seen them naked. They now imitate that. Death used to be a mystery. When they buried someone, children would not get close to the grave. But now, there is no effort to see a dead person. Death has become banal; life has become banal.

Speaking about the recrudescence of cases of rape by civilians in South Kivu, Arsene Lumpali, the lawyer of the CDJP-Bukavu, also spoke about the contamination of evil: "You cannot focus only on the survivors raped by the rebels or armed groups. Since the beginning of the wars, it looks like people have learned how to rape women. Even regular people in society are now raping women."

These stories of the spread of atrocities in society are rightly disturbing, because they point to one of the common consequences of wars: the spread of violence into everyday life, even after the war has officially ended. Once rapes, assassinations, torture, and death become so common as to look like a part of ordinary life, even ordinary members of the community are likely to find it banal to commit those atrocities. Evil can still be recognized as such, but it might no longer shock some members of the community.

Another consequence of this ubiquity of acts of violence on the lives of communities in the DRC is that the language used by the people often reflects a situation of war. Stories told by survivors, even when not directly related to war, show the impact that war has had on the thinking of

---

30. This Kinyarwanda term means, "those who work together" or "those who fight together." It is often used interchangeably with FDLR.

individuals. Cathy Caruth has shown that the wounds inflicted by traumatic events do not disappear, and they have an endless impact on the survivors. They can intrude into everything that the survivor does.[31] We see that impact of traumatic violence on the people of eastern DRC. I will illustrate this by telling the story of the impact of war on the drawings of some children from Kaniola.

Maria Masson from BDOM-Bukavu has been looking for funds to help children born of war and children living in poverty in South Kivu. During one of Masson's trips to Belgium, children from one Belgian elementary school sent donations and drawings to the children of Kaniola. The drawings of Belgian children showed trains, cars, buses, houses, and multi-story buildings. After giving the children of Kaniola the gifts from their Belgian friends, Masson asked them to make some drawings to send back to the Belgian children. No instructions were given about the kinds of drawings the children were to make. To Mason's surprise, almost all the drawings of the Kaniola children showed people running, houses burning, or men carrying weapons. The drawings of the children of Kaniola reflected the realities of war and violence. For Masson, "these children have been traumatized, and the first thing that comes to their mind is the violence that their community has endured."

One could argue that these children simply reproduced what they saw, and they could have done that even if the violence of war had not traumatized them. That is possible. Masson simply invited the children to make some drawings to send to the children in Belgium so it was natural for them to reproduce what was readily available to them. The problem with this explanation is that, according to Masson, there had been more than a year since assailants last made raids on Kaniola, so scenes of war and violence would not have been the closest thing the children could imagine and represent. Some other events could have happened in the village or in individual families since the last time the children saw acts of violence by militiamen (e.g., births, Christmas parties, or liturgical celebrations), and they could have made drawings about those events. Also, since they were at school, they could have made drawings about school, about Masson's visit, or about something they saw at the moment of drawing. They could have even imitated the drawings sent them by the Belgian children. But they drew about something that was long past. That they represented their experiences of war and violence might suggest that

---

31. Caruth, *Unclaimed Experience*, 7.

these experiences have become part of the lives of these children in a way that they do not fully comprehend. The scars of war have become part of who these children are. The memories of war and violence seem to live inside the children, and they intrude into their behaviors and thinking. These drawings became the means through which the wounds of past events were expressed.[32]

Even though all these children drew pictures about war and violence, I am not arguing that violence affects all people in the same way, or that every time a person experiences a violent event that person is automatically traumatized. Some people can have a higher degree of resilience than others. But not being personally traumatized does not mean that one does not live with the impact of war in the community. Even if someone could personally have a high degree of resilience, nonetheless, as a member of a disrupted community, that person is implicated in the suffering of other members of the community. Traumatic events do not only break individuals; they also break social beliefs and customs and alter the collective memories and identities of communities.

My own life has been an example of how an apparently unharmed individual can bear the wounds of the community. Even though I lived in the DRC during some of the most violent years in the recent history of the country, I neither was personally harmed nor lost any member of my family as a result of wars. And yet, the memories of summary executions and abandoned corpses, the images of wounded soldiers and civilians, the experience of uncertainty and chaos during the wars continue to affect me to such an extent that these experiences also inform the way I view the world.

The interviews that I have just analyzed highlight some of the questions and concerns that I bring to my conversation with the book of Nahum in this book. How can Congolese society prevent the rape of its women? How should Congolese society treat women who have already been raped, helping them own their past, and yet without excluding them from social life? How can churches, NGOs, and the government attend to the wounds of survivors of wars? How can Congolese communities care for children born of war? How can Congolese society reduce the likelihood of violent conflicts and transform existing ones? How can we reestablish trust between individuals and communities? How can churches and schools form children and adults in building a more peaceful DRC?

---

32. Caruth, *Unclaimed Experience*, 4.

More immediately, what vision does the Bible offer that can bring former enemies together, to recall their past and to imagine possibilities of reconciled communities in the DRC?

Conclusion

In this chapter, I have drawn a context for the interpretation of the book of Nahum in the DRC. I have considered the way the violence of war has affected communities in the DRC, especially in the provinces of North Kivu and South Kivu. I have described how experiences of violence and trauma shape the questions and the assumptions that I bring to the book of Nahum. Consideration of these experiences of violence and trauma is necessary, because it offers the potential for generating a better reading of Nahum, a reading that can bring healing to these same broken communities. However, claiming that this text can bring healing to the community also implies that the text offers something that is independent from the community, something the community does not have or might not want to have. The text, in the words of Jonathan Draper, has to be recognized as "a significant *other*" with which I enter into conversation.[33] As I noted in chapter 1, unless I take into account the otherness and independence of the text of Nahum, my reading of this book runs the risk of becoming simply the echo of my fears, worries, and joys. It is then necessary to explore the genre and literary data of the book of Nahum as well as the world from which and within which the book emerged. Thus, the following chapter will focus on the study of the genre and form of the book of Nahum.

---

33. Draper, "African Contextual Hermeneutics," 15. Italics in the original.

3

On the Genre, the Form, and the Poetics of the Book of Nahum

> What a lyric poet does is to imagine for us a certain state of mind and soul and then to invite us into that imagined (re-created, refined), dynamic inwardness in order to let us contemplate for ourselves our own memories of our inward motions of mind and soul.... What a good lyric enables and encourages us to say is, "I feel something like that, but that is not exactly how I feel."[1]

Introduction

THIS CHAPTER STUDIES THE genre and form of the book of Nahum. I show that the book is a lyric poem in the form of a modified city lament. It uses lyric poetry so as to evoke the experience of war in the memories of its audience and also to reveal the assuring presence of YHWH in the midst of violence. It presents that revelation by adapting two traditional literary forms, the biblical OAN and the ANE city lament.

The poet, as has been acknowledged by the majority of Nahum scholars, was a superb artist, using a wide range of poetic and syntactical devices in such a way as to give the reader the impression of finding herself within a battle scene.[2] Because the poet speaks to an audience that is afflicted (1:12), under a yoke and in bondage (1:13), invaded

---

1. Johnson, *The Idea of Lyric*, 74.
2. Spronk, *Nahum*, 6.

(2:1), and ravaged (2:3), this vivid depiction of the war scenes is likely to evoke in the audience personal memories of war. However, the book does not simply take the reader back to the past. Rather, it brings the reader imaginatively into the presence of YHWH, whose voice, character, and action dominate the book. In the midst of total destruction, YHWH is revealed as the only enduring presence, the only reliable refuge (1:7), despite YHWH's own involvement in violence. Just as he vividly depicts the conditions of war, the prophet also depicts YHWH with such power that Israel's Deity becomes visible to the eyes of the mind.

The Genre Question in Nahum

Herman Gunkel's seminal work made the study of genre central to biblical interpretation, with a primary concern for the social context (*Sitz im Leben*) in which forms of oral literature were supposed to have originated and circulated.[3] My own focus here is not on *Sitz im Leben*. Rather, I focus on the communicative potential of lyric as a poetic form, as distinct from the literary forms of epic (narrative) and drama, which may be more familiar to biblical scholars and other students of ancient literature.

Epic and dramatic poems tend to be lengthy compositions, characterized by an argument, a plot line, and developed characters.[4] Lyric poetry, by contrast, is often brief, without a plot or a discursive argument. In lyric, we may find no clear storyline connecting the various parts of a poem. The structure is often paratactic; verses and images are juxtaposed without clear connections and transitions. In order to overcome "the fragmentation produced by its paratactic flow so as to achieve a sense of cohesion," lyric poetry uses "other means, most notably the address of voice(s), musicality, imagistic and/or stylistic use of language."[5] This type of poetry is also characterized by direct addresses between the poet and his audience. W. R. Johnson says that one of the most important characteristics of lyric poetry is the I-You interaction. The poet, even when he pretends to be speaking to himself or to a third party, almost always presupposes a listening you.[6] We shall return to a more detailed treat-

---

3. Mihelic, "The Influence of Form Criticism on the Study of the Old Testament," 122.
4. Heffelfinger, *I Am Large*, 38–39.
5. Heffelfinger, *I Am Large*, 37.
6. Johnson, *The Idea of Lyric*, 3–5.

ment of the characteristics of lyric poetry in a later section. At this point, it will suffice to point out that scholars have recently started to treat some poems of the Hebrew Bible not simply as "poetry," but as "lyric poetry," urging for a different way of reading those texts than has been done in the past.[7]

An important contribution in that direction has been Katie M. Heffelfinger's study of Second Isaiah according to the conventions of the lyric genre. She has shown that Second Isaiah is a lyric poem that achieves cohesion through the description of the presence of the speaking voice of YHWH throughout the book. Similarly, this study argues that Nahum uses the lyric genre to present images of a world of war and violence, where YHWH is sovereign.

Some, like Julia O'Brien, have argued that Nahum's literary artistry is key to understanding its meaning.[8] As will be shown throughout this chapter and the next, when we consider the fact that Nahum is lyric poetry and read it accordingly, we hear more than one point of view. We find for example that the book also allows the cries of the Ninevites to be heard, without specifically saying whether the reader should rejoice over those cries or feel compassion for the lamenters. In her *Readings* commentary on Nahum, Julia O'Brien acknowledges that the book uses many tropes to convey its message, especially ambiguity so as to avoid easy identification of who the enemies of YHWH are and who his friends are.[9] But, because O'Brien *chooses* to privilege the concern of "real readers" over what she calls "text-centered approaches" that "fail to take into account historical, diverse readers,"[10] she follows the lead of the text only as far as the text does not contradict her intention to give a human face to the "Other." In her commentary, meant to be a literary reading of the book, in which "appreciation of the artistry of this book facilitates an understanding of the powerful effects it has on its readers and allows us to enter into more fruitful dialogue with Nahum's ethical world,"[11] she does not discuss the question of genre. The consequence of O'Brien's reading that goes against the intention of the text is that, even though she wants to avoid easy solutions to the questions of atrocity, misogyny,

---

7. See Dobbs-Allsopp, *On Biblical Poetry*.
8. O'Brien, *Nahum*, 2.
9. O'Brien, *Nahum*, 134.
10. O'Brien, *Nahum*, 13.
11. O'Brien, *Nahum*, 2.

and "othering" in Nahum, she often reverts to conclusions that suggest that Nahum is either a story about YHWH's destruction of Nineveh or a drama reenacting that destruction and urging the Judahites to join YHWH in destroying Nineveh. So, she says, for example, that Nahum is single-mindedly focused on the destruction of Nineveh,[12] or that Nahum calls for vengeance against Nineveh.[13] We can point out, however, that Nahum never encourages anyone to take vengeance on Nineveh (YHWH has already done it) and that detailed description of violence against someone is not necessarily an invitation for others to add more violence to an already-destroyed victim. It is more plausible that the detailed description of rape, destruction, and violence functions as an invitation to the reader to have empathy for the victim or to side with Nineveh and lament the violence done to her (see Lam 1:12). O'Brien of course arrives at the conclusion that we need to lament Nineveh's destruction. But she reaches that conclusion by reading "against the intentions of an author."[14] And yet, if one integrated O'Brien's many attentive literary observations with attention to Nahum's literary genre as lyric, it would become obvious that the book does not defend a particular argument, and what O'Brien considers to be "reading against the intentions of the author" can be shown to derive from the text's own suggestions.

Another aspect of the book that can be illumined by taking into account Nahum's literary genre is the vivid depiction of the scenes of war. As we will see it in chapter 4, some scholars believe that such vivid descriptions are signs that Nahum was an eyewitness of the fall of Nineveh is 612 BCE, and the book makes a historical reference to that destruction.[15] As will be shown below, such vivid depictions of reality are part of Nahum's genre as lyric poetry. The poet certainly is familiar with the experience of war, but lyric poetry aims at evocation, not reportage. It is grounded on the experiences of the audience, but it does not merely dwell on that experience.

Within the broad genre of lyric poetry, the poem takes the particular forms of an OAN and a modified city lament. Discussion of those forms prepares us to see how Nahum's poem functions in its specific context.

12. O'Brien, *Nahum*, 129.
13. O'Brien, *Nahum*, 142.
14. O'Brien, *Nahum*, 125.
15. See Machinist, "The Fall of Assyria," 181–82; Sweeney, *The Twelve Prophets*, 422.

Nahum as an OAN and a Modified City Lament

Modern scholars have categorized the book of Nahum variously as a liturgical hymn commemorating the fall of Nineveh in 612 BCE[16] or the victory of the Jews over Nicanor in 161 BCE;[17] a pamphlet of propaganda against Assyria;[18] a refutation speech/poem;[19] a prophetic exemplum;[20] or resistance literature.[21] The book combines some elements from those genres, but it seems better to understand the book as an OAN that has close connections to the genre of lament. The introductory depiction of YHWH in Nah 1, for example, shows some similarities with biblical hymns (see Pss 47; 93; 99), which might make the book fit for liturgical use; but we have no proof that liturgy was the primary purpose of this book (let alone that the book served as commemoration song for some victory over the enemies). The book clearly has political overtones, but it does not seem to urge the Judahites to do anything or to take military actions against Assyria. The book shows that the battle will take place outside Judah: it will be between YHWH and Nineveh (with the Judahites playing no obvious role in it). Marvin Sweeney's claim that the book is a refutation speech within a situation of disputation hangs on his own interpretation of Nah 1:9. For him, this verse questions people's low estimation of YHWH's power. The book apparently presupposes that both Judahites and Assyrians held inaccurate beliefs about YHWH's power.[22] As has been shown by Michael Floyd, the book of Nahum addresses (among other things) the question of YHWH's power, but the book cannot be considered simply as a refutation speech.[23] Adrian Graffy, on whose thoughts Sweeney draws, identifies two main parts of a disputation: quotation of (or allusion to) the opinions of the prophet's opponents (or the people to whom he speaks) and the refutation by the prophet.[24] The book of Nahum does not have quotations of (or even allusions to) the opinion of the audience.

16. Humbert, "Essai d'analyse de Nahoum 1, 2—2,3," 270.
17. Haupt, "The Book of Nahum," 1.
18. Haldar, *Studies in the Book of Nahum*, 88–89.
19. Sweeney, *The Twelve Prophets*, 424–31.
20. Floyd, *Minor Prophets*, 10.
21. Wessels, "Nahum," 625–26.
22. Sweeney, *The Twelve Prophets*, 426.
23. Floyd, *Minor Prophets*, 12–14.
24. Graffy, *A Prophet Confronts his People*, 107–10.

It certainly should be granted that, in light of what the book says about the condition of the audience (1:12, 13; 2:1, 3), it is plausible that Nahum's audience grappled with the question of YHWH's power in a violent world. However, refuting beliefs about YHWH's power does not seem to be the main problem with which the book is dealing. The answer to affliction, foreign invasions, etc., is not necessarily found in affirming YHWH's power. Biblical laments show us that, when the Israelites were afflicted or oppressed, their main question was not always whether YHWH was powerful or not. Most laments acknowledge that YHWH is powerful; but the reason for lamenting is because the lamenter cannot understand why YHWH, *who is so powerful*, does not use that power to the advantage of his people (cf. Pss 44:1–23; 88:7–9; Job 7:12–14).

Michael Floyd also suggests a solution of his own to the question of Nahum's genre. He says that we should treat Nahum as the book designates itself (1:1), that is, as a maśśā'. Floyd believes that, as a maśśā' Nahum functions as an historical exemplum. After the fall of Nineveh in 612 BCE, he argues, Nahum studied some previous prophecies about the fall of Nineveh (prophecies believed to be reported in Nah 1:12–14), and then interpreted the predictions of those prophecies in light of the new reality of the fall of Nineveh. The purpose of the book of Nahum is then to urge Judah and all the nations to celebrate the fall of Nineveh and to teach a historical lesson to both Judah and Assyria that those who oppose YHWH will be destroyed.[25] Floyd's argument rests on three unproved presuppositions: the first one is that Nahum wrote after the fall of Nineveh in 612 BCE. As we will show in the next chapter, nothing from the book of Nahum requires that we treat Nahum as a *vaticinum post eventum*. The second presupposition is that when the book speaks about "the one who plots evil against YHWH" (1:11), he is referring to the departure of Sennacherib from Judah in 701 BCE (see 2 Kgs 19:36; Isa 37:37; 2 Chr 32:21). The main problem with relying on this enigmatic verse about the departure of the "one who plots evil against YHWH" is that we have no proof compelling us to believe that Nahum actually speaks about Sennacherib. The third presupposition is that Nahum studied some previously proclaimed prophecies, and then appropriated them (in 1:12–14) in light of the departure of Sennacherib from Judah and in light of the fall of Nineveh is 612 BCE. However, those verses do

---

25. Floyd, "The מַשָּׂא (Maśśā') as a Type of Prophetic Book," 413.

not indicate that here Nahum is interpreting some previous prophecies; rather, they read as divine resolutions to end the affliction of Judah.

At the end of the twentieth century, Wilhelm Wessels suggested that we read the book of Nahum as protest/resistance literature. For Wessels, Nahum resembles many (African) poetic texts that come from people living under oppression or domination. Such texts voice the dissatisfaction of the suffering people.[26] This kind of literature, Wessels continues, is *not necessarily aimed at bringing violence upon the oppressor*; its primary goal is to air the rage and frustration of the oppressed.[27] Wessels believes that the primary function of Nahum is to portray an alternative world for the Judahites, a world in which YHWH—not Assyria—holds power. By portraying this alternative world, then, the book of Nahum can give courage and faith to the oppressed and allow them to act "in constructive and creative ways that will impact on the future."[28] To assert that Nahum voices personal experiences means that Nahum's text personalizes the experiences of the members of his community. When his audience hears his poems they may recognize themselves, each one personally, in the images presented by the poet.

The function of Nahum as resistance literature corresponds to its literary form as an OAN. The book presents itself as an oracle indicting Nineveh for its violence (Nah 3:1), its oppression of other nations (Nah 3:4), and its pride and effrontery against YHWH (Nah 1:9; 3:8). The content and form of the book resemble those of some prophetic books/passages and some psalms (e.g., Isa 10:5–11; 13:1—23:18; Jer 45–51; Ezek 25–31; Amos 1–2; Obad; Pss 2; 83; 137:8–9; 149:6–9).[29] Some of the features of the OAN are important for understanding the function of Nahum within the context of Assyrian domination. First, it is notable that not all the nations condemned in the OAN are enemies of Israel. Ellen F. Davis has shown, for example, how, in Ezekiel, Tyre and Egypt are condemned, not because of their enmity toward Israel, but because of "how their wildly inflated self-estimations have given offense to God."[30] Assyria, of course, does not fall into that category because Assyria both blasphemed against YHWH (cf. 2 Kgs 18:28–36; 19:4) and oppressed

---

26. Wessels, "Nahum," 625.
27. Wessels, "Nahum," 625.
28. Wessels, "Nahum," 626.
29. O'Brien, *Nahum*, 36–39.
30. Davis, "'And Pharaoh Will Change His Mind,'" 230.

other people (Nah 3:4; Isa 10:5–11). However, even for nations like Assyria that are condemned for their violence, their offenses are ultimately offenses against YHWH and his justice. Walter Brueggemann argues that the purpose of the OAN is to proclaim to the nations the universal rule of YHWH, the God of Israel.[31] Oppressing other nations is a way of opposing YHWH. Both the nations that usurp roles attributed to YHWH (e.g., the king of Tyre in Ezek 28:2) and those that oppress others (e.g., Ammon in Amos 1:13–15) are condemned because their actions offend YHWH.

A second pertinent feature of the OAN is that their original audience was primarily *Israelite*. What the oracles proclaimed was more important to Israel than to the nations that were condemned; their purpose was to show Israel what happens to those who usurp the place of YHWH.[32] As a result, the oracles are not interested in giving specific details about the nations that are threatened. When historical details are given, such details can often come from the experience of the Israelites or from generic formulaic language.[33] Sometimes, especially when the oracles are against nations that oppress Israel, they offer consolation and encouragement that YHWH will do to the foreign nations what those nations did to Israel. The imprecation of the last three verses of Ps 137 shows this understanding of YHWH's actions against the enemy nations as the execution of divine justice:

> Impute, O YHWH, the day of Jerusalem
> to the sons of Edom;
> they who said, "Raze! Raze! To its foundation!"
> O Daughter-Babylon, the destroyed one!
> Blessed be the one who does to you the deeds you did to us;
> Blessed be the one who seizes and dashes
>   your little children against a cliff!
> (Ps 137:7–9)

What matters in this psalm is not whether the poet was aware of any force—apart from YHWH—that was about to destroy Babylon. The focus of the oracle is on what YHWH can do to those who oppress others. In order to show her audience that YHWH actually pays the wicked according to their deeds (cf. Lam 3:64–66; Exod 21:24; Deut 19:21), the poet presents the fate of the oppressor as similar to what happened to the

---

31. Brueggemann, *To Build, to Plant*, 209.
32. Davis, "'And Pharaoh Will Change His Mind,'" 229.
33. Brueggemann, *To Build, to Plant*, 266.

audience. Similarly, in the book of Jeremiah, we see how, in 50:41–46, the proclamation against Babylon repeats almost the same proclamation that was used against Judah in 6:22–24. Brueggemann observes that, in this passage, Babylon is no longer the one to destroy and to terrify; it has now become the victim:

> In 6:24 it is Babylon who devastates Jerusalem and "we" who have pain as in labor. Now [in 50:41–46] it is the "king of Babylon" (no less) who hears and who is reduced to pain and anguish. The poem deftly makes the strong one into the weak one and portrays for us the total reversal of power in public history. The first one dramatically becomes the last one![34]

The book of Nahum, in its threats against Assyria, uses the same rhetorical strategy as Jeremiah against Babylon. The poet takes the suffering experienced by Israel/Judah at the hands of the Assyrians and reverses it against Assyria. To proclaim this oracle against Assyria, Nahum draws from his personal experience; he does not need to know anything about the historical fall of Nineveh. Working within the theological tradition in which the offender is punished according to his offenses,[35] Nahum simply uses his community's memory of the invasion of Judah by the Assyrians in 701 BCE and turns Assyria's violence against Assyria itself.

As will be shown below, these oracles are based on the belief that YHWH, the sovereign ruler, does enact justice, and no earthly nation or ruler is strong enough to escape his judgment. The punishments with which nations are threatened are often a direct effect of the violence they perpetrated against Israel/Judah or other nations.[36] Nahum's proof for what he proclaims—that YHWH will indeed destroy Assyria, just as Assyria destroyed some cities of Judah—is that this is what YHWH does to proud and violent nations. This is the point made by the reference to No-Amon and its allies Kush, Egypt, Put, and Lubim in Nah 3:8–10 and the inference in Nah 3:11,

> *You too* will become drunk;
> you will disappear from people's view.
> *You too* will search for a refuge from an enemy.

---

34. Brueggemann, *To Build, to Plant*, 268.

35. This tradition continues to the New Testament time: "the measure with which you measure will be measured out to you" (Matt 7:2).

36. See Brueggemann, *To Build, to Plant*, 73.

This direct correlation between what happened to other nations and what will happen to Assyria is supported—obliquely, yet even more strongly—by the poet's description of the fall of Nineveh in a way that resembles what the Assyrians did to some Judahite cities.

Reading the book as an OAN proves more fruitful, especially when we consider the relationship of OAN with biblical laments and Mesopotamian city laments. In his 1972 commentary on Lamentations, Delbert Hillers showed that the book of Lamentations and the OAN had some resemblances with Mesopotamian city laments.[37] Twenty years later, his student F. W. Dobbs-Allsopp built upon that proposal and explored the presence of city lament features in the book of Lamentations, in some psalms, and in a number of prophetic oracles.[38] He identified nine features of city laments that he also found in the book of Lamentations and, in modified form, in some psalms and prophetic oracles, including the book of Nahum.[39] These features are:

---

37. There are five extant Mesopotamian compositions that scholars designate as city laments. Those works describe the "destruction of Sumer at the end of Ur III period and more local calamities in the following early Isin period." They are: "Lament over the destruction of Ur" (LU), "Lament over the destruction of Sumer and Ur" (LSUr), "Nippur Lament" (LN), "Eridu Lament" (LE), "Uruk Lament" (LW). See Dobbs-Allsopp, *Weep, O Daughter of Zion*, 13. Another Mesopotamian composition that is related to city laments is the "Curse of Agade" (CA), a poem in which an assembly of gods curse the city of Agade because of the deeds of its king, Naram-Sin (2261–2224 BCE). See Cooper, *The Curse of Agade*.

38. Dobbs-Allsopp, *Weep, O Daughter of Zion*, 97–153. In this early work, Dobbs-Allsopp avoids claiming direct borrowing of the genre from the Mesopotamian traditions into the Hebrew Bible. He rather surmised the possibility of the evolution of a "native" Israelite city lament genre, with uniquely Israelite motifs and images. Following criticism by Berlin ("Review of *Weep, O Daughter of Zion*," 319) (and others) of his "more radical position" about the alleged independence of the Israelite city-lament genre, Dobbs-Allsopp clarified his position in a short article in 2000, "Let me put this unequivocally and most emphatically: based on current knowledge (which can always change in light of new archaeological discoveries), the city-lament genre appears to have originated in Mesopotamia. And though I was perhaps overcautious and far too equivocating on the issue of origins in my earlier study, nothing I said there is finally incompatible with this position. What I meant by the term 'native' (and what I take Hillers to mean by it as well) was nothing less and nothing more than that we have evidence for knowledge of city laments in Israel for a period of at least two hundred years and that as encountered in the Hebrew Bible the genre shows every sign of having long been internalized within and understood as an inherited part of the Israelite literary tradition" (Dobbs-Allsopp, "Darwinism," 626).

39. Before Dobbs-Allsopp, Jack M. Sasson had already noted that the book of Nahum and the "Curse of Agade" had similar features: "Both texts include vivid, often figurative descriptions of the fortification and fall of cities, divine curses against them, and laments over their demise; see Sasson, *Jonah*, 22, note 20.

1. *Subject and mood*: city laments speak about the destruction of cities and express that destruction in a particularly somber mood.[40]

2. *Divine abandonment*: patron deities abandon the city right before destruction.[41]

3. *Assignment of responsibilities*: the gods often destroy the city without giving clear reasons for this destruction (the decision of the gods is often arbitrary).[42]

4. *Divine agent of destruction*: often the gods use foreign armies or other agents (especially a storm).[43]

5. *Detailed description of the destruction of the cities and their environs, sanctuaries, persons, and social, religious, and political customs.*[44]

6. *The weeping goddess*: the goddess of the city contests the destruction of the city and laments it.[45]

7. *Lamentation* of the people and onlookers in reaction to the destruction.[46]

8. *Restoration of the city and return of the gods.*[47]

9. *Structure and poetic technique*: the poet uses multiple points of view; he presents himself both as independent narrator and as internal observer of what he depicts; these laments (like all laments and dirges) also use the *Kontrastmotiv* (they contrast the present with a glorious past); they also depict things in an order that is the reverse of the normal one (e.g., slaves ruling over their masters, parents eating their children); they focus on the destroyed city (giving extensive details about the destruction); external and metrical structures (e.g., use of the so-called *qinah* meter); and lists (e.g., lists of deities who abandon their cities).[48]

---

40. Dobbs-Allsopp, *Weep, O Daughter of Zion*, 31–32.
41. Dobbs-Allsopp, *Weep, O Daughter of Zion*, 45.
42. Dobbs-Allsopp, *Weep, O Daughter of Zion*, 52–53.
43. Dobbs-Allsopp, *Weep, O Daughter of Zion*, 55–65.
44. Dobbs-Allsopp, *Weep, O Daughter of Zion*, 66–74.
45. Dobbs-Allsopp, *Weep, O Daughter of Zion*, 75–90.
46. Dobbs-Allsopp, *Weep, O Daughter of Zion*, 90–92.
47. Dobbs-Allsopp, *Weep, O Daughter of Zion*, 92–94.
48. Dobbs-Allsopp, *Weep, O Daughter of Zion*, 32–45.

Dobbs-Allsopp's treatment of city lament features in the book of Nahum limits itself to identifying a few of those features. He first points to the realistic nature of the depiction of the destruction of Nineveh: a feature he finds similar to the description of the destruction of Ekur in the "Curse of Agade" (CA).[49] Next, he shows that in Nah 2:8, the exile of personified Nineveh and its slave-girls takes the place of the exile of city goddesses and their devotees in city laments. He also points to dirges and lamentation in Nahum (see Nah 2:11; 3:7), the description of corpses lying on the streets and squares (3:3), and the vivid description of YHWH's stripping and exposing Nineveh (3:5).[50] A closer analysis of the book will show that Nahum adapts more city lament motifs than pointed out by Dobbs-Allsopp. In the following paragraphs, I analyze those city lament features in the book of Nahum.

Subject and Mood

The book of Nahum focuses on the destruction of the city of Nineveh. It begins with the naming of the city in the superscription (1:1); then it mentions the same city twice again (2:9; 3:7). The mood of the book of Nahum is more complex than what we find in city laments. While in city laments the mood is somber and mournful, in Nahum the moods shift. In some places the book shows excitement about what is happening to Nineveh (e.g., 1:2–8; 2:1–3; 3:19). In others, it makes references to mourning (2:8, 11; 3:7). The poet seems to lean toward excitement over the destruction of the city, but he also allows the point of views of those affected by violence to be heard.

Divine Abandonment and Return

All the city laments feature the abandonment of the doomed cities by their patron deities right before those cities are destroyed by the chief gods, An and Enlil.[51] Dobbs-Allsopp believes that the exile of Nineveh and its slave-girls in Nah 2:8 represents the exile of the city goddess and

---

49. Dobbs-Allsopp, *Weep, O Daughter of Zion*, 128.
50. Dobbs-Allsopp, *Weep, O Daughter of Zion*, 130–31.
51. For example, the description of the abandonment of the city by its gods in LU (LU 1–35); see Kramer, *Lamentation over the Destruction of Ur*, 17–21.

her attendees.[52] The book of Nahum, however, does not assume that Nineveh was protected by any god/goddess or that Nineveh itself had some divine characteristics. The protector of Nineveh, according to Nahum, is the king of Assyria and his ministers, who all prove to be worthless as defenders of a city (see Nah 3:18). Even when Nahum speaks about the gods of the king of Assyria, those gods are not called gods: they are *pesel* and *māsēkāh* (1:14). The only God in the book of Nahum is YHWH. Reference to the exile of the city and its slave-girls in Nah 2:8 seems to function as a synecdoche to speak about the exile of Nineveh's population (2:9) rather than as a reference to the exile of Ishtar or some other deity. However, even though the motif of divine abandonment is not stated in relation to the city of Nineveh, it is assumed in relation to Judah: YHWH seems to have abandoned Judah and, in Nahum, he has returned to restore it (2:3).

Assignment of Responsibility

In Mesopotamian city laments, the destruction of cities is presented as the action of capricious gods. Usually, it is An and Enlil who bear most of the responsibility for the destruction.[53] No obvious reasons are given for the destruction of the city. In Nahum, on the contrary, YHWH is presented as taking vengeance, enacting justice (1:2–3): that is, YHWH brings about destruction because he is provoked, not because he is a capricious god. Nineveh's transgressions are given as the reasons for YHWH's actions against her (2:1, 3, 12–13; 3:1–4, 16). In this regard, Nahum differs from the Mesopotamian city laments and most biblical laments where YHWH is often accused of destroying the lamenter for no cause (Ps 44:18–23; Job 2:3) or those where the lamenter recognizes having sinned, and yet protests against the harshness and the degree of YHWH's punishment on her (Lam 1:9, 11, 12; 2:20–22; 4:6; 5:1, 20, 22).[54]

---

52. See Dobbs-Allsopp, *Weep, O Daughter of Zion*, 129–30.
53. Dobbs-Allsopp, *Weep, O Daughter of Zion*, 52.
54. Dobbs-Allsopp, *Weep, O Daughter of Zion*, 55.

Divine Agent of Destruction

In Mesopotamian city laments, the chief agent of destruction is the storm (see LU 90; 170-75[55]; LW 3.6[56]).[57] In addition to the storm, we also hear of floods (see LW 3.3), and foreign armies (LE 4:10; LU 244; LSUr 75; CA 155). These agents, however, do not act on their own. It is Enlil who directs their actions against the cities.[58] In Nahum, YHWH is presented as the sole agent of the destruction of Nineveh. We find the motif of storm in Nah 1:3 and that of floods in 1:8, but those elements are not presented as direct agents of destruction. We do not find the motif of a foreign army as agent against the city of Nineveh.[59] In the OAN, YHWH often makes use of other nations in order to punish the nations that show opposition to him (see Isa 21:1–10; Jer 49:2; 50:8; Obad 18; Zeph 2), but it also happens that YHWH acts without needing agents (cf. Isa 14; Amos 1), as he does against Nineveh. Nevertheless, unlike in the case of the destruction of Nineveh, where YHWH himself takes vengeance, the book of Nahum also suggests that when YHWH afflicted Judah (1:12), he did it through intermediaries. We see in Nah 1:12 that YHWH claims the responsibility for afflicting Judah; and yet, in the next verse, he states that Judah's yoke came from some other source (1:13). Also, in Nah 2:1 and Nah 2:3, YHWH says that Judah was invaded, laid waste, and ravaged by *běliyaʿal* and ravagers. Because of the references to Nineveh (1:1; 2:9; 3:7) and to the king of Assyria (3:18) as the targets of YHWH's vengeance, it seems that the book is claiming that the affliction of Judah was the work of YHWH; but YHWH used the Assyrians, who transformed themselves into ravagers and invaders (cf. Isa 10; 2 Kgs 18:25).

---

55. Kramer, *Lamentation over the Destruction of Ur*, 27, 35.
56. Green, "The Uruk Lament," 269.
57. Dobbs-Allsopp, *Weep, O Daughter of Zion*, 55–57.
58. Dobbs-Allsopp, *Weep, O Daughter of Zion*, 57–59.
59. Nah 2:2-10 seems to depict the invasion of an army. However, on close analysis of how the term *mēpiṣ* ("chatterer," Nah 2:2) is used elsewhere in the Hebrew Bible in connection with the theme of Divine Warrior (Hab 3:14; Zech 13:7; Pss 18:15; 68:31), one realizes that the army depicted here is, as has been shown by Julia O'Brien, not a foreign human army, but YHWH's own army. See O'Brien, *Nahum, Habakkuk, Zephaniah*, 45–46.

Destruction

City laments give very detailed descriptions of the destruction of the city, its sanctuaries, its environs, its people, and its institutions.[60] The Lament over Nippur,[61] for example, begins with the description of the complete destruction of the city and its shrines: the city is haunted with no one to restore it (LN 1); it is emptied, its main shrine is now laid waste (LN 10). We hear the same description of total destruction in Lamentations: YHWH has destroyed Israel and its palaces (2:5); he has destroyed altars and sanctuary, walls and gates, etc. (2:7–8); young and old men have been killed by the sword (2: 21). In Nahum, the poet both presents the destruction of Nineveh as a live scene and evokes the destruction of Judah (and Egypt) by the Assyrians. Throughout the book, we see YHWH attacking and laying Nineveh and its environs to waste. Already in the beginning of the book, we see YHWH drying up rivers and sea; making agricultural regions of Bashan, Carmel, and Lebanon languish (1:4); shaking mountains and hills; destabilizing the land and the entire world (1:5); shattering rocks (1:6). Dobbs-Allsopp has noted how, in Isaiah's oracle against Moab (Isa 15–16), the attacking army first moves through other regions before reaching the intended place of onslaught.[62] The effect of this move through various regions is that the destruction of the targeted city is presented as inevitable. Nahum presents YHWH's actions as meant to undo the city and make a complete end of it (1:8, 9). By starting with the drying of the sea and rivers, the destabilization of forests and mountains, Nahum prepares the reader to realize that the destruction of Nineveh was inevitable. Finally, in Nah 2–3, the poet vividly shows us YHWH's shattering of Nineveh. The army attacks the city in all its parts: through the meadows/streets, through the city squares, into the palace (2:5, 7). The city is plundered; its chariots and beasts are burned in fire (2:10, 14). Personified as a woman, the city is shamed and disfigured (2:8; 3:5–6). The gate bars of the city are consumed in fire; its people are scattered on the mountains (3:13, 17). The carnage is such that *any* onlooker can realize that Nineveh is devastated beyond consolation (3:7); its wound cannot be healed (3:19). The sanctuaries of the city are also emptied of their

---

60. Cooper, *The Curse of Agade*, 20.

61. Translated into French by Attinger, *La Lamentation sur Nippur* (2010, 2015; http://www.iaw.unibe.ch/e39448/e99428/e122665/e122821/pane122850/e122917/2_2_4.pdf, accessed April 20, 2017).

62. Dobbs-Allsopp, *Weep, O Daughter of Zion*, 101.

idols; in their stead, YHWH makes a grave for the king of Assyria (1:14) and overwhelms both Nineveh and Judah with his majestic presence. The exile of Nineveh's population, the captivity of the nation's leaders, and the dashing of the babes against the corners of streets (3:10) seal the fate of Nineveh as a city that used to resemble a pool full of water, but that has now been emptied (2:9). The destruction of Nineveh evokes the violence Assyrians imposed on other nations, especially Judah: they laid Judah waste and ravaged it (2:3); their violence left piles of dead bodies (3:3). What YHWH is doing against Nineveh will make her fate resemble that of the nations that Nineveh itself destroyed: Judah and Egypt:

> Are you better than No Amon (Thebes) who sat by the Nile with water all around her?
> For whom the sea was an army and water a wall,
> Ethiopia and Egypt were her strength, and without end,
> Put and Lubim were her helpers?
> Even (*gam*) she went into exile; she went into captivity.
> Even (*gam*) her little babes were dashed against every street corner;
> and on her nobles, lots were cast;
> and her great ones were bound in fetters.
> You too (*gam*) will be drunk; you will hide yourself.
> You too (*gam*) will look for a refuge from the enemy
> (Nah 3:8-11)

The repetition of *gam* in Nah 3:11 (following its use in 3:10) emphasizes the fact that the depiction of the scenes of the destruction of Nineveh is meant to evoke what happened to those nations that Assyria herself destroyed. Here, we see that YHWH is paying Nineveh with the same violence with which it destroyed other nations.[63]

The poet does not directly speak about the destruction of Assyrian religious, social, and political customs. He alludes to the destruction of idols in Nah 1:14, but nothing is said about how/whether the Assyrians even held any religious services for those idols. The political and military institutions are not destroyed; they are simply exposed for what

---

63. The same idea is expressed in Obad 15-16:
For the day of the Lord is near against all the nations.
As you have done, it shall be done to you;
   your deeds shall return on your own head.
For as you have drunk on my holy mountain,
   all the nations around you shall drink;
they shall drink and gulp down,
   and shall be as though they had never been. (NRSV)

they actually are as unreliable (2:6; 3:13, 16–18). In Judah, however, the interruption of the celebration of festivals is presented as a major concern within the community, because the resumption of the celebration of festivals and of keeping vows is presented as the hallmark of YHWH's restoration of Judah. Indeed, resuming those celebrations is the only action that YHWH's messenger commands Judah to do (2:1). Unlike in Mesopotamian city laments and in Lamentations—both places where the poets often lament the destruction of customs within the destroyed city (see LU 117; Lam 1:4; 2:6–7)—in Nahum, it is not the destruction of *Nineveh's* customs that is mourned, it is *Judah's* destruction that is indirectly lamented.

Lamentation over the Destruction of the City

One of the most important features of Mesopotamian city laments is the lamentation over the destruction of the city. The chief lamenter is the city goddess, who often challenges the decision of the divine assembly and bewails the destruction of the city (see LW 3.22; LU 115–20; LE 25).[64] In addition, those laments depict people bewailing the fall of their cities and the destruction/death of their friends and relatives.[65] In the Hebrew Bible, most lamentations are carried out by the suffering people themselves, by onlookers, or, in rare cases, by YHWH himself. In Lamentations, we see personified Zion and its people weeping day and night (see Lam 1:2, 16). In Jeremiah, we see the prophet Jeremiah weeping because of the suffering of his people (Jer 8:18–23); we see YHWH also joining in weeping (see Jer 9:16–18). It should be noted that, when YHWH joins the community in weeping, he joins those *he himself* destroyed—unlike Mesopotamian goddesses, who weep because other gods destroyed the goddesses' cities. In Nahum, we see the maidservants of Nineveh moaning like doves and beating their breasts (2:8); onlookers acknowledge the affliction of Nineveh and wonder whether such affliction can be adequately lamented (3:7). Mentions of laments over Nineveh are but a small part of the book. The book is dominated by the description of the destruction of Nineveh by YHWH (see Nah 2:1; 3:19). That description functions as the reverse of lamentation. As was said above about the depiction of the destruction of Nineveh, the poet's celebration over the fall

---

64. Dobbs-Allsopp, *Lamentations*, 7–9.
65. Dobbs-Allsopp, *Weep, O Daughter of Zion*, 90.

of Nineveh likely evokes the laments of the Judahites over the destruction of their cities by the Assyrians. John H. Hayes writes about the use of OAN in contexts of warfare against foreign nations and shows that, in the Hebrew Bible, these oracles were used in the context of lamentation services. The oracles were given as YHWH's response to the cries of the people.[66] One way Hayes illustrates his point is by analyzing the combination of lament and oracle against an enemy in Ps 60. This psalm begins with a long superscription explaining the context in which David sings it:

> For the leader, on the Shushan of Testimony. A Mitcham of David (in order to teach); when he fought against Aram-Naharaim and with Aram-Zobah; and Joab returned and smote twelve thousand Edomites in the Valley of Salt.
> (Ps 60:1–2)

After the superscription, the psalmist presents his plea to YHWH, who has abandoned and broken his people (v. 3), has destroyed the land (v. 4), etc. In v. 8, YHWH appears and speaks,

> I will triumph, I will divide Shechem
>   and measure out the valley of Succoth.
> Gilead is mine, and Manasseh is mine;
>   Ephraim is the helmet of my head;
>   Judah has been prescribed to me.
> Moab is my wash basin;
>   over Edom I will cast my shoe:
>   Philistia, shout for joy because of me.
> (Ps 60:8–10)

John Hayes shows that God's appearance and threat against these foreign nations are direct responses to the laments of the people in vv. 3–6. Destroying these nations is shown to be the way YHWH brings about salvation longed for by Israel.[67] Even though I do not espouse Hayes's whole idea about the cultic use of the OAN, his point about their function as a response to the lament of the people helps us see the relationship between Nahum and laments. We do not hear the Judahites lament in the book of Nahum. But the terms used to describe their condition are drawn from the lament repertoire or from contexts of suffering and oppression: *'ānāh*/to afflict (Nah 1:12; cf. Isa 53: 7; Pss 88:1, 7; 90:15; 102:24; Job 30:11; Lam 3:33; 5:11); *maṭṭeh* /yoke (Nah 1:13; cf. Isa 9:4; 10:5); *mōsēr* /

---

66. Hayes, "The Usage of Oracles against Foreign Nations," 86–87.
67. Hayes, "The Usage of Oracles against Foreign Nations," 88.

bond (Nah 1:13; cf. Isa 28:22; 52:2; Jer 2:20; 5:5; 27:2); *bāqaq* /to ravage or empty (Nah 2:3; cf. Isa 19:7; 24:1, 3; Jer 19:7; 51:2). It is important to note that it is YHWH (the instigator of their affliction) who names the condition of the Judahites. One aspect of laments is that the lamenter wants YHWH (and other people) to notice the affliction of the lamenter (see Pss 25:18; 86:1; Lam 1:9, 11, 12, 18, 20; 2:20; 3:59, 60). Therefore, that it is YHWH who names the affliction of the Judahites in Nahum suggests that YHWH has noticed what happened to Judah, and the proclamations contained in Nahum are a way for YHWH to respond to the concerns of the Judahites. The book of Nahum then becomes, as will be shown later, a way for the poet to invite the audience to see what YHWH sees and communicates to them through his prophet, that is, through the book itself.

In summary, following the hypothesis that YHWH is paying Nineveh in her own currency, we can surmise that the scenes of destruction the poet imagines happening in Nineveh evoke what Nineveh did against Judah. Also, the celebration of the doom of Nineveh evokes the cries of the Judahites. The book of Nahum then, though not directly lamenting the destruction of Judah, by celebrating the fall of Judah's attacker, indirectly voices the concerns of the Judahites. This connection between the proclamation against the enemy and the lament of the victims is one way of explaining the pervasive use of features drawn from laments in the book of Nahum. The book draws from this lament form, because the book is meant to address a situation of affliction and violence. As will be shown below, the style of the book works in such a way as to evoke in the minds of an audience the memories of their struggle with Assyrian violence.

The Poetics of Lyric

The book of Nahum, as was said above, is a lyric poem. F. W. Dobbs-Allsopp identifies the "lack of narrativizing devices" and "strong reliance on the naked properties of language as its basic means for making meaning" as the two main characteristics of lyric poetry.[68] Unlike narratives or dramas, where the author relies on a storyline, arguments, characters, or plot in order to convey meaning, lyric poetry employs only the lexical and syntactical properties of language. Lyric poems are paratactic. There are no obvious devices connecting verses or strophes; the reader must discover the logic of the text and imagine how parts are connected. Lyric

---

68. Dobbs-Allsopp, *Lamentations*, 12.

poems rely on wordplay and play on sounds; they use evocative images and extravagant language. The book of Nahum has been praised by most scholars for its use of a wide variety of poetic devices.[69] Those devices are anchored around two foundational poetic techniques: parataxis and an extravagant use of language. The result of the use of those poetic techniques is that the poet is able to represent the image of war and also make visible to the mind of the readers/hearers emotions and passions: we hear/see slave-girls moaning and beating their breasts (2:8); we are told that the spirits of the Ninevites sank and their loins trembled, and we have the impression of watching them (2:11b).

Parataxis

Parataxis has been defined by biblical scholar Alan J. Hauser as

> the placing side by side of words, images, clauses, or scenes without connectives that directly and immediately coordinate the parts with one another.... Parataxis does not present a complete picture, but normally selects only certain elements which often at first glance do not appear to correlate well with one another. This does not mean that the adjacent parts lack a common unity or exist in a vacuum separate from one another. The unity that is present is subtle, implicit, indirect, and below the surface. It comes to expression not so much in the words of the writer as in the thoughts the writer creates in the mind of the audience.[70]

Paratactic arrangement of verses, images, and ideas is the way lyric poetry remedies its lack of plot and argumentation. It should be noted that, in the Hebrew Bible, both narrative and poetic texts use parataxis at the grammatical level as a way of connecting thoughts or ideas. However, while narratives often have a storyline and argument and focus on the logical succession of events, lyric poems more often present only images that the reader/hearer is expected to connect.[71]

The book of Nahum shows no narrative logic. It presents images and actions without specifying which ones chronologically come before and which ones come later. Despite efforts by some scholars to look for

---

69. Spronk, *Nahum*, 6.
70. Hauser, "Judges 5: Parataxis in Hebrew Poetry," 26.
71. See Lichtenstein, "Biblical Poetry," 112–13; Heffelfinger, *I Am Large*, 39.

an argument or for narration in the book of Nahum,[72] the book tells no obvious story. We have a general understanding that the poem presents the battle between YHWH and Nineveh. The book however does not give us the story of that battle; rather, it makes us live it. It projects series of scenes without explaining how they are connected. We see for example the army dashing and rushing around city streets and squares, but we are not given an explanation about what it is doing and how it ended up in those places (see 2:4–5). We need to associate those images with the description of Nineveh and its inhabitants in 2:7–9 in order to form an image of what is happening.

The book of Nahum also refrains from directly stating its goals. Readers might infer from YHWH's actions against Nineveh that YHWH feels compassion for afflicted Judah and intends its restoration. Yet this is not stated, and the reader's own emotional response may be complicated by the poetic images of destroyed Nineveh, and the articulation of its citizens' desolation and devastation (2:11). The display of such devastation leaves the book open to compassion, indifference, or celebration over the destruction of Nineveh. The poet for example presents "those who see her" fleeing from the scene of Nineveh's devastation and wondering whether Nineveh can find a comforter (3:7); but he also says that "everyone who hears" about the devastation of Nineveh claps his hands (3:19). Parataxis invites us to consider all those points of view (that of those who feel compassion, that of afflicted Ninevites, and that of those who celebrate the fall of Nineveh), each reaction and emotion at a time. Adele Berlin notes that when multiple points of view are presented within a text, each point of view claims to be the legitimate one, and the reader misses part of the message of the text if she does not listen to all the points of view or if she privileges one point of view at the outset.[73]

Another way of understanding the use of parataxis and the combination of multiple disjointed/contradictory images and ideas has been suggested by M. L. Rosenthal and Sally M. Gall in their study of lyric sequences. For Rosenthal and Gall, lyric poems are often created as a way of trying to deal with an "intractable situation."

> This need becomes an energizing element in the aesthetic of any given work. It presents itself as a sense of being balked, or of

---

72. See Roberts, *Nahum, Habakkuk, and Zephaniah*, 65; Spronk, *Nahum*, 91–92; Maier, *The Book of Nahum*, 243–47.

73. Berlin, *Poetics and Interpretation of Biblical Narrative*, 52.

being beset by an engulfing flood of circumstance that can be stayed only momentarily. The counter-efforts of sensibility lead to clarifying an inner state and relating it somehow to the intractable principle—the irresistible torrent of fatality, the sheer mass of sensations and memories and feelings, the impersonal sweep of history, the uncontrollable forces of political life, the cycles of existence, the unpredictable working of the psyche, the erosion of cherished values—through poetic equilibrium.[74]

We have already shown that the situation with which Nahum's implied audience grapples is the problem of Assyrian violence against Judah. The book presents YHWH's violence against Nineveh and shows various reactions to that violence. Those contradictory reactions show how the poet does not intend to present one single argument or point of view, but explores the problem from multiple competing perspectives.[75]

Extravagance of Lyric and the Sublime

Using the example of Percy B. Shelley's "Ode to the West Wind" (1820), Jonathan Culler writes about what he calls the "extravagance of lyric"—the lyric's predilection for hyperboles, the tendency of poets to be carried away, to exaggerate, and to create scenes that evoke otherworldly experiences:

> Not only do lyric poems seem willing to address almost anything in preference to an actual audience (the wind, a tiger, my soul); they do so in hyperbolic accents. Exaggeration is the name of the game here: the tiger is not just orange but "burning"; the wind is the very "breath of Autumn's being" and, later in the poem, saviour and destroyer.[76]

---

74. Rosenthal and Gall, *The Modern Poetic Sequence*, 101.

75. See Rosenthal and Gall, *The Modern Poetic Sequence*, 11; Heffelfinger, *I am Large*, 67.

76. Culler, *Literary Theory*, 77. It should be noted that, in biblical poetry, the idea that lyric poetry seems willing "to address almost anything in preference to an actual audience" is not supported by all the theorists and poets. W. R. Johnson, as we saw it above, shows that lyric poems almost always presuppose the presence of a listening You. Since lyric poems have their origins in songs sung in front of an audience, even when the poem does not mention an actual audience, such an audience is presupposed. See Johnson, *The Idea of Lyric*, 7–9. Also, as we will see it below, biblical poets, even when they speak about mountains, seas, etc., they do so as a way of speaking directly to an actual audience (even when that audience is not specified).

The main reason for this predilection for exaggeration is

> a paradox that seems to lie at the core of lyric poetry. The extravagance of poetry includes its aspiration to what theorists since classical times have called the "sublime": a relation to what exceeds human capabilities of understanding, provokes awe or passionate intensity, gives the speaker a sense of something beyond the human.[77]

The book of Nahum's aspiration to the sublime was recognized by eighteenth-century British scholar Robert Lowth:

> None of the Minor Prophets, however, seem to equal Nahum, in boldness, ardour, and sublimity. His prophecy too forms a regular and perfect poem; the exordium is not merely magnificent, it is truly majestic; the preparation for the destruction of Nineveh, and the description of its downfall and desolation are expressed in the most vivid colours, and are bold and luminous in the highest degree.[78]

Before showing how the book of Nahum relies on the sublime as a way of addressing its audience, I will give some of the features of texts that the classics called "sublime." The first known classical theoretical treatment on the sublime in literature was (Pseudo-)Longinus's *On the Sublime* (ca. first–third centuries CE). For Longinus,

> the Sublime, wherever it occurs, consists in a certain loftiness and excellence of language. . . . A lofty passage does not convince the reason of the reader, but takes him out of himself. That which is admirable ever confounds our judgment, and eclipses that which is merely reasonable or agreeable. To believe or not is usually in our own power; but the Sublime, acting with an imperious and irresistible force, sways every reader whether he will or no. Skill in invention, lucid arrangement and disposition of facts, are appreciated not by one passage, or by two, but gradually manifest themselves in the general structure of a work; but a sublime thought, if happily timed, illumines an entire subject with the vividness of a lightning-flash, and exhibits the whole power of the orator in a moment of time.[79]

Longinus identifies five characteristics of sublime texts:

---

77. Culler, *Literary Theory*, 77.
78. Lowth, *Lectures on the Sacred Poetry of the Hebrews*, Kindle locs 7253–55.
79. Longinus, *On the Sublime*, Kindle locs 252–60.

1. grandeur of thought (the ability for the poet to let himself be carried by thoughts and images that transcend ordinary experience);
2. a vigorous and spirited treatment of the passions;
3. a certain artifice in the employment of figures;
4. dignified expression;
5. majesty and elevation of structure.[80]

These are features that we easily encounter in the book of Nahum. This book carries the reader to celestial realms, takes her to the sea, lifts her upon the mountains, and even makes her watch the shaking of the loins of the Ninevites. The book begins with the majestic depiction of YHWH riding in the storm, in the whirlwind, above the clouds, drying the sea and rivers, making vegetation languish, and shattering rocks (1:3–6). The poet does not recount the story of God's journey through the sky: he carries his reader around, to watch YHWH's actions. At once YHWH is majestic in the storm and whirlwind, above the clouds (1:3b); then he is shown fighting the sea and rivers (1:4a); then up to the forests and mountains (1:4b–5a); then finally his actions encompass the entire world (1:5b). Unlike other prophetic books, which begin with direct address, either God's words or people's/the prophet's words to God,[81] Nahum begins with a description of YHWH. From this very beginning of the book, even though the poet gives no physical description of YHWH, we have the impression of seeing YHWH deal with the world and of hearing him rebuke the sea!

In addition, the book powerfully presents the emotions of those involved in the battle. YHWH is angry and passionate (1:2); Judah is afflicted (1:13); Nineveh's spirit is sinking and there is a sick trembling in its loins (2:2, 11); the slave-girls of Nineveh moan and beat their breasts (2:8); the intoxicated king of Assyria, grievously wounded (3:19), seeks refuge from his enemy (3:11); the onlookers flee from the scene of Nineveh's destruction, wondering whether the city can be properly mourned (3:7). In contrast to the emotions of anger and affliction, we also see the poet imagine Judah celebrating the end of suffering (2:1); we see nations that suffered under Assyrian domination celebrate the fall of their oppressor (3:19). In every instance, the poet dwells on each emotion

---

80. Longinus, *On the Sublime*, Kindle locs 361–62.

81. The book of Habakkuk is the only prophetic book that begins with the prophet's address to God (Hab 1:1).

to such an extent that we are tempted to believe (however briefly) that *this* emotion is the only one that matters in the book. Dobbs-Allsopp speaks about lyric's "quintessential *occasionalness*, its tendency to give expression to one particular mood or idea at a time and to do so with verve and excitement."[82] One danger of momentarily yielding to one emotion at a time is that the reader might be tempted to forget that the emotion itself is momentary, and thus she might stay on it to the point of ignoring other emotions that also vie for her attention.[83] We saw above how Julia O'Brien often suggests that the main purpose of Nahum is to depict the fall of Nineveh and call for vengeance against the Assyrian city.[84] When we consider the book as lyric, we see that the book presents multiple points of view to which the reader is supposed to listen, without privileging some at the outset.

The book of Nahum also uses images and figures of speech in order to make visible to the mind of the reader the scenes that it depicts. Presenting YHWH's anger like burning fire (1:6) makes the reader imagine all the danger involved in approaching YHWH and in experiencing his anger. Summoning Judah to behold the *footsteps* of the messenger of glad tidings (2:1) focuses the attention of the reader to the fact that the messenger is coming (walking), rather than simply on the messenger's existence or presence. Metaphorically associating Assyria/Nineveh with a lion's den and the king of Assyria with the image of a lion (see 2:12–13) makes the irony about Assyrian impotence poignant, for, as we will see in the following chapter, the Great King of Assyria is the supreme "Lion" who vanquishes all the other lions. And here, the den is described as the place from which the lions hunt their prey. The question about the whereabouts of the lion's den suggests that we do not know where the den is. Since we now do not know where the lion's den is, the poet suggests that the king of Assyria has disappeared without a trace.

The poet overwhelmingly uses nonfinite verbs and verbless clauses to give a sense of immediate presence to the event being described. It takes place neither in the past nor in the future, but here and now, in front of the reader. It is worth noting the example of Nah 3:2:

> Qôl šôṭ wĕqôl ra'as 'ôpān
> (Crack of the whips and sound of rattling wheels);

---

82. Dobbs-Allsopp, *On Biblical Poetry*, 213; Johnson, *The Idea of Lyric*, 74–75.
83. Dobbs-Allsopp, *On Biblical Poetry*, 214.
84. O'Brien, *Nahum*, 142, 146–47.

> *Wĕsûs dōhēr ûmerkābāh mĕraqqēdāh*
> (and horses galloping and chariots bounding).

We are not told about something that has already taken place or that will take place in the future; we are shown an army of horses and chariots invading Nineveh.[85] The book also uses ambiguity and confusion as a way of making the scene of war alive in the mind of the reader. Pronouns are often used without indication of their antecedents (see 1:10–14). Imperatives and direct speeches are sometimes used without indicating the speaker or the person to whom commands are issued. Note especially the use of such imperatives and direct speeches in 2:9b–10:

> Nineveh used to be like a pool of water in former days;
>   but they are fleeing.
> "Stop! Stop!" (*'imdû 'amōdû*)
>   But no one turns.
> "Plunder (*bōzzû*) the silver!
>   Plunder (*bōzzû*) the gold!
> There is no end to treasures!"

The poet seems to step aside to let the reader experience the chaos of war. An unidentified speaker commands those fleeing to stop; but no one turns back (2:9). We hear another voice encouraging the plunder of Nineveh's treasures (2:10). The confusion of speakers and those acting here mimics the confusion of war and places the audience in the very heat of the battle, to listen to the shouting and to watch fugitives run from Nineveh, while the place is being plundered by the invaders. For an audience that lived through an experience similar to what Nahum depicts, there is the possibility of feeling directly addressed, and, as we saw above in the epigraph, realizing that they too feel something similar to the experience described by Nahum, even though the text is not exactly a reproduction of their experience.[86]

This vivid presentation of reality is not unique to Nahum. Many other prophetic books use such techniques to address their audiences. One text deemed one of the most sublime texts by Lowth[87] is the scene of the fall of the king of Babylon in Isa 14, where we not only hear the rejoicing of the earth after the fall of the Babylonian monarch (vv. 7–8), but we are even given an internal view of Sheol, with former victims now

---

85. For a similar observation, see Spronk, *Nahum*, 91–93.
86. See Johnson, *The Idea of Lyric*, 74.
87. Lowth, *Lectures*, Lecture XII; Kindle loc 4293.

deriding the one who used to oppress them (vv. 9–11). We even hear what the king of Babylon used to think about himself before his fall (v. 13):

> The earth has rested and is quiet;
> > they break into shouts of joy.
> Even the cypress trees rejoice because of you;
> > yea, even the cedars of Lebanon:
> "Since you have been put down,
> > no one has come up to cut us."
> (Isa 14:7–8)

> Sheol from below is stirred up because of you,
> > to meet your coming.
> It raises against you the spirits of the dead,
> > that is, all the leaders of the earth;
> it raises from their thrones
> > all the kings of the earth.
> All of them will respond
> > and say to you:
> "You too have been weakened like us;
> > you have become like us!"
> (Isa. 14:9–10)

> And you had said in your heart:
> > "I will go up to the sky;
> I will raise my throne
> > above the stars of God;
> I will sit on the mountain of the assembly,
> > to the recesses of Zaphon.
> (Isa 14:13)

The poet's ability to convey reality in such vivid depiction seems to suggest that the poet shares with his audience what he has seen himself.[88] But the claim here is not purely historical in the sense that the poet reports on what he saw in historical terms. What lyric poetry does is to create an experience (often drawing upon the poet's experience, and yet going beyond it) and present to the audience the depiction of that experience in such vivid terms as to make one believe that we are reliving the event spoken about. In the Hebrew Bible, this is particularly true of the prophets. Their ability to bring both God and human experience visible to the mind of the audience derives from the theological belief

---

88. See Longinus, *On the Sublime*, Kindle loc 565.

about the nature of prophetic ministry and witness, which Ellen F. Davis summarizes as

> the practice of standing mud-spattered (see Jer. 38:6) amid the ruins of life—not just an individual life, but the life of a people, one's own people—while speaking honestly to God and truthfully for God. Prophetic ministry and witness entails making God real, present, and necessary in situations that seem to deny that God exists, that God has any power in our lives, that God's will for us is not death but life.[89]

Prophets are visionaries who bear witness to what they *see* in the divine realm and in the created world (both human and non-human): they see God (see Isa 6:1a), stand in his presence (see Jer 15:19), and want to show his "inescapable involvement in the world";[90] they also stand in the midst of their people and see and experience the conditions of the people and the world around them (see Jer 4:23–26). That the book of Nahum is called a "vision" (*ḥazôn*) shows us an explicit connection between its content and the theological assertion about the nature of prophetic ministry as witness to what one has seen. When Nahum depicts YHWH in the whirlwind, in the storm, or battling the sea, we are led to believe that he shows his audience what he sees, and so he invites that audience to *see with* him.[91] But the point here is not about historical reportage, as if Nahum was telling us what he saw in Nineveh. He certainly sees and shares the affliction of his audience (he is part of the people), and so part of what he presents to his audience is drawn from the affliction experienced by that very audience. As we shall see, he repeatedly evokes the affliction of the Judahites (1:12–13; 2:3); he directly addresses his audience (see 2:1); he also uses rhetorical questions (e.g., 1:6, 9; 3:8, 19) to invite his addressees (both those he directly addressed and those who later continue to read his poems) to consider what he presents, inducing them "to mentally agree that the implied assertion is true."[92] But as art, Nahum's prophecy does not indulge in reproducing what is seen. As W. R. Johnson puts it, art

---

89. Davis, *Biblical Prophecy*, 144–45.

90. Davis, *Biblical Prophecy*, 8.

91. For a similar observation about sublime poetry, see Longinus, *On the Sublime*, Kindle locs 564–65.

92. Moshavi, "What Can I Say?" 97.

is not a reproduction of what is seen: it is a highly complex action (action both by artist and audience) in which what is outer and what is inner—things, perceptions, conceptions, actualities, emotions, and ideas—are gathered into and made manifest by emotive and intelligible forms.[93]

In Nahum therefore, we see a combination of things experienced, things learned, and the poet's own contribution. Such a combination of experience, tradition, and personal imagination has the effect of creating a dialogue between the poet and his audience. Murray Lichtenstein has pointed to biblical poetry's "genius for effecting the direct, immediate involvement of its audience in a kind of emotional dialogue with both its form and its content."[94] Lichtenstein even remarks that biblical poetry is primarily "traditional poetry," and, as such, never exists without dialogue with someone, whether it is the poet with his religious and literary tradition or the poet with his audience, who shares that tradition.[95]

American poet Wendell Berry, writes that a poem

has the power to remind poet and reader alike of things they have read and heard. Also—and this is partly why the subject is so complex—it has the power to remind them of things that they have not read and heard, but that have been read and heard by others whom they have read and heard. Thus the art, so private in execution, is also communal and filial. It can only exist as a common ground between the poet and other poets and other people, living and dead. Any poem worth the name is the product of a convocation. It exists, literally, by recalling past voices into presence. . . . Poetry can be written only because it has been written. As a new poem is made, not only with the art but within it, past voices are convoked—to be changed, little or much, by the addition of another voice.[96]

As we saw above, the book of Nahum draws from literary traditions of the ANE. It shares features with texts from both inside and outside the Hebrew Bible. The poet also consciously draws from Israelite religious traditions. It should certainly be noted that Nahum does not simply repeat ANE or Israelite traditions; he adapts various elements of those traditions in the context of his audience. But Nahum, though writing in a

93. Johnson, *The Idea of Lyric*, 14.
94. Lichtenstein, "Biblical Poetry," 120.
95. Lichtenstein, "Biblical Poetry," 120–21.
96. Berry, "The Responsibility of the Poet," 88–89.

specific context, draws from and adds to those traditions. The use of the so-called "YHWH creed"[97] in Nah 1:3 is illustrative of how Nahum draws from Israelite larger religious tradition: "YHWH slow to anger, but great in power; he surely does not leave the guilty unpunished." The creed that we find in many Hebrew Bible texts (Exod 34:6–7; Num 14:18; Joel 2:13; Jonah 4:2) is used in Nahum with modifications. The full version of that creed is found in Exod 34:6–7:

> YHWH passed before him, and proclaimed, "YHWH, YHWH, a God merciful and gracious, slow to anger, and abounding in covenant loyalty and faithfulness; keeping covenant loyalty for the thousandth generation, forgiving iniquity, transgression, and sin; yet by no means clearing the guilty, but visiting the iniquity of the parents upon the children and the children's children, to the third and the fourth generation."

The use of a common tradition shows us that, when writing his poetry, Nahum speaks to an audience that he believes to be steeped in some common traditions and that can adopt Nahum's own addition to the tradition. The acknowledgement of the participation of biblical texts in a common ongoing tradition means that, when Nahum addresses eighth-seventh centuries BCE Judahites in their affliction, the poet also addresses all the generations that later identify with Israelite tradition. The book of Nahum apparently spoke to generations later, as shown by the use of part of it by the anonymous sixth-century poet, Second Isaiah:

> How beautiful upon the mountains
>   are the feet of the messenger who announces peace,
> who brings good news,
>   who announces salvation,
>   who says to Zion, "Your God is King."
> (Isa 52:7)

> Behold, on the mountains the feet of him
>   who brings good news,
>   who announces peace!
> "Celebrate your feasts, O Judah;
>   Pay your vows.
> For never again will Belia'al pass through you;
>   He is cut off completely."
> (Nah 2:1)

---

97. For a discussion on this creed, see Kelly, "Joel, Jonah, and the Yhwh Creed," 805–26.

Both Nahum and Second Isaiah address the question of comfort. Even though the two poets wrote in different historical contexts, it seems that, because the contexts of the two poets were somewhat similar—both dealing with affliction—Second Isaiah could adapt and use Nahum.

The direct consequence of Nahum's participation in a common tradition on my book is that, even though I focus on the book of Nahum, I assume that the other texts with which Nahum shares themes and literary features are important in understanding this book. Among those texts, the eleven prophetic books with which Nahum forms the so-called "Book of the Twelve" hold a special place.

In the last three decades, scholars have increasingly treated the Twelve Prophets as one book, rather than as independent books.[98] Scholars retrace the first treatment of the Twelve as one book to the Greek Old Testament, where the book of Sirach names the Twelve Prophets together: "May the bones of the Twelve Prophets send forth new life from where they lie, for they comforted the people of Jacob and delivered them with confident hope" (Sir 49:10, NRSV).[99] Some scholars believe that the Twelve could have circulated as independent books, but they came to be redacted into a unified book.[100] Others deny any redactional intention within the Book of the Twelve.[101] In this book, I follow the moderate position of David Petersen, who considers the Twelve to be, not a book like Jeremiah or Isaiah, but a "thematized anthology."[102] By that, Petersen means that these small books are organized around one theme: all of them, except Jonah and Nahum, speak about the theme of the Day of YHWH (*Yôm YHWH*). And while Nahum does not use that expression, Nahum's poem speaks about the day YHWH will exact punishment on Nineveh.[103] A similar position seems to have been adopted by the author of Sirach, who considered the Twelve to be about the theme of comfort

---

98. See Sweeney, "The Latter Prophets and Prophecy," 243–46; Nogalski and Sweeney, *Reading and Hearing the Book of the Twelve*.

99. See Redditt, "The Production and Reading of the Book of the Twelve," 26–27.

100. See for example the position of Nogalski, "Joel as 'Literary Anchor' for the Book of the Twelve," 91–109.

101. See Ben Zvi, "Twelve prophetic books or 'the Twelve,'" 125–56; for caution about avoiding fixity and absolute assumptions about intentional redaction in the Twelve, see Jones, "The book of the Twelve as a Witness," 65–74.

102. Petersen, "A Book of the Twelve?" 10.

103. Petersen, "A Book of the Twelve?" 10.

for the people of Judah. The depiction of the punishment on Nineveh then can be understood as a source of comfort and hope for the Judahites.

Conclusion

This exploration of Nahum's poetic features has shown us that the book of Nahum is particularly interested in *showing* the conditions in which the lamenters find themselves and in engaging them in dialogue. The choice of sublime lyric poetry is a consequence of that interest in bearing witness to the situation in which the audience finds itself; it is also a way of making YHWH present amid the catastrophes of the life of the prophet's community. In order well to read the book of Nahum, it is important to imagine the world from which this text could have emerged and in which it would have made sense.

4

The Historical Context of the Vision of Nahum

Assyrian Invasions and Judah's Collective Memory

Introduction

PREVIOUS DISCUSSIONS ON THE historical context of the book of Nahum have focused on the identity and geographical origin of the prophet, the dating of the book, or the events that led to the composition of the book. Since the book opens with a superscription that names Nineveh as its subject (1:1), discussions about the setting of Nahum have tried to find connections between the destruction of this Neo-Assyrian capital city and the events depicted in the book of Nahum.[1] The textual sources upon which they have heavily relied in this historical reconstruction have often served to decide whether the book of Nahum precedes or follows the fall of Nineveh in 612 BCE.[2] Even though there is no conclusive evidence about the relationship between the fall of Nineveh and the scenes depicted in the book of Nahum, scholars continue to focus on that historical event as central to the production of the book of Nahum, and indeed, it is often asserted that the book is an eye-witness account.

In this chapter, I reformulate the question of the historical context of the book of Nahum by arguing that the genre of the book requires that we focus on the kind of audience to which this book would have spoken

1. Sweeney, *The Twelve Prophets*, 419.
2. See for example the discussion in O'Brien, *Nahum*, 19.

(rather than focusing on the historical fall of Nineveh). I analyze both texts and icons related to Judah and the Neo-Assyrian Empire. This combination of textual and iconographic materials draws our attention away from the fall of Nineveh to the land of Judah in the seventh and eighth centuries, where many survivors of Assyrian violence would still have vivid recollection of Assyrian onslaught on Judahite cities. Nahum's depiction of the fall of Nineveh, rather than being an eyewitness account of that fall itself, is a *poetic evocation* and likely a reflection of other events, one that would have spoken powerfully to the collective memory of those Judahites who had survived the Assyrian violence of the eighth century BCE.

To such an audience, Nahum would not offer *information* about the destruction of a foreign city. Rather, through his text, the poet-prophet dialogues with his audience in such a way as to take them back to the events that destroyed their own community, to help them reckon with trauma and imagine an alternative to Assyrian domination. As was just shown, in order to achieve this goal of conversing with an audience familiar with traumatic events, the poet-prophet draws from the traditional forms of OAN and city laments, and shows his audience that the fall of Nineveh is YHWH's way of effecting justice and vindicating the cause of wronged victims. That is, YHWH repays the oppressor for what he did to other nations (cf. Ps 137:8–9).

I explain how I imagine Nahum's model audience in four stages. The first section of this chapter summarizes the current debates on the historical context of Nahum. The second part focuses on Neo-Assyrian palace art and royal propaganda. It starts with an explanation of how an iconographic approach to biblical texts[3] can illumine the study of the context of Nahum. Then I use as a case study the lion-hunt reliefs discovered by British-Assyrian archaeologist Hormuzd Rassam in the North Palace of Ashurbanipal, Assyrian bas-reliefs depicting the conquest of the Judahite city of Lachish by Sennacherib (705–681 BCE) in 701 BCE,[4] and archaeological excavations at Tel ed-Duweir (ancient Lachish). The third part considers the psychological consequences of the Assyrian invasion on the inhabitants of Lachish and how Nahum speaks to the collective trauma brought about by the conquest of Judahite towns by the Assyrians. The last part places the book of Nahum side-by-side

---

3. See Keel, *The Symbolism of the Biblical World*.
4. Russel, *Sennacherib's Palace Without Rival*, 39.

with the Neo-Assyrian bas-reliefs to show that the book may well evoke the destruction of the city of Lachish by Sennacherib in 701 BCE.

It should be noted that this is a heuristic choice, to focus attention on the Assyrian icons as an indirect witness to the kind of audience to which the book of Nahum would have spoken "prophetically," and to identify the survivors of the destruction of Lachish as a model audience. It is impossible to prove that the Judahite prophet-poet Nahum was himself an inhabitant of Lachish or its environs in the period of Assyrian destruction; moreover, it is unnecessary. What I intend to show here is that the oracles of Nahum bear some resemblance, in literary form, to the iconographic representation of the conquest of Lachish, and that that resemblance is itself useful in understanding how the biblical text may have functioned in the context of eighth and seventh-century Judah.

Scholarly Discussions on the Historical Context of Nahum

We saw in chapter 3 that one of the distinctive features of the book of Nahum is its vivid depiction of scenes of battle. Some scholars view such vivid descriptions as an indication that the prophet was writing right after the fall of Nineveh. Peter Machinist's argument evidences two related problems with such an approach:

> This graphic quality [of the description of the fall of Nineveh] indicates not prophecy of things to come, but a report—from the messenger already introduced—of things happening now or that have already happened, thus furnishing one indication that Nahum should date after, but probably not too long after, the actual conquest of Nineveh in 612 BC. What the prophet recounts is a Nineveh flooded out by water (2:7, 9) and stripped, like the prostitute she is (3:5), of her glory, riches, and power—her officials and army taken away and consumed.[5]

The first problem is Machinist's use of sources to establish that there was a flood, as Nahum supposedly "reports." Machinist relies too heavily on a much later source, a fifth-century account by the Greek physician Ktesias, whose books are available to us only through fragments preserved by other historians. The part that Machinist uses about the destruction of Nineveh was preserved by Diodorus Seculus:

---

5. Machinist, "The Fall of Assyria in Comparative Ancient Perspective," 181–82; see Sweeney, *The Twelve Prophets*, 422.

> Now there was a prophecy which had come down to him [the king of Assyria] from his ancestors: "No enemy will ever take Ninus by storm unless the river shall first become the city's enemy." Assuming, therefore, that this would never be, he held out in hope, his thought being to endure the siege and await the troops which would be sent from his subjects. The rebels, elated at their successes, pressed the siege, but because of the strength of the walls they were unable to do any harm to the men in the city; for *neither engines for throwing stones, nor shelters for sappers, nor battering-rams devised to overthrow walls had as yet been invented at that time*. Moreover, the inhabitants of the city had a great abundance of all provisions, since the king had taken thought on that score. Consequently the siege dragged on, and for two years they pressed their attack, making assaults on the walls and preventing inhabitants of the city from going out into the country; but in the third year, after there had been heavy and continuous rains, it came to *pass that the Euphrates, running very full, both inundated a portion of the city and broke down the walls for a distance of twenty stades* (II, 26:9—27:1).[6]

Ktesias does not cite his sources, and no earlier source corroborates his account. Furthermore, there seem to be problems even with some of the historical details, such as the statement that "neither engines for throwing stones, nor shelters for sappers, nor battering-rams devised to overthrow walls had as yet been invented at that time." There is ample evidence that these weapons had in fact been invented before the time of the destruction of Nineveh (612 BCE) and were widely used in Mesopotamia, even as early as the ninth century BCE.[7] Further, the Babylonian Chronicles recount the fall of Nineveh, but their account is quite different from that of Ktesias. The Chronicles recount that Median and Babylonian troops, after a three-month siege, attacked the city, "carried off the rich spoil of the city and the temple, (and) [turned] the city into a ruin heap."[8] Nothing is said of a flood. Archaeological excavations, as Machinist himself acknowledges, have not confirmed the hypothesis of the destruction of Nineveh by a flood.[9]

---

6. Diodorus, Siculus, *Complete Works of Diodorus Siculus*, Kindle loc 2637. Emphasis added.

7. Eph'al, *The City Besieged*, 82–85.

8. Cogan, *The Raging Torrent*, 192.

9. Machinist, "The Fall of Assyria," 193.

The second problem is Machinist's assumption that Nahum is offering a literal description of a flood. In 2:7, we read:

> The gates of the river are opened!
> The palace is dissolved (*nāmôg*).

Machinist considers *nāmôg* as a reference to literal flooding. The first colon of the verse speaks about the "gates of the rivers," so it seems that the verb *mûg* here might be a reference to literal flooding. The problem with translating *mûg* as "to flood" is that this verb nowhere else refers to literal flooding. The only place where *mûg* is associated with water is in Ps 65:11,

> You water its furrows, you settle its cuttings;
> You soften it (*těmōgěgenāh*) with showers;
> You bless its growth.

Note that, even when it is associated with water, *mûg* does not refer to literal flood. Other occurrences of this word have to do with either human beings (Exod 15:15; Josh 2:9, 24; 1 Sam 14:16; Isa 14:31; Jer 49:23; Ezek 21:15; Job 30:22) or inanimate objects (Amos 9:5, 13; Nah 1:5; Ps 46:7; 75:4; 107:26) melting away before YHWH. More telling is that the other occurrence of the same word in Nahum (1:5) has nothing to do with flooding: "mountains quake before him and the hills melt away (*hitmōgāgû*)."

The second verse used by Machinist is Nah 2:9:

> (Now Nineveh used to be *like a pool of water in her days*).
>   But they are fleeing!
> "Stop! Stop!"
>   But no one turns back!

Machinist takes this comparison to mean that Nineveh actually became a *pool of water because of flooding*.[10] But the two verses on either side of this one speak about a situation in which people are fleeing from the city because it is under attack. It seems clear that the reference to a pool of water is a *metaphor*, not a historical report.[11] Nineveh is being drained of its inhabitants, like a pool whose waters are drying up.

---

10. Machinist, "The Fall of Assyria," 191.
11. See O'Brien, *Nahum, Habakkuk, Zephaniah*, 47.

Other scholars date Nahum before the fall of Nineveh,[12] pointing out that the book represents Assyria as an active threat, with Judah still under the Empire's yoke (1:13).[13] Some of those scholars maintain that prophets "do not wait until destruction is evident before making their predictions";[14] it makes little sense, they claim, that Nahum would have offered an elaborate "prediction" or description of the fall of an already fallen empire/city.[15] Walter Maier's point is similar to that of Machinist, namely, that Nahum knew about the fall of Nineveh. They are different only because, while Machinist says that Nahum knew about the fall of Nineveh after the fact through human means, Maier argues that he knew about it beforehand through divine revelation.

Marvin Sweeney's position lies between that of Machinist and the one that dates the book before the fall of the city. He believes that the book was written either after or shortly before the fall of Nineveh, when it was obvious that the city was about to fall. His reason for dating Nahum around the fall of Nineveh is that predicting the fall of a strong empire that was still standing would lack rhetorical power, because the poet would have nothing with which to support his claim that YHWH was going to do what he announced: "Clearly, the prophet's rhetorical strategy depends upon the ability to point to Nineveh's fall as a demonstrable event that has already taken place or is imminent."[16]

What both sides of the debate take for granted is that Nahum writes in response to something external to Judah: information or stimulus that comes to him from *outside* Judah. They do not consider the text as a response to the concerns of Nahum's Judahite audience. They also do not take into account the fact that the book of Nahum is written in poetry and therefore does not report, but evokes. Further, they do not treat the book as an OAN. As was shown above, most OAN are not interested in reporting facts *about the nations that they threaten*. They can draw from historical events (e.g., Nah 3:8–10), but the driving force behind the text itself is the experience of the prophet's community. The text aims at *countering* the message sent by the oppressor (through the invasion and devastation of Judah), namely that YHWH will not save his people (see

---

12. Maier, *The Book of Nahum*, 31; Weigl, "Current Research on the Book of Nahum," 81–82.

13. Lanner, "Who Will Lament Her?" 7.

14. Maier, *The Book of Nahum*, 32.

15. Maier, *The Book of Nahum*, 10.

16. Sweeney, *The Twelve Prophets*, 422.

2 Kgs 18:32–35) with a vivid depiction of how YHWH actually takes on the oppressor and delivers those who are oppressed.

When we read the book of Nahum in conversation with Assyrian bas-reliefs depicting Assyrian conquest of Judahite towns, we find that the book of Nahum likely takes the reader, not to the ruins of *Nineveh*, but to the scenes of the conquest of *Judahite* towns by the Assyrians. While voicing the sufferings of the Judahites who survived the Assyrian invasion in 701 BCE (in a way similar to what we find in expressions of national and personal sufferings in the book of Lamentations or in some psalms of lament), the book also imagines a future in which YHWH will put an end to Assyrian pride and violence by making Assyria pay for what it did to Judah. The book conveys the message that violence against Assyria will be a response to what she did to Judah by presenting a tableau that would have made it clear to his audience that what the prophet declared for Assyria was a reproduction of the violence perpetrated against Judah. In addition, the threefold repetition of the participle *nōqēm* (avenging) in 1:2 makes it clear that the reader's attention should be drawn to YHWH's vengeance.[17] The rhetorical power of the book becomes clearer when we place it within the larger context of Assyrian ideologies of domination and royal propaganda.

Assyrian Palace Art and Royal Propaganda

Modern biblical scholarship largely focuses on Near Eastern *texts* related to the Bible and on finding parallels between those texts and the Bible. The seals and icons that have been recovered by archaeologists over the last century and more have largely been ignored by exegetes, or used simply for the sake of confirming information that is already available in texts. They have not been treated as sources of information in their own right about the culture and social life of the ancient Near East.[18] The reason might have to do with (over-)specialization in scholarship, for art has its own language, which requires training.[19] Not having the appropriate training, biblical scholars are often inept with complex images, just as art historians can be inept with complex texts (e.g., biblical texts). Thus, that images have not been very much used in biblical studies does not have to

---

17. See O'Brien, *Nahum*, 48–49.
18. de Hulster and LeMon, "Introduction," xix.
19. Uehlinger, "Clio in a World of Pictures," 225.

be attributed to any intentional refusal by scholars to deal with images.[20] It might be due to the lack of familiarity with the language of icons.

However, because the Bible comes from a culture and a society that is not familiar to modern men and women—and metaphors, which are extensively used in the Bible, are rooted in their places and time of origin[21]—the study of icons becomes very important because icons show the reader, in artifacts, the world that underlies the metaphors used in biblical texts.

One important methodological premise of iconographic exegesis is that images should be analyzed according to artistic/aesthetic principles. Uehlinger writes,

> We shall posit that in order to correctly use and evaluate a pictorial source in historical terms, the modern interpreter not only has to learn the particular "language" of images . . . but also to inquire into the rules which governed their commissioning, production and display in antiquity.[22]

To avoid conflating images with texts, iconographic exegetes have suggested that interpreters follow distinct steps that pay due attention to both texts and images. Izaak J. de Hulster suggests that the interpreter first determine the date or the approximate date of the text that she intends to study. Once the date is determined, the interpreter should look for images related to the period and locale from which the text came, and analyze them *as images*.

In addition to illumining the study of biblical metaphors, Near Eastern icons also teach us about past events and the organization of society in antiquity. The Neo-Assyrian palace art that I analyze in this section gives us a vivid depiction of the image that Neo-Assyrian kings made of themselves and of other beings (human and non-human). Beginning with the period of apogee under Tiglath-pileser III (744–727 BCE), during which the Neo-Assyrian Empire started keeping a standing army, Assyrian monarchs embarked on an expansionist program aimed at transforming the whole known world into one large empire. Central to the political and military project of expanding the empire and "assyrianizing" the world was the ideology of kingship and the work of propaganda, of spreading the image—literally and figuratively—of the Assyrian king. "The Great

---

20. As suggested by Brown, *Seeing the Psalms*, 3–4.
21. de Hulster, *Iconographic Exegesis and Third Isaiah*, 114.
22. Uehlinger, "Clio in a World of Pictures," 224–25.

King" was proclaimed as both the representative of the gods and the symbol of civilization, and through both those roles, as protector of his realm against dangers. As I shall show, the iconography of empire established the king's reputation as "protector" of the empire chiefly through depiction of two activities: war and (curiously to most moderns) hunting, especially hunting lions and wild bulls.

The Neo-Assyrian kings built and embellished enormous palaces that functioned, in their own right, as means of propaganda. Thus Sennacherib (or his royal chroniclers) explains his palace renovation project:

> At that time, after I had completed the palace in the midst of the city of Nineveh for my royal residence, had filled it with gorgeous furnishings, *for the astonishment of all the people*, (I found that) the side-palace, which the former kings, my ancestors, had built for the care of the camp, the standing of the horses, and the storing of things in general had no terrace, that its site was too small . . . .[23]

Many of the walls of Assyrian royal palaces were adorned with reliefs depicting victories and achievements of the monarchs. In this section, I analyze the "lion hunt" reliefs from the North Palace of Ashurbanipal (668–627 BCE) and the Lachish reliefs from the Southwest Palace of Sennacherib. While the former offer us a generic example of royal propaganda, the latter depict a particular historical instance of the performance of the ideology of Assyrian kingship.

Lion Hunt Reliefs from the North Palace of Ashurbanipal

Since the third millennium BCE, Assyrian kings were associated with hunting wild animals, especially lions, bulls, and serpents.[24] In the first millennium BCE, hunting lions became a sport, a political activity, and a religious duty for the Assyrian monarch.[25] Lion hunting was so central to Assyrian royal administration that the seals of Assyrian kings depicted the king slaying a lion.[26] How hunting lions became almost an obsession for some Assyrian kings had to do with the characteristics associated with the lion in the ancient Near East. One of the oldest motifs associated with

---

23. Luckenbill, *The Annals of Sennacherib*, 128. Emphasis added.
24. Cassin, "Le Roi et le Lion," 356.
25. Cassin, "Le Roi et le Lion," 375–81.
26. Strawn, *What Is Stronger Than a Lion?* 171.

the lion was that of the lion as wicked, as enemy, and as threat to order.[27] Lions attacked other animals, people's domestic animals (e.g., sheep), and human beings. As predators *par excellence*, lions came to be viewed as the greatest danger. Their actions were understood to be crimes in the same category as human crimes.[28] They seem to have been perceived as a danger not only to humans and animals, but also to gods and to world order. It is because of the threat that lions represented that they were considered prime enemies of the Assyrian king.[29] From this perspective, then, the lion was considered as the representation of everything that was *not* Assyrian. The lion was the beast of the fields and the image of the uncivilized world that needed to be conquered and tamed.[30] In short, the lion stood for the forces of chaos and disorder.

Yet, from another perspective, the lion *was* Assyria. This unstoppable beast, while appearing as the first enemy of the Assyrian king, also represented everything the Assyrian monarch claimed to be. It represented ultimate power. Kings often referred to themselves as lions, thus appropriating the characteristics associated with lions.[31]

Hunting and killing those animals became then, for the king, a means of attesting his role as protector of his realm and destroyer of every agent of disorder in his empire. By killing the lion, the king showed that he—not the lion—was the supreme power of the world. For that reason, it was illegal for an ordinary person to kill a lion.[32] Since killing lions was seen as a heroic task that only the king could fulfill, allowing ordinary citizens to kill that animal would have suggested that the king was but an ordinary Assyrian. It would have also removed the fear of the beast against which the world *needed* the Great King. The lion-hunt reliefs from the North Palace of Ashurbanipal that I analyze in this section are some of the most memorable examples of palace art serving royal proclamation and propaganda. They bring to the viewer the image of the king as he wished to be perceived inside and outside his empire.

27. Strawn, *What is Stronger Than a Lion?* 134.
28. Cassin, "Le Roi et le Lion," 385.
29. Strawn, *What is Stronger Than a Lion?* 145.
30. Watanambe, *Animal Symbolism in Mesopotamia*, 87.
31. See for examples, Hammurabi, who calls himself "a young lion" or Sennacherib and Esarhaddon, who identify their actions with those of lions (Cassin, "Le Roi et le Lion," 360, 370).
32. Cassin, "Le Roi et le Lion," 375.

Ashurbanipal's North Palace at Nineveh (Kuyunjik) was discovered in 1853 by a British expedition led by Hormuzd Rassam. The palace contained remains of Ashurbanipal's library and numerous bas-reliefs on the walls of its rooms, many of which are in excellent condition. Over one hundred slabs from the walls of that palace have been kept in the British Museum.[33] The sculptures featured two main themes: war and lion hunt, where we see "the king shown proudly victorious over powerful enemies, whether royal beasts or men."[34] Archaeologists imaginatively reconstructed the palace, assigning letter numbers to the reconstructed rooms. We will focus on Room C, labeled the "Lion-Hunt Room" by the British Museum.

This room was entirely decorated with slabs depicting a lion-hunting expedition.[35] In addition to lion-hunt reliefs, part of Ashurbanipal library was found in this room.[36] Although in the condition of its discovery the room apparently was being used for storage,[37] it is very likely that this room was designed and decorated for other, more important purposes. Its position in the palace complex and its size (small and hallway-like) suggest that this room is connected to rooms A, S, and R. All the four rooms seem to have been parts of an alleyway that visitors and palace insiders would have used going from the western portal into the great court J.[38] Those walking through rooms S, R, and A would have seen general hunting scenes and images of people going to and coming from hunting expeditions. Arriving in Room C, which served as ante-chamber leading to the court, one had reached what mattered the most: the royal hunting of lions. These are the images that were meant to stick to the minds of the visitors. The twenty-nine extant slabs in this room paint the hunt itself as

---

33. See the catalogue in Barnett, *Sculptures from the North Palace of Ashurbanipal at Nineveh*, 66.

34. Barnett, *Sculptures from the North Palace of Ashurbanipal at Nineveh*, 12.

35. Barnett, *Sculptures from the North Palace of Ashurbanipal at Nineveh*, 12.

36. Barnett, *Sculptures from the North Palace of Ashurbanipal at Nineveh*, 32.

37. Barnett, *Sculptures from the North Palace of Ashurbanipal at Nineveh*, 32.

38. Barnett suggests that, in order for this most plausible explanation to work, we need to allow for the existence of a door leading from Room C into court J. Note that Boucher, the artist whose drawings of the palace have been the standard drawings for the British Museum, does not leave a door connecting Room C and court J. But without such a door, as Barnett suggests, it makes little sense why the ascending passage that starts in room S (at the western portal) would simply lead to such a small room as Room C.

the focus of massive public organization and palace machinery designed to display the bravery and power of the king.

On the wall directly opposite the entrance to the room, those entering were confronted by three slabs (15–17) giving a summary of the hunt:[39] dead lions, guards, servants, and a lion being released from a cage. The lions are depicted as ferocious, but also helpless in face of the power of the king. Other slabs placed around the room show the royal attendants preparing for the hunt and managing the horses and the weapons at the hunt site; the citizens of Nineveh are seen rushing through a wooded area to view the spectacle. The presence of these spectators suggests that the hunt was a staged performance, but it also depicts the citizens' approval of what the king was doing. As public transcripts of the Assyrian empire, this scene creates what James C. Scott calls "the appearance of unanimity among the ruling groups and the appearance of consent among the subordinates."[40] The image is of a monarch supported by loyal servants and a willing and enthusiastic public. This official image of "typical Assyrians" did not need to coincide with reality. The image was designed to speak to both outsiders and insiders, proclaiming national unity to the former and reminding the latter of what they needed to be.[41] This representation then encouraged national unity and loyalty.

The most interesting and poignant "characters" in the reliefs are the lions themselves. Another set of slabs (10, 11, and 12; plate VII) depicts a scene full of lions doomed to death: some have fallen to the arrows of the king; others are vomiting blood; still others are pierced by arrows and walk in pain and rage to the servants standing with hounds.[42] These lions had been caged and released in order to be massacred by the king. In another slab we see, just behind the chariot of the king, two dead lions covered in arrows. Another lion that seems to have been left for dead springs up to attack the chariot. The king's two attendants strike the springing lion with their spears. A third dead lion lies under the king's chariot. This scene shows a king surrounded by danger, and yet vanquishing every danger. The massacre seems to have been a *mise en scène* of what the artist wanted the viewers to believe about the world: a place full of danger, in which the king was much needed.

---

39. Barnett, *Sculptures from the North Palace of Ashurbanipal at Nineveh*, 37.
40. Scott, *Domination and the Arts of Resistance*, 55.
41. Weissert, "Royal Hunt and Royal Triumph," 356.
42. Barnett, *Sculptures from the North Palace of Ashurbanipal at Nineveh*, 37.

These scenes of the king facing the most ferocious beast intend to show the visitor a monarch who is ready to risk his own life for the sake of his kingdom. The reliefs encourage any possible enemy of the king (both inside and outside the empire) to imagine in their own person the defeat and pain that was the inevitable result of opposition to the Great King.[43] The poignancy with which the pain and death of the lions is represented underscores the king's capacity to subdue the worst of enemies, the beasts who represent the threat of disorder, chaos to the Assyrian world.

The image of the king presented in Ashurbanipal's lion-hunt reliefs helps us better understand the destruction of the city of Lachish by his grandfather, Sennacherib, as an episode in the Assyrian king's performance of the image that he made of himself.

Sennacherib's Invasion of Judah and the "Lachish Reliefs" at Nineveh

When Sennacherib invaded Judah in 701 BCE, the kingdoms of Israel and Judah had been feeling the weight of Assyrian domination for more than a century. The first known contact between Israel/Judah and Assyria happened at the battle of Qarqar (853 BCE), during which, according to the Kurkh Monolith, King Ahab of Israel (ca. 871–852 BCE) joined a coalition of twelve kings to mount opposition against Shalmaneser III (859–824 BCE).[44]

Interactions between the Assyrian empire and Israel/Judah led first to the conquest and destruction of the Northern kingdom of Israel by Shalmaneser V (727–722 BCE).[45] Twenty years later, Sennacherib invaded the kingdom of Judah and destroyed many of Judah's fortified cities. The Hebrew Bible states that all the fortified cities of Judah were taken by the Assyrians: "In the fourteenth year of King Hezekiah, Sennacherib, king of Assyria, went up against all the fortified cities of Judah and

---

43. Cassin, "Le Roi et le Lion," 400 ; Weissert, "Royal Hunt and Royal Triumph," 350. Compare this to the statement about YHWH in Nah 1:9, "No opposition rises up twice."

44. Cogan, *The Raging Torrent*, 14–15.

45. See 2 Kgs 17:1–6.

captured them" (2 Kgs 18:13; Isa 36; 2 Chr 32:2).[46] Only Jerusalem seems to have survived destruction by Sennacherib.[47]

The discovery of bas-reliefs in Sennacherib's XXXVI palace ("Palace without Rival") at Nineveh (today's Kuyunjik) by British archaeologist Austen Layard has shed light on one of the cities that Sennacherib besieged in 701 BCE, the garrison of Lachish, located about sixty kilometers southwest of Jerusalem, in the Shephelah. Sennacherib himself does not mention Lachish in his official account of his campaign to Judah. However, the inscription placed upon one of the slabs does make this identification, which is confirmed by the details on the bas-reliefs (e.g., the clothing worn by the captives, the booty carried by the captives, the vegetation) and the discovery by archaeologists at Lachish of a palace-fort similar to the one shown on the reliefs. Remarkably, the Hebrew Bible does not speak directly about the siege or fall of Lachish.

What we read from the Hebrew Bible is that Sennacherib resided in Lachish when he besieged Jerusalem (2 Kgs 18:14; Isa 36:2; 2 Chr 32:9).[48]

Lachish before Sennacherib

The city of Lachish had been inhabited since the Late Bronze Age.[49] The book of Chronicles (2 Chr 11:5–12) mentions Lachish among the cities fortified by Rehoboam (ca 931–915 BCE). Ussishkin has identified this fortified city with the archeological Level V of Lachish. It is possible that, after the division of the United Kingdom, Lachish became a Judahite fortress city under Asa (908–867 BCE) or Jehoshaphat (870–846 BCE).[50] At

---

46. Scholars disagree on how many times Sennacherib invaded Judah. However, they all agree that Sennacherib invaded Judah (once or twice) and his invasion(s) had a massive impact on Judah and Judahites. In this book, I will not address the question of the number of times Sennacherib invaded Judah. It suffices to know that his invasion(s) brought massive destructions to Judean lives. For full discussions on the question of Sennacherib's campaign(s) in Judah, see Evans, *The Invasion of Sennacherib in the Book of Kings*; Childs, *Isaiah and the Assyrian Crisis*.

47. Cogan, *The Raging Torrent*, 114–15.

48. The closest we get to a description of the conquest of Lachish is the prediction of its punishment by YHWH in Mic 1:13, "Attach the chariots to the steeds, woman inhabitant of Lachish; you are the beginning of the sin of Fair Zion, because in you are found the crimes of Israel." But even though Lachish is threatened with attack in this passage, we hear nothing about how that punishment was carried out by YHWH.

49. Ussishkin, "Lachish," 555; see Josh 10:31–32.

50. Ussishkin, "Lachish," 558.

this time (Level IV), Lachish gained in importance, as evidenced by the fact that when rebellion broke against him in Jerusalem, King Amaziah of Judah (796–767 BCE) took refuge in Lachish (2 Kgs 14:19). The city was surrounded by massive fortifications. It had a large outer wall, an inner wall, a large city-gate, and a large palace-fort.[51] This level of the city had only government houses (with no domestic buildings). It was eventually destroyed by an earthquake around 760 BCE.[52] However, even after the earthquake, life seems to have continued in the city.[53] During the time of Hezekiah, repair works were undertaken. A large number of Judahite military personnel stayed at Lachish, which was rebuilt as a government center, to watch over the southwest of the kingdom, while Jerusalem watched over the northeast.[54] Lachish's military importance must have been one of the motivations for Sennacherib to target it. This level of the city of Lachish (Level III) is the most important for this study, because it was this level that was destroyed by Sennacherib in 701 BCE. Level III Lachish was distinguished by a massive palace-fort, city walls with a defensive wall and a revetment wall supporting the defensive wall and a large city-gate complex made of two gatehouses, an outer and a massive inner gatehouse.[55] The many civilian houses and shops indicate that the population of Lachish increased before the invasion of the city by Sennacherib in 701 BCE.

Sennacherib at Lachish

According to Ussishkin, "It is clear that upon arriving in Judah, Sennacherib's attention was focused primarily on the city of Lachish. Lachish was the most formidable citadel in Judah, and its conquest and destruction seemed the paramount task facing Sennacherib when he came to crush the military powers of Hezekiah."[56] Archeology and Assyrian documents confirm the importance of Lachish in defending Judah against Assyrian invasion.

   51. Ussishkin, "Lachish," 558.
   52. Ussishkin, "Lachish," 558.
   53. Ussishkin, *The Conquest of Lachish*, 30.
   54. Ussishkin, *The Conquest of Lachish*, 27.
   55. This gatehouse is the largest known of its kind. See Ussishkin, *The Conquest of Lachish*, 31.
   56. Ussishkin, *The Conquest of Lachish*, 17.

Archeological Perspective

In 1929, W. F. Albright identified Tel ed-Duweir with the biblical city of Lachish.[57] In 1932, British archeologist James Leslie Starkey (in collaboration with Olga Tufnell and Lancaster Harding) started excavations at Tel ed-Duweir. The excavations ended when Starkey was murdered in 1938.[58] Between 1966 and 1968, Professor Yohanan Aharoni of Tel Aviv University carried out limited excavations at the mound.[59] Since 1973, excavations at Tel ed-Duweir have been carried out by the Institute of Archeology of Tel Aviv University under the direction of David Ussishkin.[60]

Excavators identify Lachish III with the city that was destroyed by Sennacherib in 701 BCE.[61] Ussishkin reconstructs the attack of the city by Sennacherib by studying the topography of the mound.[62] He shows that the first thing the Assyrians did was to pitch their camp on one hilltop on southeast Lachish.[63] This location allowed the Assyrians to attack the city without much danger.

Starkey's and Ussishkin's teams found evidence of fire and destruction of houses and shops—charred wood and ashes; the city was evidently burned to the ground.[64] Hundreds of arrowheads (many of which were unused) and iron and bronze armor scales as well as sling stones that must have been used by both attackers and defenders during the battle, have also been discovered.[65] Large heaps of stones are identified as the remains of the Neo-Assyrian siege ramp. This is the oldest such ramp found in the ancient Near East and, more importantly, the only Assyrian ramp found to date, a point to which we shall return below.[66] Ussishkin estimates that between 13,000 and 19,000 tons of stones were used to build a ramp some 50–60 meters wide.[67]

---

57. Ussishkin, *The Conquest of Lachish*, 19.
58. Ussishkin, *The Conquest of Lachish*, 22.
59. Ussishkin, *The Conquest of Lachish*, 23.
60. Ussishkin, *The Conquest of Lachish*, 23.
61. Tufnell, *Lachish III*, 55.
62. Ussishkin, *The Conquest of Lachish*, 49.
63. Ussishkin, *The Conquest of Lachish*, 49.
64. Ussishkin, *The Conquest of Lachish*, 50; Tufnell, *Lachish III*, 56.
65. Tufnell, *Lachish III*, 55.
66. Ussishkin, *The Conquest of Lachish*, 54.
67. Ussishkin, "Sennacherib's Campaign to Philistia and Judah," 345.

Ussishkin and his team have also discovered cheap pottery and ordinary utensils in burned houses, but no evidence of valuables or human remains in those burned houses. Ussishkin concludes that

> the city was set afire immediately after its conquest rather than during the battle. Once the city was taken by the invaders it was ransacked and looted and the inhabitants were forced out. Allowed to take with them only what they could carry on their backs, they naturally discarded all the heavy, cheap and easily replaceable objects, such as stone utensils and pottery vessels.[68]

Another important archeological finding has been the discovery of a number of mass graves (some of which can be dated to 701 BCE) where a population of mostly children and women were buried without much ceremony. Starkey and his team estimated the number of skulls to about 1,500.[69] Even though some of the skeletons show signs of burning—which might suggest that they perished in fire—Tufnell attributes the death to their inability to stand the siege.[70] It is then possible that these people died because of the siege (famine, diseases, etc.) and were taken, after the battle had ended, to be buried *en masse*.[71] Because most of the skeletons belonged to women and children, it is possible that the people buried in these mass graves were civilians.[72]

These archaeological findings bear witness to a situation of utter destruction in Lachish around 701 BCE. They have also helped us better interpret the account of the destruction of Lachish as given in the Assyrian bas-reliefs.

The Perspective of Assyrian bas-reliefs

In 1847, Austen H. Layard discovered a number of bas-reliefs in Room XXXVI of Sennacherib's "Palace without Rival."[73] The walls of Room XXXVI are believed to have been entirely covered with reliefs depicting the siege and fall of the city of Lachish.[74] The room was built in the

---

68. Ussishkin, *The Conquest of Lachish*, 54.
69. Tufnell, *Lachish III*, 62.
70. Tufnell, *Lachish III*, 62.
71. Ussishkin, *The Conquest of Lachish*, 56.
72. Ussishkin, *The Conquest of Lachish*, 56.
73. Uehlinger, "Clio in a World of Pictures," 221.
74. Ussishkin, "The 'Lachish Reliefs' and the City of Lachish," 177.

rear end of the palace. Before one reached Room XXXVI, one passed through three doorways: the first one led from the Court XIX to Room XXIX (outer hall); the second led from the outer hall to Room XXXIV (central hall); then the third led from the central hall to Room XXVI at the rear.[75] At each doorway were erected two colossal winged bulls whose sizes decreased the farther one entered the palace, starting with approximately 18 foot bulls at the outer hall, down to approximately 12 foot bulls at the entrance of Room XXXVI.[76] Ussishkin, following Layard, has remarked that the placement of these bulls created an imposing vision to anyone who looked to the inner room standing from the court: because the bulls were placed in decreasing sizes, one had the impression that the palace was very deep and that the chambers were quite distant from one another.[77]

Inside Room XXXVI, each wall was covered with the Lachish Reliefs. Unfortunately, the reliefs on the left wall are missing.[78] Only twelve slabs[79] have been recovered; they are now housed in the British Museum. The slabs were arranged in the room in such a way as any visitor entering the room would be struck by the impressive power of the Assyrian monarch. The back wall facing the visitor was covered with six slabs (I–VI). Slabs III and IV, which depict the storming of the city of Lachish by Sennacherib's army, were placed, in Ussishkin's words, "exactly in the centre of the rear wall of the room, opposite the entrance. Given good lighting conditions, anyone who passed through the main entrance could see the storming of Lachish as he proceeded through the three doorways flanked by the colossi."[80] The twelve extant slabs depict the siege of and victory over Lachish with details that give one the impression of watching the battle unfold. No other Assyrian campaign received such attention from an Assyrian monarch. Clearly, for Sennacherib, the victory over Lachish was one of the most important achievements of his reign.

75. Ussishkin, "The 'Lachish Reliefs' and the City of Lachish," 176.
76. Ussishkin, "The 'Lachish Reliefs' and the City of Lachish," 176.
77. Ussishkin, "The 'Lachish Reliefs' and the City of Lachish," 176.
78. See Fig. 6 in Ussishkin, "Sennacherib's Campaign to Philistia and Judah," 347. Layard and Ussishkin have suggested that these slabs depicted large bodies of "horsemen and charioteers." See Ussishkin, "The 'Lachish Reliefs' and the City of Lachish," 178.
79. There are various ways of numbering the slabs. I follow Ussishkin in numbering the extant slabs from I to XII.
80. Ussishkin, "The 'Lachish Reliefs' and the City of Lachish," 178.

Slab I, placed to the left corner of the back wall (opposite the entrance), depicts the attacking infantry. As on the other slabs, the background of this slab looks rocky, with plants (olive trees, grape vines, fig trees) behind and between the soldiers. The presence of these valuable crops suggests that, in addition to being militarily important, Lachish was also an important economic center. This economic factor would have been another motivation for the conquest of the city by Sennacherib. There are three columns of soldiers (archers and slingers) advancing in pairs—the image of a well-organized and disciplined Assyrian army.[81] All the archers and slingers on this slab are standing with their weapons in hands.[82] Slab II depicts foot soldiers rushing in three rows to attack the city. The central and lower rows depict spearmen, swords stuck into their belts, holding shields as they advance. Arrows coming down from defending Lachishites stick to the shield of the leading spearman.[83] The upper row depicts pairs of archers and slingers. Heaps of sling stones are shown in front of the slingers. This slab also depicts city walls with defenders manning them from towers. Some sling stones and arrows appear to be flying from the Assyrians to the defenders, who are perched above the walls, while Assyrian soldiers climb onto ramps placed against the walls of the city. Defenders are shooting arrows and stones or are simply throwing stones with bare hands.[84]

Slab III was placed in the center of the wall. It depicts the storming of Lachish. It shows the city gate, disconnected from the walls of the city. Many Judahite soldiers fight from the walls and from the roof of the gatehouse. Meanwhile, battering rams on ramps[85] and siege machines are pounding against the walls in order to breach them. The defenders are attempting to throw fire on the machines in order to destroy them, but Assyrian soldiers extinguish fire with water and continue to attack. To the left of the gatehouse are two battering rams, while to the right of the gatehouse five battering rams are shown ascending on ramps. If this number is accurate, then Lachish was attacked with at least seven battering rams. Ussishkin has remarked that this is the largest number of

---

81. Uehlinger, "Clio in a World of Pictures," 277.
82. Ussishkin, *The Conquest of Lachish*, 94–96.
83. Ussishkin, *The Conquest of Lachish*, 97.
84. Ussishkin, *The Conquest of Lachish*, 80, 99.

85. There seem to be two siege ramps, although only one has been archaeologically attested.

battering rams shown in any Neo-Assyrian relief.[86] Spearmen, slingers, and archers directly attack the defenders perched above the walls and the gatehouse. Ladders are thrown down, along with fire and missiles by defenders. Three bodies of soldiers are falling to the ground from the top of the wall. In the midst of this confusion, columns of deportees are shown leaving the city through the city-gate.[87] One can see four women and two men carrying bags on their shoulders and walking away from Lachish. At the bottom of the siege ramp, near the city gate through which the deportees are leaving, three naked prisoners are impaled on poles while two Assyrian soldiers secure the poles. The location where these prisoners are impaled must have been chosen for the sake of instilling fear and dissuading the deportees from rebelling.

On slab IV, we see the continuation of the battle scene from slab III. We also see columns of booty-bearers and deportees advancing towards Sennacherib, who is sitting on the camp right outside Lachish. Battering rams are shown on ramps, with soldiers climbing and shooting. Three Judahite military chariots are set afire by defenders and thrown on the attacking Assyrians.[88] To the right of the city are shown two rows of people. Judahite families heading for exile are shown in the lower row. They walk camels loaded with goods or carrying women and babies. Assyrian soldiers are depicted on the upper row, carrying booty. Slab V continues the scene from slab IV. On it we see Assyrian soldiers carrying booty (cultic objects and a Judahite government chariot).[89] On the upper row, we see a man leading a bullock and prisoners with raised hands, begging for mercy. On the lower row, we see a spearman leading two prisoners, while two other prisoners (probably dead) are lying naked on the ground.[90] On slab VI, placed to the right corner of the wall, we see deportees walking towards Sennacherib on the upper row. On slab VII, placed on the right-hand wall, on the lower row, we see one soldier leading a prisoner, while another soldier is stabbing a half-naked prisoner seated on the ground.[91]

86. Ussishkin, *The Conquest of Lachish*, 102.

87. David Ussishkin points out that these deportees are leaving the city after the battle has ended, not during the battle. This means that the slabs are not necessarily giving us a chronological account of the unfolding of the battle. They sometimes combine scenes that happened at different moments. See Ussishkin, *The Conquest of Lachish*, 102.

88. Ussishkin, *The Conquest of Lachish*, 105.

89. Ussishkin, *The Conquest of Lachish*, 84.

90. Ussishkin, *The Conquest of Lachish*, 86.

91. Ussishkin, *The Conquest of Lachish*, 86.

Slab VIII shows Sennacherib sitting on his throne. Two eunuchs stand behind the king with fans. The king looks towards the defeated city of Lachish, from which come Assyrian soldiers leading prisoners and deportees. Some prisoners are kneeling and begging for mercy. Above the king is placed an inscription that reads: "Sennacherib, king of all, king of Assyria, sitting on his *nemedu* throne while the spoil from the city of Lachish passed before him."[92] Uehlinger has commented on the presence of the *nemedu*[93] throne on the reliefs:

> Although Sennacherib's [*nemedu*] is not strictly speaking a divine throne, it seems that his sitting on the *nemedu* chair could be perceived as a quasi-divine, and certainly ever-protected manifestation of the royal persona, to which Sennacherib and his contemporaries may well have attached some kind of battle-winning significance.[94]

Slab IX depicts the royal tent and chariots. Above the tent we read a short inscription, "Tent of Sennacherib, king of Assyria."[95] Below the tent stands a ceremonial chariot. More royal chariots appear on slab X, and the final extant slabs, XI and XII depict the Assyrian camp.

Lachish is one of the rare cases where archeological excavations match Assyrian textual or iconographical descriptions of an ancient city.[96] Archeological digs and the Assyrian bas-reliefs have offered us the picture of a city whose inhabitants suffered major losses at the hands of the Assyrians. In light of the data that we have analyzed in this section, it is now important to consider the psychological impact of such violence on the Lachishites in particular and on Judahites in general.

Trauma and the Inhabitants of Lachish

The scenes depicted in these bas-reliefs and the findings from archaeological digs show that the conquest of Lachish (with other fortified cities)[97]

---

92. Ussishkin, *The Conquest of Lachish*, 109.

93. A royal throne "characterized by three rows of anthropomorphic genies" (see Uehlinger, "Clio in a World of Pictures," 288).

94. Uehlinger, "Clio in a World of Pictures," 288.

95. Ussishkin, *The Conquest of Lachish*, 109.

96. Ussishkin, *The Conquest of Lachish*, 118–19; see Layard, *Discoveries among the Ruins of Nineveh and Babylon*, 128–29.

97. Cogan, *The Raging Torrent*, 114.

was a traumatic event for both the surviving inhabitants of Lachish and many other Judahites. From a military standpoint, the fall of a highly fortified city had the potential of disrupting, among Judahites, belief in Hezekiah's power to stand up to Assyrian leaders or to protect the people against external threats. The description of Hezekiah's preparation measures (2 Chr 29–32; 2 Kgs 18; 20) suggests that he was a good military leader. Those preparation measures would have boosted the trust of the Judahites in Hezekiah and his military expertise. However, that trust in the power of Hezekiah and his army to avert Assyrian invasions would also have made people more likely to become traumatized by the shaking of the system in which they had believed. That is, Hezekiah's preparation measures made Judahites less prepared for what was going to happen to them.[98]

The taunt of the Rabshakeh in 2 Kgs 18–19 (cf. Isa 36–37) might reflect a historical speech, but it might also be the expression of the disillusionment of the Judahites in the face of the Assyrian destruction of Judahite cities:

> Tell Hezekiah, "Thus says the great king, the king of Assyria: what is this trust that you have?"
> (2 Kgs 18:19; Isa 36:4)

> Do not let Hezekiah make you trust in YHWH, saying, "YHWH will surely rescue us, and this city will not be handed over to the king of Assyria."
> (2 Kgs 18:30; Isa 36:18)

The last verse also shows that the destruction of Judahite cities was seen as more than failure of political and military leadership. It was also a moment of trial for faith in YHWH, the God who was supposed to rescue the people of Judah. YHWH, according to the Rabshakeh, is no different than the gods of the nations who were not able to rescue their protégés from the hands of the king of Assyria (2 Kgs 18:32c–35; Isa 36:19–20).

The perspective of the Hebrew Bible is that survival did not depend only on military strategy. Victory over Assyria depended on faith in YHWH. The prophet Isaiah, a contemporary of Hezekiah (see 2 Kgs 19), made it clear that Assyria was only an instrument of YHWH (Isa 10:5–6). The Rabshakeh also claims that the king of Assyria was sent *by YHWH* to punish Hezekiah (2 Kgs 18:22). The same kind of theological interpretation is given to the fall of the Northern Kingdom that happened

---

98. See Caruth, *Unclaimed Experience*, 62.

twenty years before: Israel fell because they did not give up their evil ways and did not follow the statutes of YHWH, their God (2 Kgs 17:13–23). From a theological standpoint, in order to avert Assyrian violent invasion, Hezekiah and Judah needed to turn from their evil ways and follow the ways of YHWH. According to the books of Kings and the Chronicler, Hezekiah turned from his evil ways (2 Kgs 18:3–6) and the people of Judah welcomed his reforms aimed at restoring proper worship of YHWH in Judah (2 Chr 30:12). However, the same books show that, despite that massive conversion,[99] not everyone experienced rescue by YHWH. Only Jerusalem survived, but other towns were exterminated. What then went wrong? For those who were in Jerusalem, hope in the power of YHWH to rescue them from Sennacherib still made sense. But for the inhabitants of a city like Lachish, the Rabshakeh's words would have sounded more reliable than the prophet Isaiah's "Do not be frightened by the words you have heard, by which the deputies of the king of Assyria have blasphemed me" (2 Kgs 19:6).[100]

Peter Machinist has studied the challenge that Assyrian conquest of Judahite cities posed to the theology of the Deuteronomistic Historian. Analyzing the speech of the Rabshakeh, Machinist asserts that it is "an open and extensive attack on an author's own fundamental institutions and ideology."[101] He argues that the presence of such an embarrassing text within the Deuteronomistic History is not simply a record of an event that took place in the past. More importantly, it testifies to the impact of the Assyrian invasion on Judahites and to the efforts of biblical writers to come "to terms with Assyria."[102] The notion of coming to term with Assyria points to the fact that Assyria became, in the lives of those who survived the invasion of 701 BCE, a permanent concern. That is to say, the experience of violence suffered at the hands of the Assyrians affected the lives and the subsequent actions of the survivors.

---

99. The descriptions of massive conversions under Hezekiah may be tainted with exaggerations, but it is likely that they are based on a historical nucleus. See Rosenbaum, "Hezekiah's Reform and the Deuteronomistic Tradition," 23–43; Miller and Hayes, *A History of Ancient Israel and Judah*, 354.

100. Machinist, "The Rab Šāqēh at the Wall of Jerusalem," 163.

101. Machinist, "The Rab Šāqēh at the Wall of Jerusalem," 159.

102. Machinist, "The Rab Šāqēh at the Wall of Jerusalem," 166.

Nahum and the Destruction of Lachish

That Nahum lived in Lachish or its immediate vicinity cannot of course be demonstrated with certitude. However, the similarities between the fall of Nineveh as described in Nahum and the fall of the city of Lachish, as described in the Neo-Assyrian bas-reliefs and confirmed by archeological excavations, show that the audience for which Nahum wrote was familiar with an event similar to the fall of Lachish. Even though most features of both Nahum and the Assyrian reliefs can be found in other books, it is telling that many features from the Lachish reliefs can be encountered in the book of Nahum, and that can allow us to imagine that Nahum assumes that his audience has familiarity with an event like the fall of Lachish. We hear for example of rocks beings shattered before YHWH (Nah 1:6). Within the context of the destruction of Lachish, where massive rocks were used to construct a siege ramp—a formidable weapon of mass destruction at this time—this rock shattering could have echoed other instances where God breaks weapons of war in order to save his people or to punish the evildoers (e.g., Jer 49:35; 51:56; Hos 1:5; Pss 37:15; 46:9; 76:3); it could also echo the destruction brought about through the siege ramp. The multiple mentions of fire in Nahum (1:10; 2:14; 3:13, 15) would have spoken powerfully to those who would have survived the fire of Lachish. Also, the image of defenders rushing to walls to protect the city in vain (Nah 2:6) would have spoken to the survivors of Lachish who watched soldiers hopelessly defend a city that eventually falls into the hands of the Assyrians.

Conclusion

As was said above, the suggestion about the destruction of Lachish as the context to which Nahum speaks is *heuristic* in nature. The tentative status of that proposal, which is plausible but probably not susceptible to definitive proof, is congruent with the purpose of this project, the focus of which is not in the first instance to re-evaluate archaeological data and reach new historical conclusions. Rather, the primary aims are exegetical, theological, and pastoral—to consider how Nahum may be read with empathy and (historically enriched) insight, with particular attention to readers who have experienced the trauma of war.

5

Imaging God amid Chaos

Introduction

CHAPTER 3 SHOWED THAT Nahum's choice of genre and form is determined by the book's interest in addressing the conditions of affliction and the need for restoration and comfort in which its audience finds itself. Chapter 4 described an historical context in which Nahum's poetry would have made sense. Chapters 5 and 6 are exegetical; building upon the literary observations made in chapter 3 and upon the analysis of the historical context in chapter 4, they will show how the poet chooses images and themes around which to focus. Both chapters will show that, for the book of Nahum, depicting the active presence of YHWH amid the conditions of war is the response that Judah's affliction and need for restoration and comfort require. To that purpose, the book centers on two interdependent themes: the description of YHWH and the evocation of memories of war. Both themes are interwoven through careful literary artistry so as to help the book achieve its objective.

The book is a long poem with two major parts, each part more or less focusing on one of those two major themes. The first part, which begins with the superscription (1:1) and ends in 1:11, gives a majestic and cosmic depiction of YHWH. The second part (1:12—3:19) is presented as a speech of YHWH. It evokes war memories by depicting YHWH's attack on Nineveh. The scenes of war in this speech are likely intended to evoke in the Judahite audience memories of the Assyrian invasion of

701 BCE. Thus, the book functions as an indirect lament on behalf of a Judahite audience that suffered Assyrian violence.

The division of the book in two parts, however, does not correspond exactly with the presentation of the two themes. Because YHWH is the main actor in both parts of the book, and because the second section is presented as divine speech (1:12; 2:14; 3:5), this second part indirectly reflects the characterization of YHWH begun in the first part.

Over the last two centuries, Nahum scholarship has largely considered the violent destruction of Nineveh to be the sole focus of Nahum. The book is often characterized as devoid of forgiveness, misogynistic, nationalistic, and hostile toward foreigners (excluding the "other"), and celebrating violence. An early twentieth-century British-American interpreter, J. M. P. Smith, made a scathing observation that is representative of that view:

> [The prophecy of Nahum] concerns itself with only one theme—Nineveh is on the brink of destruction; there is no possibility of escape for her. In ecstatic contemplation of this "consummation devoutly wished for," the prophet is wholly consumed. He can, will see nothing else. . . . There appears a certain fiery form of indignation against Judah's ancient foe, which exhibits a degree of animosity for which the great ethical prophets furnish no parallel. The pent-up feelings of generations of suffering patriots here burst forth into flame. The whole prophecy is a paean of triumph over a prostrate foe and breathes out the spirit of exultant revenge.[1]

The recent treatment of Nahum by Julia O'Brien has echoed ideas from Smith's view that the book is single-mindedly focused on the destruction of Nineveh.[2] The purpose of the book, according to O'Brien, is to draw a sharp line between the self and the other; to celebrate Judah's restoration and render Nineveh faceless by celebrating its downfall.[3] She finds theological value in the book of Nahum only as a venue for readers to reflect on their relationships with others *by rejecting the*

---

1. Smith, *A Critical and Exegetical*, 280–81; cf. Smith, *The Book of The Twelve Prophets*, 90. The reference to the "great ethical prophets" is to Isaiah, Jeremiah, and Zephaniah, who, according to Smith, focused on condemning the sins of their own people, rather than focusing on the sins of other nations. It should be noted that some of the books attributed to the so-called "ethical prophets" also contain large sections focusing on the destruction of foreign nations (see Isa 13–23; Jer 46–51).

2. O'Brien, *Nahum, Habakkuk, Zephaniah*, 23; cf. O'Brien, *Nahum*, 129.

3. O'Brien, *Nahum*, 122.

rhetoric and (presumed) ideology of the book, rejecting its strategies of "Othering-for-the-Sake-of-Annihilation," its depiction of violence (especially violence against women and children), its characterization of God, and its exultation over the suffering of others.[4] One of the ways O'Brien envisions reading against the intention of Nahum is to urge the reader to treat others as self and give them a human face, rather than keeping them faceless, as she believes Nahum does. In her "responses" to the "problems" of Nahum, O'Brien seems to imagine solutions to the problems of violence, misogyny, and othering as primarily a human-to-human matter: she does not speak about the role to be played by God in dealing with violence and atrocity, even though the poem places YHWH at the center of its rhetoric. This absence of the mention of God is explained by the fact that O'Brien believes that the image of God in this book is not helpful for healing (because it is violent, exclusionary, and misogynistic), so one has to read the book "against the intentions of [the] author."[5]

Some scholars have challenged the focus on Nineveh and have drawn attention to the theme of God as central to the book. One such scholar is Elizabeth Achtemeier, for whom

> Nahum is not primarily a book about human beings, however—not about human vengeance and hatred and military conquest—but a book about God. And it has been our failure to let Nahum be a book about God that has distorted the value of this prophecy in our eyes.[6]

For Achtemeier, contrary to the allegations that Nahum calls for human vengeance and violence, the book focuses on showing the power of YHWH. We fully understand the value of Nahum's prophecy only when we realize that the book's rhetoric aims at convincing readers of the power of *YHWH*, and its depiction of the vengeance of YHWH is a theological statement that, because YHWH is a just God, he must avenge wrongdoing.[7]

The assertion by Achtemeier that Nahum concerns itself with the theme of the power of YHWH and his care for rights and justice tells only part of the story. The book of Nahum certainly speaks vividly about YHWH and his actions in the world and against those who oppose him.

4. O'Brien, *Nahum*, 18, 124.
5. O'Brien, *Nahum*, 124–25.
6. Achtemeier, *Nahum–Malachi*, 5–6.
7. Achtemeier, *Nahum–Malachi*, 10.

We see and hear YHWH throughout the poem, and we also hear of his destroying enemies (1:8) and knowing those who seek refuge in him (1:7). However, even though Nahum gives a powerful presentation of God, this book does not only defend YHWH's justice and power, as suggested by Achtemeier.[8] Justice and the defense of those wronged is part of what YHWH does. But, as has been pointed out by Julia O'Brien, *not everyone* who suffers YHWH's violence suffers violence as consequence of wrongdoing.[9] The book, as will be shown below, presents multiple images of YHWH so as to comfort and assure its audience of YHWH's restorative presence in their midst. The poet invites the reader to explore *all* the images of YHWH presented in the book as (taken together) icons of YHWH's presence within the conditions of violence.

As I hope to show in the following two chapters, we need to consider both the description or self-revelation of YHWH and the scenes of war within which YHWH's presence is affirmed. Each chapter will focus on one of those two themes. In chapter 5, I begin with the theme of divine presence as portrayed by the poet, not only because it is the first theme we encounter in the book, but also because it is the most important aspect of Nahum. In chapter 6, I will treat the theme of war memories by analyzing the scenes of YHWH's attack on Nineveh.

The theme of divine presence is the most important in the book, because in Nahum YHWH is the main actor, threatening, destroying, comforting, and restoring. The book depicts YHWH as both cosmically present in the world and immediately present in the midst of war. It begins above the earth, in celestial realms, and ends on the earth, where we see YHWH dealing with and speaking to human beings and personified cities. YHWH is first depicted as the only God, who gets angry and takes vengeance when provoked (1:2–3a), and as the cosmic divine warrior whose power destroys every opposition, every threat to world order, and even elements that are not presented as opposing him (1:3b–6). Then he is described as responding to human actions, discriminating between his enemies and those who take refuge in him (1:7–8), afflicting particular human beings, both in Judah and outside Judah (1:12; 2:4—3:19), and restoring Judah and ending its affliction (1:12–13; 2:1, 3).

Within this depiction of YHWH, we encounter multiple tensions. YHWH is depicted in Judah's traditional creedal language (1:2–3a) yet is

---

8. Achtemeier, *Nahum–Malachi*, 10.
9. O'Brien, *Nahum*, 65.

never identified as Judah's God. There is tension between the poet's efforts to make YHWH visible to the mind of the reader/hearer and his hesitation to portray YHWH directly (in 1:3b–16 we do not see YHWH as such, but rather his *traces* in the clouds, the whirlwind, and the storm). We see tension between the insistence on YHWH's vengefulness in 1:2 and the fact that some of YHWH's victims never oppose or provoke him (1:5). YHWH's attack on Nineveh is described in vivid language, with YHWH himself confronting this international foe (2:4–14; 3:4–6), but then we are told that there is nothing special about Nineveh; YHWH is doing what he does with any nation that behaves as Assyria does (3:8–11). In the lyric mode of the book, the poet guides the reader through all these images, not privileging any, but considering each one in turn. The effect is that we are given glimpses of a God who exceeds simple characterization by "heroic epithets" and therefore escapes moralistic appropriation ("God is on our side").

Because Nahum is an indirect city lament, this multifaceted presentation of YHWH functions as an affirmation of YHWH's return to Judah, where affliction might have suggested that YHWH had abandoned the Judahites. YHWH is shown to be present, because divine presence, despite its involvement in violence against both Judah and Nineveh, is viewed as the basis for restoration and comfort to the audience. That is, what matters most to *this* audience is *not* that YHWH is destroying another nation, but that he is *present* amid the conditions that vividly bring back their memories of war and affliction and that he is capable of restoring them. The poet is careful in the presentation; he chooses poetic devices and structures in a way that requires more than an uncontrolled outburst of emotions. This artist uses verbal art to imagine a well-ordered world, even as he depicts war.

Since the book itself follows no storyline, and images are presented in a paratactic way, my argument does not follow the text in a linear manner. Rather, I select representative verses in order to show how the book treats its two major themes. I begin by analyzing the general depiction of YHWH as a vengeful God in Nah 1:2–3a, then I analyze the depiction of YHWH in the theophany of 1:3b–6. Finally, I comment on some verses (1:7–8, 9–11, 12c–13; 2:3) that speak about the distinction between those who present themselves as YHWH's enemies and those who seek refuge in him.

YHWH as Jealous and Vengeful—Nahum 1:1, 2–3a

The presentation of YHWH in these verses draws on Sinai and Deuteronomistic traditions and focuses on YHWH's vengeance as a means both to insist on exclusive devotion to him and to bring consolation and comfort to those who are afflicted. These verses use a number of grammatical and poetic devices to show that the emotions attributed to YHWH are not a mere free-floating outburst of anger, jealousy, and vengeance. Rather, like the text itself, they are a well-organized and controlled expression of YHWH's response to provocation.

> A jealous (*qannô'*) and vengeful (*nōqēm*) God is YHWH;
> vengeful (*nōqēm*) is YHWH and possessed of wrath (*ba'al ḥēmāh*).
> Vengeful (*nōqēm*) is YHWH toward his opponents
> and keeping [anger] for his enemies.
> YHWH is slow to anger, but great in power,
> certainly not letting anyone [guilty] go unpunished.
> (Nah 1:2–3a)

Most noticeable in these verses is the repetition of the name of YHWH (four times), a repetition that focuses attention on YHWH and has the effect on the listener of announcing YHWH's enduring presence. In 1:2a, the name YHWH occurs twice at the center of a chiasm, thus drawing further attention to it. The poet emphasizes the importance of the name YHWH by repeating it in two other instances (1:2b, 3a) rather than substituting a pronoun or another appellation, such as *Elohim*.

The name YHWH is modified by the attributes, "jealous," "vengeful," "possessed of wrath," "slow to anger," "great in power," "not letting anyone go unpunished." The three qualities highlighted in 1:2—jealousy, vengeance, and wrath—have direct bearing on our understanding of the whole book. Structurally, the most important attribute is *nōqēm* ("vengeful"). This term is repeated three times and is placed each time in close connection to the name YHWH, whose central position has already been shown. The other two attributes are *qannô'* and *ba'al ḥēmāh*.

When read within the general context of the Hebrew Bible, the term *nōqēm* speaks of actions that are the result of provocation. When *nōqēm* describes the actions done by YHWH, they are performed on behalf of people who are threatened or wronged by others (Gen 4:15, 24; Exod 21:20; 2 Kgs 9:17), against those who do not obey YHWH (Lev 26:25), and against YHWH's enemies (Deut 32: 41; Isa 1:24). In Nah 1:2–3a, the first two instances of *nōqēm* (1:2a) do not specify against whom YHWH's vengeance is directed. In the third instance, however, we are told that YHWH's vengeance is against those who oppose him (1:2b).

If we read the attribute *nōqēm* in relation to the other two attributes in 1:2 (*qannô'* and *ba'al ḥēmāh*) and the statement in 1:3a that "YHWH is slow to anger, but great in power, certainly not letting anyone go unpunished," we hear echoes of Sinai and Deuteronomistic traditions (Exod 20:3–6; 34:6, 14; Deut 4:24; 5:6–10; 6:15; 32:16, 21; Josh 24:19).[10] In those passages, the Hebrew Bible speaks of the covenant between Israel and YHWH with the phrase *'ēl qannô'*, underscoring YHWH's insistence on exclusive devotion from Israel and his refusal to be put in competition with other beings. Failure to observe that commandment can lead to experiencing YHWH's anger.[11] This general rule, however, is not always applied in a straightforward way. At times YHWH does not carry out the punishment reserved for those who violate his commandments. An important instance appears in Exodus 34, after the incident of the Golden Calf (Exod 33). Even though the Israelites *deserve* YHWH's anger, YHWH relents and makes two statements that repeat the first commandment about YHWH's insistence on exclusive devotion (34:14–15) and add a new clause about his ability to forgive evil (34:6–7, especially 34:7a):

> For you shall not worship any other god, because YHWH, whose name is jealous, is a jealous God. Lest you make a covenant with those who live in the land and, [when] they play the harlot with their gods and sacrifice to them, they will invite you and you will eat their sacrifices.
> (Exod 34:14–15)

> Then YHWH passed by in front of him and proclaimed, "YHWH, YHWH, a God who is compassionate and gracious,

---

10. Only Josh 24:19 uses the term *qannô'* with a *waw*, as in Nah 1:2; all the other instances do not have a *waw* between the *nun* and the *aleph*. In both Nah 1:2 and Josh 24:19, the term seems to have the same meaning as *qn'* without the *waw*.

11. See Exod 20:3–6:
"Let there be for you no other gods before me. You shall not make for yourself an idol, whether in the form of anything that is in heaven above, or that is on the earth beneath, or that is in the water under the earth. You shall not worship them or serve them; for I, YHWH your God, am a jealous God, visiting the iniquity of the fathers on the children, on the third and the fourth generations of those who hate me, but showing covenant loyalty to thousands, to those who love me and keep my commandments."

> slow to anger, and abounding in covenant loyalty [ḥesed] and truth ['emet]; who keeps covenant loyalty for thousands, who forgives iniquity, transgression and sin; yet, he would by no means leave [the guilty] unpunished, visiting the iniquity of fathers on the children and on the grandchildren, to the third and fourth generations."
> (Exod 34: 6–7)

When these two statements are read together, we see that, within Exodus, violating the commandment about exclusive devotion to YHWH can lead to YHWH's anger and punishment of the culprit. However, whether to carry out the sentence or not depends on YHWH (Exod 33:19). This tension between YHWH's requirement for exclusive devotion and his ability to forgive serves the function of a creedal statement in the Hebrew Bible.[12]

This creed is paraphrased four times in the prophetic books, all of them in the Book of the Twelve: Joel, Jonah, Micah, and Nahum. In all these instances, the creed is used within the context of threat of punishment by YHWH. In Joel and in Micah, the creedal statement is used as a positive communal doctrinal memory that serves as the basis for the appeal of the prophets to the people (Joel) and to YHWH (Micah).

In Joel, this creed is used as an invitation to the people to return to YHWH in order to avert the punishment that YHWH planned against them. The prophet tries to convince the people that, even though YHWH seems bent on destroying them, it is still possible to have him change his mind, because changing his mind about punishment is part of who YHWH is:

> Yet even now, says YHWH
>   "Return to me with all your heart,
> with fasting, weeping, and mourning;
>   and rend your heart and not your garments."
> Now, return to YHWH your God,
>   for he is gracious and compassionate,
> slow to anger, abounding in covenant loyalty [ḥesed],
>   and relenting (niḥām) from evil.
> (Joel 2:12–13)

The emphasis here is on YHWH's ability to forgive. The prophet does not speak about YHWH's punishment of the iniquities of parents on their children (as in Exodus), for the verses that preceded the creed

---

12. O'Brien, *Nahum*, 48.

have already made it clear that punishment is what the prophet's literary audience deserved (Joel 2:1–11). So, for Joel, it is good that, although punishment may be justified, YHWH has the capacity to relent.

The same positive use of the creedal statement takes place in Micah. Here the people of Judah are being mocked by their enemies because YHWH has punished them for their sins. The prophet then prays that YHWH will rebuild and shepherd his own people, just as he has done since the time he took them from Egypt. The "YHWH creed" is used as the basis for the prophet's pleading: he is asking YHWH to rebuild them because he knows that forgiveness accords with YHWH's nature:

> Who is a God like you, pardoning iniquity
> and passing over the transgression
> of the remnant of your possession?
> He does not retain his anger forever,
> because he delights in covenant loyalty [ḥesed].
> He will return and have compassion upon us;
> he will tread our iniquities under foot.
> You will cast all our sins
> into the depths of the sea.
> You will show faithfulness (ʾemet) to Jacob
> and covenant loyalty [ḥesed] to Abraham,
> as you have sworn to our ancestors
> from the days of old.
> (Mic 7:18–20)

In this passage, divine forgiveness of sins and the abating of divine anger are not seen as in tension with YHWH's requirement of exclusive devotion. The prophetic voice recognizes that the people's harsh punishment is due to their shocking transgressions. Yet the appeal to YHWH to forgive is presented, not as asking for a concession but as something that YHWH can willingly do. What sets YHWH apart from other gods is YHWH's ability to balance both the requirement for justice and a commitment to mercy and clemency.

Unlike these two books (Joel and Micah), Jonah uses the creedal statement of Exod 34:6–7 in a negative sense, as an attribute of YHWH that undermines Jonah's mission. YHWH threatens to punish Nineveh, but Jonah knows YHWH too well to believe that YHWH will carry out the sentence. He is displeased that, even though both YHWH and Jonah know that YHWH can change his mind and relent from doing evil against Nineveh, YHWH still sends Jonah to prophesy against Nineveh:

And he prayed to YHWH and said, "Please, YHWH, was not this what I said while I was still in my country, and therefore I started to flee to Tarshish, for I knew that you are a gracious and compassionate God, slow to anger and abounding in covenant loyalty [ḥesed], and relenting [niḥām] from evil?"
(Jonah 4:2)

Jonah's concern is with YHWH's forgiving nature and his capacity to relent [nḥm] from bringing about calamity, because the fact that YHWH forgives sins undermines missions like the one on which he sent Jonah. Jonah protests against YHWH, not because he does not believe in the fact that YHWH is "slow to anger" and "relenting from evil," but because, while knowing his own capacity to forgive, YHWH still sent Jonah on a mission he knew would have undermined Jonah's credibility as a prophet predicting disaster.

In Nahum, the creed takes the form of a statement of YHWH's patience in anger and determination to punish the guilty. Nahum omits an important element, ḥesed ("covenant loyalty"), which appears in the other attestations of this creed. In its stead is the statement that YHWH is "great in power." Like Joel, Micah, and Jonah, Nahum rereads a traditional creed and adapts it within the context of Judah's affliction (1:12), where there could have been doubts about YHWH's power to enact justice.[13] However, the poet has not yet told us that Nineveh or Assyria are the target of YHWH's anger and vengeance. The foe here is still anyone who challenges YHWH and provokes him to anger. Despite the mention of Nineveh in the superscription, the characterization of YHWH in 1:2–3 is universal, not necessarily bound to any specific historical foe. The poet withholds the name of the foe from the reader, and it seems that anyone who acts as an enemy of YHWH can experience YHWH's vengeance, because YHWH does not let the guilty go unpunished. Therefore, the view of J. M. P. Smith and others that Nahum is entirely consumed by the fall of Nineveh[14] seems to be based on an excessive focus on the superscription and on the few mentions in Nahum of Assyria, the Assyrian king, or Nineveh (1:1; 2:8; 3:7, 18). Close attention to the book shows that if Nahum could be characterized as consumed by any theme, it would be the theme of *the presence of YHWH, as active agent and as speaker.*

---

13. Sweeney, *The Twelve Prophets*, 420–22.

14. For people holding that opinion, see Smith, *A Critical and Exegetical Commentary*, 280–81; Smith, *The Book of The Twelve Prophets*, 90.

The identity of a particular target of YHWH's anger and vengeance is secondary.

This focus on YHWH's presence and activity can be explained by the needs of the book's audience. As was shown in chapter 3, affirming the presence of the deity within a destroyed city is a way of assuring restoration for that city. In Nahum's context of affliction, bondage, invasion, and ravages, the most pressing needs of Judah would be not the destruction of Nineveh *per se* but the end of affliction and the removal of the enemy's yoke from upon Judah by YHWH himself (1:12–13), the restoration of Judah to its former glory (2:3), and the resumption of Judah's traditional celebrations (2:1). Granted, cutting off Judah's destroyer is part of the process of restoring Judah (2:1), but its purpose is not simple vengeance or retribution. It signifies a return to peace and a just order.

The name of the prophet to whom the visions recorded in this book are attributed, *nḥm* ("comfort"), suggests such a connection between YHWH's vengeance and assurance for the audience. The following verses, in which YHWH describes Judah's condition and promises to restore her (1:12, 13; 2:1, 3), bear out this connection:

> Although I afflicted you,
>   I will afflict you no more.
> Now I will break his yoke from upon you
>   and I will tear off your fetters.
> (Nah 1:12c–13).

> Look, upon the mountains the feet of the bringer of glad tidings,
>   the messenger of wellbeing:
> "Celebrate your festivals, O Judah!
>   Fulfill your vows!
> For never again will the worthless one pass through you.
>   He has been completely cut off."
> (Nah 2:1)

> For YHWH has restored[15] the glory of Jacob,
>   as the glory of Israel.

---

15. The LXX translated this verse as, "For the Lord has turned away the insult of Jacob as the insult of Israel; for the destroyers have destroyed them and have spoiled their branches." The assumption here is that YHWH is removing the sin/insult of Jacob, so that the moment of prosperity is about to begin. However, the MT seems to suggest that what YHWH is doing is not turn away the insult, but to bring back that which was ravaged. The use of *kî* shows that what comes after *kî* explains why what comes before it takes place. For a similar explanation, see Sweeney, *The Twelve Prophets*, 437–38.

> For ravagers have ravaged them
>   and have ruined their branches.
> (Nah 2:3)

In all instances, we see that YHWH's restorative actions are consequent to previous violent actions against Judah. In 1:12c–13, YHWH himself is both the cause of Judah's affliction and the one who ends that affliction. YHWH will remove the yoke and tear apart the cords of Assyrian domination (1:13). In 2:1, we are told that the "worthless one" has been passing through Judah but that YHWH is stopping those invasions and cutting off the unidentified perpetrator. In 2:3, we are told that ravagers have been ravaging Judah but that YHWH is restoring the glory of Judah. In all these verses the poet does not use the term comfort (*nḥm*) to speak about YHWH's actions. He does, however, use terms of reversal: no . . . more (*lō'. . . 'ôd*), break (*'eshbōr*), tear off from (*'ănattēq*), and restore (*šāb*). This vocabulary conveys to the prophet's Judahite audience that restoration comes only through YHWH's reversal of the actions that destroyed Judah (including reversing their affliction by YHWH himself; 1:12c). We see in 3:7 that for the poet, when a city is destroyed its most pressing need is consolation and comfort. After Nineveh has been devastated, onlookers ponder whether there can be consolation and comfort for this city:

> And it will happen that all who see you will retreat from you and say:
> "Nineveh is devastated; who will lament (*yānûd*) her?
> From where should I look for comforters (*mĕnaḥămîm*) for you?"
> (Nah 3:7)

The poet here implies that it is difficult (or impossible) to find comforters for Nineveh. By raising the issue of comfort, however, he shows that it is a primary need for this city in ruins.

Building upon the assertion that Nahum is an indirect lament over the destruction of Judah, it is plausible to say that the question about comforters for Nineveh also points to the afflictions of Judah. If comfort is a needed response to devastation, YHWH's reversal of Judah's affliction, which entails the suppression of Judah's foe, brings comfort to Nahum's audience in Judah.

The connection between destruction, affliction, vengeance, and comfort is more explicit in other (chronologically later) Hebrew Bible texts. Such texts can help us better understand why YHWH's vengeance against his foes in Nahum has more to do with bringing comfort and restoration to Judah than with the celebration of violence. An example comes from the sixth-century BCE poet, Third Isaiah, who associates YHWH's vengeance with YHWH's consolation of those who mourn:

> The Spirit of YHWH God is upon me,
>   because YHWH has anointed me
> to bring good news (*lĕbaśśēr*) to the afflicted ('*ănawîm*);
>   he has sent me to bind up the brokenhearted,
> to proclaim liberty to captives,
>   and an opening to prisoners;
> to proclaim the favorable year of YHWH,
>   and the day of vengeance (*nāqām*) of our God;
> to comfort (*lĕnaḥēm*) all who mourn.
> (Isa 61:1–2)

It is not possible to prove direct borrowing from Nahum by Third Isaiah, yet, the use of similar vocabulary (*nḥm, nāqām, 'ănawîm, lĕbaśśēr, lĕnaḥēm*) makes it plausible that this anonymous prophet drew from the same tradition of YHWH's vengeance against Judah's enemies as a sign of comfort and consolation for the afflicted people.

Thus far I have shown how in Nah 1:2–3a the poet focuses on YHWH's vengeance as a means both of insisting on exclusive devotion to YHWH and bringing consolation, comfort, and restoration to the afflicted. This view of YHWH as avenger at the beginning of the book seems to be in tension with the later assertion that the suffering of Judah, just like the impending suffering of Assyria, comes from *YHWH himself* (Nah 1:12).[16] The yoke of Assyria (1:13) and its invasion of Judah (2:1) seem to have been instigated by YHWH himself (1:12b–13). The book of Nahum does not state explicitly that Assyria was used by YHWH to destroy Judah. However, the combination of YHWH's responsibility with the accusation of a foreign nation echoes a larger Hebrew Bible motif of YHWH's punishment of his people through flawed intermediaries and the violation by those intermediaries of reasonable limits to the violence used against another nation. Assyria and Babylon, especially, function as YHWH's agents of punishment against YHWH's people and as prototypes of empires that usurp divine prerogatives (2 Kgs 17:6–23; 18:25;

---

16. In both 1:12 and 1:13, Judah and Assyria are not named; only pronominal suffixes are used. However, as we continue reading the poem, we come to realize that the one that was afflicted (second person feminine suffix) is Judah (2:1, 3) and the one whose yoke was on Judah (second person masculine pronominal suffix, 1:13) is the king of Assyria (3:18).

Isa 10:5; 36:10; Mic 3:6–7). Terence E. Fretheim notes that when YHWH assigns some nations the task of punishing others, he (YHWH) assumes that those nations know of universal moral norms that cannot be exceeded. Unfortunately, the agents almost always "exceed the mandate, going beyond their proper judgmental activities in vaunting their own strength at the expense of Israel and in making the land an 'everlasting waste' (Jer. 25:14)."[17] Usurpation of power is not simply a sign of arrogance and pride: it is a direct challenge to YHWH's universal rule. YHWH punishes those nations because, just as he does not tolerate competition with other beings in the area of Israel's worship, he does not accept competition from any other power. The book of Isaiah gives a detailed example of the motif of nations going beyond what YHWH commands them to do:

> Woe to Assyria, the rod of *my* anger
> > and the staff in whose hands was *my* indignation.
> Against a godless nation *I* sent it,
> > and against the people of *my* fury *I* commissioned it;
> to capture booty and to seize plunder;
> > to trample them down like mud on the streets.
> But not so did it think;
> > and in its heart, not so did it plan.
> For, in its heart, it is to destroy
> > and cut off many nations.
> For it says, "are not *my* princes all kings?"
> . . .
> So will it happen that when YHWH has finished all his work on
> > Mount Zion and on Jerusalem: "*I* will visit the fruits of the
> > arrogant heart of the king of Assyria and the glory of his haughty
> > eyes.
> For he said,
>
> "by the power of my hand have *I* acted
> > and by *my* wisdom, for *I* have understanding."
> > (Isa 10:5–8, 12–13b; emphasis added)[18]

17. Fretheim, "'I was Only a Little Angry,'" 173–74; see also Isa 10:5–10. On how proclamations against foreign nations assume the notion of universal justice, see Lanner, *Who Will Lament Her?* 34.

18. It should be noted that the notion of YHWH using these foreign nations to punish his people is not a notion of which those nations were conscious. Even though we find the claim that the Assyrian Rabshakeh believed that Assyria was sent by YHWH to destroy Judah (2 Kgs 18: 25), since 2 Kings is a Judahite text (and we have no Assyrian version of the same belief), it is more plausible that the speech in the mouth of the Rabshakeh reflects more Judahite belief than a record of Assyrian belief.

In addition to the attributes of YHWH presented in Nah 1:2–3a, it is important to consider the poetic and grammatical techniques used in these verses. These techniques show us the image of YHWH as immediately present and active. No finite verbs are used to indicate whether the poet is placing YHWH's acts in the past or in the future. Participles predominate, giving the impression of something that is taking place at the moment of speech. We are not told that YHWH *was* angry or that he *will* take vengeance on his enemies: we seem to see YHWH in anger, taking vengeance on his foes. Further, since habitual actions/qualities are often expressed in participles,[19] the use of participles here may suggest that the attributes of YHWH are not uncontrolled outbursts of emotion. Rather, they are part of YHWH's longstanding mode of action when provoked.

Two structural techniques govern these verses: chiasm and alliteration. I briefly mentioned the use of chiasm in the beginning of this section, when I spoke about the centrality of the theme of YHWH and vengeance in Nah 1:2–3a. Another aspect of chiasm that we need to consider here is its function in characterization. Eli Assis's observation about the function of chiasmus in biblical Hebrew, though dealing with biblical narrative, proves instructive on how we can understand the presentation of YHWH in Nah. 1:2–3a:

> Composing a unit chiastically requires careful planning, determination of all components in advance, and word choice that is concordant with its context while resembling the parallel component of the chiasmus. The reader who apprehends such structures will appreciate the skillfulness of the author and the well-planned design of the composition. Awareness of the reader's response led biblical authors to employ chiasmus to reflect the inner world of a character. *This structure was applied when the author wanted to present the deeds or the character's discourse as deliberate and premeditated. Chiasmus appears especially where one would otherwise regard the character's actions or discourse as spontaneous or unaccounted for.*[20]

Assis uses numerous examples to support his argument.[21] I will mention two of them. His first example comes from Jonah. In Jonah

19. See Waltke and O'Connor, *An Introduction to Biblical Hebrew Syntax*, 613–14.
20. Elie Assis, "Chiasmus in Biblical Narrative," 274–75. Emphasis added.
21. Some of those examples are: Jonah 1:3 (about Jonah's planned decision to go to Tarshish, rather than going to Nineveh); Josh 2:9–11 (about Rahab's belief in God as well-thought and logical statement); 2 Sam 19:27–28 (about Mephibosheth's accusation against Ziba as well-crafted accusation against David for condemning the

1:2–3, we read about what Jonah did after YHWH told him to arise and go to Nineveh to preach against its wickedness:

> But Jonah rose up to flee to Tarshish from the presence of YHWH. So, he went down to Joppa, found a ship which was going to Tarshish, paid the fare, and went down into it to go with them to Tarshish from the presence of YHWH.

Assis shows the chiastic structure of this verse as follows:

> A But Jonah rose up to flee to Tarshish from the presence of YHWH.
>   B So he went down to Joppa,
>   C found a ship
>   D *which was going to Tarshish*
>   C' paid the fare
>   B' and went down into it
> A' to go with them to Tarshish from the presence of YHWH

Assis shows that by casting Jonah's actions in chiasm, the writer intends to show us that everything Jonah does here is well-planned and well thought-out; his going to Tarshish is not simply the result of a spontaneous reaction. The speech of Jonah in 4:1–5 is further support to the claim that Jonah's response to YHWH's command to go to Nineveh was carefully considered and logical: he knew that YHWH is compassionate, so he doubted that YHWH would carry out the sentence against Nineveh.

The second example comes from the words of Rahab in Josh 2:9–11 expressing her belief in YHWH:

> A I know that YHWH has given you the land,
> B and that dread of you has fallen upon us, and that all the inhabitants of the land melt in fear because of you
> C for we have heard how YHWH dried up the water of the Sea of reeds before you when you came out of Egypt

---

wrong person); 2 Kgs 5:3 (about Naaman's apology as a premeditated speech); 1 Sam 3:7 (about Eli's request to Samuel to tell him what YHWH told Samuel: seen as a result of meditation and reflection); Judg 18:16–17 (about the theft of Micah's ephod and theraphim by the Danites); 1 Sam 23:22–23 (Saul's instruction to the Ziphites to watch David's movements and catch him).

> C' and what you did to the two kings of the Amorites that were beyond the Jordan, Sihon and Og, whom you utterly destroyed.
> B' As soon as we heard it, our hearts melted, and there was no courage left in any of us because of you.
> A' YHWH your God is God indeed in heaven above and on earth below.

By presenting Rahab's speech in chiastic structure, the writer of Joshua intends to show that her conversion to Israel's faith is something she does only because she has analyzed Israel's previous history with other people and she understands what YHWH can do for those who believe in him.[22]

Following Assis's theory about chiasm, we can infer that the use of chiasm in Nah 1:2–3a intends to show that the poet carefully selected the attributes with which to represent YHWH and that when YHWH is vengeful, jealous, or angry, he acts on those qualities in a deliberate and controlled way.

In addition to chiasm, we see that the attributes are arranged in such a way as to create alliteration with the succession of *nun* and *qop*. The repetition of these two sounds can imprint to the mind of the reader the words *nqm* and *qnw'* (both of which are formed with those two sounds). It also shows that the poet is deliberate in his description of YHWH in these verses.

The combination of these morphological and poetic techniques shows that the text is carefully crafted and that the book of Nahum does not simply express an outburst of the animosity by the poet against the enemy of his people, as was argued by J. M. P. Smith.[23] It also shows that YHWH's coming vengeance against his enemies is not the reflex reaction of an impatient, nationalistic God. Rather, YHWH requites in an orderly way and according to the demands of justice.

YHWH's Storm Theophany—Nahum 1:3b–6

In these verses, the poet takes the reader above the earth (1:3b). The image of YHWH is majestic: he is shown in the storm and the whirlwind, behind the clouds, rebuking the sea and rivers, drying up forests, and

---

22. Assis, "Chiasmus in Biblical Narrative," 278–79.
23. Smith, *A Critical and Exegetical Commentary*, 280–81.

shaking mountains, hills, and the whole world. YHWH's presence reaches to all the parts of the cosmos, where YHWH destroys everything that opposes him and impacts even those that neither oppose him nor present any threat to world order. However, the figure of YHWH seems to elude the reader despite the impression of watching him:

> YHWH—in the whirlwind and the storm is his way,
>   and the clouds are the dust of his feet.
> He rebukes the sea and he dries it up;
>   he dries all the rivers.
> Bashan and Carmel wither,
>   and the blossoms of Lebanon wither.
> Mountains quake before him,
>   and hills dissolve.
> The land heaves before him,
>   the world and all who dwell therein.
> Before his indignation, who can stand
>   and who can endure the heat of his anger?
> His wrath pours out like fire,
>   and rocks are shattered before him.
> (Nah 1:3b–6)

The movement of YHWH in these verses is remarkable: his presence is seen through the clouds, whirlwind, and storm. He is depicted facing the sea and rivers, shaking mountains and hills, and instigating earthquakes. We even have the impression of seeing YHWH's anger in the form of fire shattering rocks. The poet uses multiple images to show the lambent presence of YHWH in all parts of the world so that it is impossible to imagine anyone standing against him. We see here one aspect of the genius of lyric poetry, its ability to take the reader to multiple places at the same time.[24] In prose, the writer might show the reader how YHWH goes from one place to the other and how he deals with one element after the other. In lyric, YHWH's presence in the world and his actions in the world seem to happen all at once, with no clear transition. Moreover, God seems to act simultaneously in the heavenly realms (clouds, whirlwind, storm) and the regions of earth.

This poetic presentation of YHWH in Nah 1:3b–6 weaves Nahum's theological ideas together with motifs drawn from the ANE traditions of divine warrior and storm theophany, especially the Canaanite myth

---

24. See Lichtenstein, "Biblical Poetry," 110–15.

of the battle between the storm god, Ba'al, and the deified Sea, Yamm.²⁵ This myth assumes that worship of Ba'al is normative in Canaan and that Ba'al is indispensable to defending world order against the power of destruction represented by the sea. The myth suggests that the order observed in the world is the result of a battle that took place a long time ago. However, despite the victory of Ba'al over Yamm in primeval time, that order still looks precarious and needs to be constantly defended: the sea and the rivers still appear as dangerous to other beings. The cult of Ba'al in that context becomes a means through which the worshipers take part in that primeval battle, reenact Ba'al's victory, and maintain order in the world.²⁶

The Hebrew Bible uses the motifs of the divine warrior and storm theophany in many texts speaking of the manifestation of YHWH and of the creation of the world. For example, the Priestly creation account in Genesis 1 is believed to have borrowed from the motif of primeval combat between the deity and the sea and sea monsters.²⁷ Genesis, of course, does not speak of creation as a battle between the sea and YHWH. YHWH gathers the waters and contains them, without any opposition. But the existence of the mass of water above which the spirit of God hovers in Gen 1:2 suggests that, even though YHWH is the one who created everything, this water needed to be separated and gathered to create order in YHWH's creation. Other texts echo more explicitly the

25. Their struggle begins when Yamm sends his messengers to declare to the divine assembly his intentions to become their king and demands that he be given Ba'al as a captive. Since the divine assembly seems afraid to challenge Yamm's wishes, Ba'al decides to go on his own to battle and defeat Yamm. After his victory over the deified Sea, Ba'al returns to the divine assembly and "appears in glory," to the rejoicing of all the other gods. Ba'al then rightly claims kingship over the gods. Some of Ba'al's weapons are lightning bolts, thunder, storms, and rain. On his return from the battle, Ba'al rides on the clouds. His very presence is accompanied by meteorological, ecological, and geological disruption. At his approach, trees and forests wither; he shakes the earth and makes the mountains quake. Conversely, that return is also the beginning of a moment of prosperity: rain and dew fall, to water vegetation and bring about fertility for the land. See Cross, *Canaanite Myth and Hebrew Epic*, 93, 147-49.

26. Brevard S. Childs writes that, "In the drama of the cult an actualization of the original cosmic events takes place in which that which once occurred is again realized *hic et nunc*. The reality of the mythical, timeless event enters into the present moment of time. As in the primeval age, the participant shares directly in the elemental powers of the creation. In the cultic drama he partakes of the power of the primeval age which is loosed from all time sequence. 'Everything is just as it was on that first day.'" *Myth and Reality in the Old Testament*, 19.

27. See Childs, *Myth and Reality*, 31-43.

motif of creation through battle (Pss 74:13–14; 77:16; 89:9–10; 104:7). In Ps 74:13–14, for example, the psalmist praises YHWH for having split open the sea and for killing the sea monsters and giving them as food to his creatures. There are also examples of YHWH's appearance following the pattern of storm theophany (Exod 19:16–21; Judg 5:4–5; Jer 10:1–16; 51:15–19; Amos 1:2; Nah 1:3b–5; Hab 3:3–4; Pss 18:9–14; 68:7–8; 77:16–19; 104; Job 38:1). It has already been shown by Brevard Childs that even though the Hebrew Bible draws from a common cultural stock, as do other ancient Near Eastern myths, whenever it uses the language, ideas, and motifs from those traditions, it breaks the myths and then strives to make the broken myth fit into its own way of presenting reality.[28]

In Nah 1:3b–6 we see a combination of many motifs from ancient Near Eastern myths. In 1:3b we hear the echo of a theophany in the clouds and the storm. In 1:4–6, we see the imagery of the divine warrior, battling the sea and shaking the world. Nahum does not tell us that here YHWH is battling the sea or the rivers. The myth of the primeval battle has been, to use Childs's language, broken and incorporated into a new context. YHWH is the only agent in the theophany. Unlike in the Ba'al myth and other Hebrew Bible texts, where the deity actually rides in the storm and on the clouds (Isa 19:1; Ps 68:4), in Nahum, there is no depiction of an actual divine journey. The clouds are not a chariot but the dust of YHWH's invisible feet; the storm and the whirlwind do not carry YHWH: they are his pathway. We do not see YHWH actually passing, we only see the traces of his passing (see Ps 77:20). We have the impression of missing YHWH just when we get close to seeing him physically.

This presentation of YHWH touches on something similar to what theologians mean when they speak of God's iconic presence in the Bible. Carey Walsh develops the idea that the mode of God's self-revelation in the Hebrew Bible is analogous to the function of an icon. She draws on the view of French phenomenologist Jean-Luc Marion that the icon "attempts to render visible the invisible," without the invisible "ever being reproduced in the visible."[29] In her study of theophanies, where God's presence is attended by fire, storm, or clouds, Walsh has shown that the biblical writers invite readers to look beyond these visible phenomena, which, like icons, point to something beyond themselves.[30]

---

28. Childs, *Myth and Reality*, 31–72.
29. Marion, *God Without Being*, Kindle locs 617–20.
30. Walsh, "Iconic Presence," 88.

This understanding of iconic presence may illumine the poetics of Nahum, which uses both direct description of YHWH (naming divine attributes) and indirect description (identifying divine actions and speech) as windows, invitations to perceive an invisible presence that exerts its hold upon the reader.

After the presentation of clouds, storm, and whirlwind as traces of YHWH's presence, the poet shows us YHWH's actions. His only direct action in this theophany is his rebuke of the sea (1:4a). YHWH is the subject of the verbs *ybš* and *ḥrb*, which convey his drying up of the sea and rivers, but these actions seem to flow from his initial rebuke of the sea. We see here some vestige of the myth of the battle between Baʻal and the Sea in the Canaanite Baʻal cycle. In that myth too the prime enemy of the deity is the sea, but the consequences of the battle extend to other elements of nature. In Nahum, we do not see YHWH engaged in battle, rather his rebuke (his words) dries the sea and the rivers. One consequence of making the voice of YHWH central to this theophany is that, within Judah's context of destruction and lament, where the presence of YHWH is vital as sign and signal for the restoration of Judah, Nahum's words represent the divine voice. Through these words YHWH reveals himself to Judah, and the reader hears YHWH thunder against the forces that threaten peace and order.

Another element of the difference between Nahum and the Baʻal myth is that, even when YHWH dries up the sea and the rivers, those water sources do not function as active forces offering resistance to YHWH: they are not shown to be YHWH's real enemies. YHWH acts upon them without any resistance. This is unlike the Baʻal myth, where, as we saw it above, Yamm, the eventual loser of the battle, is the one who provokes Baʻal; it is active. In Nahum, the sea is not YHWH's equal or even an active being. As noted above, YHWH's actions can be seen as a reaction to provocation. But the theophany seems to stand in tension with that reading of YHWH's actions. Many of the elements subdued by YHWH are not enemies (1:5b). They are diminished as a consequence of YHWH's multi-faceted, and powerful, yet elusive, appearance. The drying of the sea and rivers or the withering of forests evoke what YHWH did in primordial time and point to what he can do now. They are used here as icons rather than depicting an actual battle of YHWH against cosmic elements.

Jon Levenson has shown that the images of YHWH's battles against primordial forces (sea and monsters) are often evoked in the Hebrew

Bible as a way of reassuring Israelites that YHWH is capable of destroying those who threaten his creation:

> The events of the primordial era, God's defeat of the monster and creation of the world, are not locked away in the vanished past. They are still available. That power, that energy, that unassailable mastery is still needed. It can be reactivated yet. The enemy is now human and historical, but the challenge to YHWH is not new or different in essence from the challenge he met *in illo tempore*. . . . In this predicament the proper posture of a faithful YHWHist is to keep his eye upon the inevitability of the defeat of YHWH's adversaries and to wait patiently and confidently for his master's reactivation of his infinite power to deliver. The benevolent, world-ordering side of God may be eclipsed for a while, but it can never be uprooted or overthrown.[31]

For readers living under the Assyrian yoke, speaking of YHWH's presence in the cosmos might turn their attention to what YHWH could do with the empire to which they were subject. Images of the sea and rivers drying up would assure Nahum's audience that, even though they are still afflicted, YHWH will at last defeat the power that holds sway over them. Some of the elements subdued in 1:3b–5 are referred to later in the book as part of the means of defense or refuge for YHWH's enemies. In 3:8 we hear that No-Amon used the sea as a defense, but the sea was not able to help her. In 3:18 we see the Assyrians taking refuge on the mountains with no one to gather them. In both cases, these human efforts are futile, because the force of YHWH's presence does not spare mountains or sea (1:5).

The theophany in 1:3b–5 not only makes YHWH visible to the mind of the audience, but also shows that nothing can oppose YHWH. It shows the reader/hearer how, after the earth has been shaken, the mountains and the hills have fallen apart, the seas and rivers have disappeared, and the whole world is shaken, the only standing agent is YHWH. He has not been shaken or vanquished by anyone, and there is no prospect that he ever will be. This depiction of YHWH prompts the rhetorical question in 1:6a, "Before his indignation, who can stand and who can endure the heat of his anger?" The indignation of YHWH is such that trying to oppose him is futile and self-destructive. His fury is like a fire that destroys even rocks (1:6b).

---

31. Levenson, *Creation and the Persistence of Evil*, Kindle locs: 771–74, 799–801.

The imagery of rock-shattering may be used here to express the power of YHWH; but it can also speak in a more specific way to the experience of Nahum's hearers. Rocks can function as protection against danger (Exod 33:22; Deut 32:7; 1 Sam 2:2; Ps 18:32), but rocks also serve as raw materials for constructing weapons of war, especially Assyrian siege ramps.[32] The phonological proximity between ṣurîm (rocks) and ṣārîm (adversaries) may suggest that here ṣurîm is used as a pun: rocks can play the role of adversaries or at least support the efforts of the enemies to stand up to YHWH. From that perspective, the destruction of rocks also can imply the destruction of YHWH's adversaries.

It is significant that the presentation of YHWH in this theophany concludes with a question: "Before his indignation, who can stand and who can endure the heat of his anger?" (1:6a) According to Adina Moshavi, biblical writers use rhetorical questions in order

> to induce the addressee to mentally agree that the implied assertion is true. The rhetorical question accomplishes its goal by means of the implication of obviousness: the question exerts psychological pressure on the addressee by implying that any reasonable person would agree with the implied assertion.[33]

There are at least five rhetorical questions in Nahum (1:6a; 2:12; 3:7bc, 8–9, 19),[34] implying that the poet is interested in appealing to his audi-

32. See Ussishkin, *The Conquest of Lachish*, 54.
33. Adina Moshavi, "What Can I Say?" 97.
34. "Where is the lion's den
      and the cave of the young lions,
    where the lion walked, the lioness is there,
      and the young lions, with no one to disturb?" (2:12)

   And it will happen that all who see you will retreat from you and say:
   "Nineveh is devastated; who will lament her?"
   From where should I look for comforters for you? (3:7)

   "Are you better than No Amon (Thebes)
      who sat by the Nile
    with water all around her,
      for whom the sea was an army
      and water a wall,
    Ethiopia was her strength,
      and Egypt, without limit?" (3:8–9a)

   "All who hear news about you
      will clap their hands against you;

ence as a conversation partner. In 1:6 for example, he does not simply tell the audience that YHWH's fury cannot be opposed; he makes the audience believe that both they and the poet have arrived at this conclusion together, after observing YHWH deal with the world.

This powerful depiction of YHWH, who acts even against elements that do not provoke him, raises the question of what is needed to escape/avoid YHWH's anger. It stands in tension with both the assertion in Nah 1:2–3a that YHWH's vengeance is against his enemies and what seems to be a sharp distinction between enemies and those whom YHWH knows (Nah 1:7–11, 12c–14; 2:3; 3:8–11). In the following section, I will treat the way YHWH discriminates between enemies and those whom he knows.

YHWH's Enemies and Protégés—
Nahum 1:7–8, 9–11, 12c–14; 2:3; 3:8–11

In this section, I would like to consider some of the ways the poem presents the character of YHWH *vis à vis* his enemies and his protégés (those who seek refuge in him). Since the next chapter focuses on war memories, I do not dwell here on the details of the war scenes. Rather, I focus on the presentation of YHWH. In the book of Nahum, YHWH is not identified as the God of Israel or Judah. The characterization of YHWH is more universal, and his actions towards protégés and enemies are not static, in the sense of always favoring certain nations or peoples.

Some scholars have argued that the book of Nahum intends to present YHWH's battle against Nineveh as a battle between the protector of Judah (YHWH) and the protector of Assyria (king of Assyria). Julia O'Brien, for example, shows that in the book of Nahum we see a battle between two males (YHWH and the king of Assyria), each protecting his female.[35] In Nahum, however, the line between YHWH's enemies and protégés is not drawn with ethnic or national terms. The poet shows that even Judah was once treated as an enemy of YHWH (1:12). The setting of Nahum's prophecy is the threat against Nineveh, but no nation can presume to escape from YHWH's punishment when it behaves as his enemy (3:8–11).

---

for upon whom has not passed
your unending evil?" (3:19).

35. O'Brien, *Nahum*, 88.

The first passage that makes a distinction between protégés and enemies is 1:7–8

> YHWH is good
>   as a refuge on the day of opposition,
>   and the one who knows those who seek refuge in him.
>   And with a flood-tide
> he makes an end of its place;
>   and his enemies he pursues into darkness.

It appears here that YHWH is an open refuge. In order to benefit from YHWH's protection during the time of opposition, there are no additional requirements beyond the act of seeking refuge in "him." The statement that YHWH is a good refuge in times of opposition (1:7a) is made first; then we are told that he knows those who seek refuge in him (1:7b) and destroys and chases those who do not into darkness (1:8).

Key to understanding how the poem distinguishes between protégés and enemies is the way one translates 1:7a, *"tôb YHWH lĕmāʿōz."* The LXX renders this verse as "The Lord is kind to those who rely on him on the day of tribulation and knowing those who trust him" (*chrēstos kyrios tois hypomenousin auton en hēmera thlipseōs kai ginōskōn tous eulaboumenous auton*). It is clear that the LXX translation has *tois hypomenousin auton* ("to those who rely on him"), which we do not find in the MT. Some scholars believe that the LXX's version is superior/earlier to the MT.[36] Jon Levenson explains that position by claiming that the original text had *"tôb YHWH lmqw(y)w,"* but the copyists of the MT confused *lmqw(y)w*/למקו(י)ו ("to those who hope in him") with *lĕmāʿōz*/למעוז ("as a refuge"). Levenson views the initial *lamed* before *māʿōz*/מעוז (which he replaces with *mqwyw*/מקויו) as a *lamed* of advantage or attribution (the "benefactive dative"); that is, it designates those who benefit from YHWH's goodness (those who hope in him).[37] Another position (currently the dominant one) is that we maintain the MT and treat the *lamed* as a *lamed* of emphasis, thus rendering the colon as, "Good is YHWH, *indeed,*

---

36. See Smith, *A Critical and Exegetical Commentary*, 300; Levenson, "Textual and Semantic Notes on Nah. I 7–8," 792.

37. An expression similar to what the LXX has in this colon is found in Lam 3:25, *"tôb YHWH lqww."* Levenson then suggests that in Nah. 1:7a we find *lmqwyw*/למקויו instead of *lqww*/לקוו because Nahum used the piel form of the verb, while Lamentations used the qal form. See Levenson, "Textual and Semantic Notes," 793. For the use of the *Lamed* of advantage, see Waltke and O'Connor, *An Introduction to Biblical Hebrew Syntax*, 208.

a shelter in the day of distress."[38] A third position consists in reading the initial *lamed* in 1:7a as a *lamed* of specification:[39] YHWH is called "good," not in the moral sense of being good[40] nor in the sense of being favorable to his protégés, but in the sense of being good/fitting in the function of a refuge in time of opposition. Considering this *lamed* as a *lamed* of specification seems to fit best the context. The verse builds upon the image of YHWH shown in Nah 1:2–3a and in Nah 1:3b–6 and addresses the question of whether YHWH has what it takes to be a reliable refuge on a day of opposition. The preceding verses showed that YHWH can be angry and vengeful, that he is exceedingly powerful and slow to anger; and that his presence can be indiscriminately destructive for humans and nature. When YHWH appears, the whole world and everything within the world feel the impact of his power. Everything is shaken and YHWH remains the only secure being, and thus a source of security for humans (both Judahites and others). It is this depiction of YHWH that allows the poet to assert in 1:7 that YHWH can be trusted as a refuge in the time of opposition.

The distinction between those whom YHWH knows and those whom he chases into darkness[41] is that the former seek refuge in him, while the latter do not. Later in the book we are shown intoxicated Nineveh looking for a refuge in vain (3:11–18). That futile search for a refuge contrasts with the immediate availability of YHWH as a refuge for those who look to him to find shelter (1:7).[42] It seems that even those

---

38. Spronk, *Nahum*, 46–47; Becking, "Is God Good for His People?" 621–23; also assumed by O'Brien, *Nahum*, 40–41. On the use of the *emphatic lamed*, Huehnergard, "Asseverative *la and Hypothetical *lu/law in Semitic," 591; Waltke and O'Connor, *An Introduction to Biblical Hebrew Syntax*, 212; Pss 89:19; 119:91; Qoh 9:4.

39. For a discussion on the *lamed* of specification, see Waltke and O'Connor, *An Introduction to Biblical Hebrew Syntax*, 207.

40. See for example Maier: "God is good, the only Source of absolute, perfect goodness. There is nothing good besides Him. Men are evil and treacherous; but God is 'good,' not only in the moral sense of his sinlessness, but here chiefly in His faithfulness, as He fulfills His pledges; in His mercy, as He remembers His ungrateful children; and in His help, as He hastens to support and defend His own" (*The Book of Nahum*, 175–76).

41. J. J. M. Roberts shows that "chasing into darkness" possibly echoes the motifs of chasing enemies to the underworld, to the realm of the dead. See Roberts, *Nahum, Habakkuk, and Zephaniah*, 52.

42. The Hebrew Bible (especially in the Psalms and Lamentations) often depicts YHWH as people's refuge or salvation on the day of opposition or distress (e.g., Pss 17:7; 37:40; 46:2; Lam 3:25):

who happen to be YHWH's enemies can change their status once they seek refuge in him. This is not to suggest that YHWH is neutral or that YHWH does not pay attention to how people behave: he does not let the guilty go free (1:2). What it means is that, according to these verses, there is no a particular people that is inherently a protégé or an enemy of YHWH.

In 1:9–11 the poet presents YHWH's enemies in general terms as those planning evil against him and experiencing his destruction:

> Whatever you would plan against YHWH;
>   he makes a total end.
>   Opposition would not rise twice.
> For like entangled thorns
>   and drunk drunkards
>   they will be consumed like thoroughly dried up stubble.
> From you has departed
>   the one planning evil against YHWH,
>   the worthless counselor.

The depiction of YHWH in these verses continues the theme of the divine warrior. The deadly effects of YHWH's action in anger evident in 1:2–3a and 1:3b–6 seem to fall now on those who oppose YHWH. The poet relies on sound and vocabulary, combined with images of war (making a complete end, chasing, darkness, burning) to create a battle scene. We do not know who is addressed in 1:9, but the use of "you" speaks directly to listeners and draws attention to YHWH's utter destruction of his enemies.

The reference of 1:10 is obscure, but the alliteration, with repeated sounds of *samekh* and *bet*, conveys to the reader a sense of order within a context of total destruction (1:9a). Julia O'Brien has argued that the "concatenation of similes" in this verse intends to intrigue and confuse readers so as to make them focus on the beauty of the text and momentarily forget which historical enemies are threatened with burning here.[43] This claim seems to ignore the fact that, up until this point in the poem, the

---

> YHWH is good to those who wait for him
>   to the person who seeks him. (Lam 3:25)

> And YHWH helps them, and delivers them;
>   he delivers them from the wicked, and saves them,
>   because they take refuge in him. (Ps 37:40)

43. See O'Brien, *Nahum*, 42.

poet has not yet named YHWH's enemies and those who take refuge in him. It would have made very little sense to focus on making the reader forget something that has not been named. It seems that Nahum uses these similes to underscore the inevitability of the destruction: just as it is natural for thorns to be entangled and drunkards to get drunk, so will it be with those who stand as YHWH's enemies and their destruction.

If YHWH's enemies are utterly destroyed, those who find favor with him are restored. In 1:12c–13 YHWH is depicted as the one who "afflicted" the addressee and also as the one who will change her situation. In 2:3 YHWH is not the perpetrator of violence against Judah, but rather comes to restore what the ravagers destroyed:

> For YHWH has restored the glory of Jacob,
>   as the glory of Israel.
> For ravagers have ravaged them
>   and have ruined their branches.

YHWH and the ravagers stand in antithetical parallelism. Both terms are subjects of verbs that have Jacob/Israel as direct objects, but verbs that lead to opposing results: the ravagers destroy, while YHWH restores. The actions of the ravagers precede those of YHWH, since YHWH restores what has been devastated. In this verse, however, restoration by YHWH comes first. Only after this are we told why YHWH needs to restore. The poet draws the attention of the hearer first to what YHWH is about to do (or is already doing), and then to what happened to Judah in the past.

Conclusion

This chapter has attempted to show how the book of Nahum paratactically presents multiple images of YHWH and invites the reader to consider each image at a time. In the following chapter, we shall treat the presentation of war memories and how YHWH's presence and the destruction of Nineveh together may bring comfort to afflicted Judah.

6

The Destruction of Nineveh and Judah's Memories of War

Introduction

IN THE PREVIOUS CHAPTER, I showed how affirming the presence of YHWH responds to the needs of Judahites in conditions of destruction and affliction. In this chapter, I address the second theme of the book of Nahum—Judah's memories of war. Taking into account the form of Nahum as an indirect lament over the destruction of Judah by the Neo-Assyrian empire (701 BCE), this chapter will analyze the scenes of war between YHWH and Nineveh to argue that the depiction of the fall of Nineveh intends to evoke in Nahum's Judahite audience the memories of war and to allow them to lament their conditions of destruction and affliction at the hands of the Assyrians. Nahum's choice of words and images, its vivid depiction of war, and the association of this war with the empire that destroyed Judah in 701 BCE make it that the book can evoke those memories of war in Judah's survivors of the Assyrian violence. That is, even though the battle is imaginatively taking place in Nineveh, the rhetorical goal of these scenes of war is to reach to the concerns of a Judahite audience wrestling with the sequels of Assyrian violence.

I begin this chapter by analyzing verses in which YHWH indicts Nineveh for her crimes. This section will show that, in light of the characterization of YHWH as vengeful and following the requirements of justice, YHWH does not simply attack Nineveh without explaining to her (and indirectly to the audience) the reasons for her destruction. In the second section, I will analyze the depiction of the war between YHWH and Nineveh. I will show especially how the vividness of the depiction of the war is due to the poet's and the audience's familiarity with war on their Judahite soil, rather than being a historical account of the fall of Nineveh. I will show how those scenes evoke (without attempting to report on) Assyrian attacks on cities like Lachish in 701 BCE.

YHWH's Indictment of Nineveh

As has been shown above, YHWH's vengeance on Nineveh is presented as a consequence of YHWH's indictment of the city. Both parts of the book of Nahum end with the word "evil" (*rāʿāh*) as a general designation of the crime committed by Nineveh. The first part of the book ends with the affirmation that the worthless counselor plots evil (*rāʿāh*) against YHWH (1:11). The second ends with the rhetorical question showing that all the nations of the earth have suffered from Nineveh's evil (*rāʿāh*; 3:19). These two mentions of the word "evil" also represent the two main kinds of evils that the book shows Nineveh to have committed. The first kind of evil is that of self-deception: Nineveh is guilty of plotting evil against YHWH (1:11) and of thinking of herself as exceptional, superior to all the nations that have faced divine judgment for their crimes (3:8–18). The second kind of evil is what can be called crimes of action: she makes her evil "pass over" (i.e., overwhelm) Judah and all the other nations through plunder, deportation, and wanton violence.

Evil Thoughts

It is common that, when a biblical writer speaks about YHWH's condemnation of a nation or its leaders, he includes quotations expressing the intent of that nation or its leaders to carry out the crimes for which YHWH is condemning them.[1] Those quotations suggest that the actions of which the nation is accused are premeditated. In Exod 15:9, while celebrating YHWH's destruction of Egypt by YHWH, the poet gives

---

1. See Exod 15:9; Isa 10:8–11, 13–14; 13:13–14; Jer 46:8; 49:4; Ezek 26:2; 27:3; 28:3; 29:3, 13; 32:2.

the reader a dramatic view of the thinking of Pharaoh as he pursues the Israelites:

> The enemy said, "I will pursue, I will overtake,
>   I will divide the spoil, my throat will fill itself with them,
>   I will display my sword, my hand will impoverish them."

Murray Lichtenstein writes that, in this verse,

> there can be no question as to the Egyptian culpability; the "foe" is unequivocally an enemy in thought, word, and deed. And the true hallmark of every enemy of God is precisely Pharaoh's short-sighted, even blasphemous reliance solely upon the might of his own "sword" and his own "hand."[2]

In the book of Nahum, we have no quotation of Nineveh's speech. All we have are reports of Nineveh's actions against other nations and YHWH's accusations of Nineveh for short-sighted thoughts and presumption. We hear about Nineveh's thinking by looking at how other nations before her had behaved and how their behavior led to their destruction. Their fate should have served as signs for Nineveh. Nineveh, however, ignored all those signs, because she believed herself to be superior to all other nations (3:8). The ways Nineveh thinks about YHWH and about herself determine how she acts towards other nations.

Planning evil against YHWH

In 1:11, we hear that the king of Assyria had evil thoughts about YHWH:

> From you has departed
>   the one planning evil against YHWH,
>   the worthless counselor.

That the antecedent of the pronoun "you" in this verse is not indicated has led scholars to two suggestions. Some suggest that the poet is speaking to Nineveh, from where the one plotting evil originated.[3] That opinion is plausible, because Nineveh is one of the two of YHWH's addressees who is feminine (3:7; Judah being the other). Other scholars say that this pronoun refers to Judah, who is addressed in 1:12 and 2:1 and

---

2. Lichtenstein, "Biblical Poetry," 111.
3. Maier, *The Book of Nahum*, 196.

to whom YHWH promises restoration.[4] Since restoration is promised to Judah (2:1) and destruction to Nineveh (see 3:5-7), it is more likely that Judah is the antecedent of the "you" in this verse. This question is connected to that of the identity of "the one planning evil against YHWH." Some scholars believe that this verse makes a clear historical reference to Sennacherib, who invaded Judah in 701 BCE and *left Judah*, after being defeated by YHWH, whom he had blasphemed (see Isa 37:23-38; 2 Kgs 19:22-37).[5] In that case, "you" refers to Judah and "one planning evil against YHWH" refers to Sennacherib. Others say that the reference is to all the Assyrian kings who had invaded Judah until the time when the book was written.[6] Sennacherib seems the most likely Assyrian king to whom Nahum would have referred, for two reasons. First, historically, Sennacherib is the Assyrian king who had the most damaging impact on Judah. Second, in the Hebrew Bible, Sennacherib is the only Assyrian king who is said to have mocked and blasphemed against YHWH (2 Kgs 18:28-35; 19:3-4, 14-19; Isa 37:3-4, 14-19). It is possible that, since Sennacherib is the most likely Assyrian to have contributed to the conditions of affliction in which Nahum's audience finds itself, the prophet primarily referred to Sennacherib and then to all the Assyrian leaders who continued his legacy in Judah. In addition, it is impossible to prove that the expression *mimmēk yāṣāʾ* refers to the specific moment of Sennacherib's departure from Judah in 701 BCE, as has been argued by Floyd and others. It is more plausible that the poet is here speaking about the consequence of YHWH's battle against Nineveh. That is, after YHWH has defeated "the one planning evil against YHWH" (Assyria), the latter will leave Judah and depart, thus signaling the end Assyrian domination.

More important than identifying the historical Assyrian monarch to whom this verse alludes is the assertion that Assyria's evil thoughts are directed against YHWH. We certainly do not hear the content of her thoughts, but we see the actions that those thoughts undergird. The poet calls the actions of Nineveh against other nations "*rāʿāh*, a term that is also used in the book to speak about what the counselor of evil is planning against YHWH (1:11). In other words, the evil that Nineveh plans

---

4. Floyd, *Minor Prophets*, 50-51; O'Brien, *Nahum*, 45-46.

5. Floyd, *Minor Prophets*, 50-51; O'Brien, *Nahum*, 45-46; Sweeney, *The Twelve Prophets*, 433; Smith, *The Book of the Twelve Prophets*, 94; Maier, *Nahum*, 196-97.

6. See Achtemeier, *Nahum-Malachi*, 14; Robertson, *The Books of Nahum, Habakkuk, and Zephaniah*, 75.

against YHWH (1:11) takes form in her deception and violence against all the nations of the world (see 3:19).

Presumption of exceptionalism and short-sightedness

In addition to having evil thoughts against YHWH, Nineveh is also accused of the presumption of exceptionalism and short-sightedness, in that she esteems herself capable of committing crimes and escaping YHWH's punishment, and yet she is unable to examine her own historical setting and realistically assess her military capabilities (3:8–18). In this lengthy indictment, the poet proceeds with a *kal v'chomer* (*a fortiori*) argument, starting with the example of No-Amon (Thebes), whose defenses and alliances seemed to render her impregnable—yet she was unable to prevent her own devastation. It then concludes with the exposition to Nineveh of how unreliable her own defense and military organization are. In the poet's imagination, No-Amon was defended beyond measure (3:8–10), while Nineveh is defended only by unreliable fortresses, wide open gates, effeminate soldiers, and slumbering leaders (3:12–18). If No-Amon, which was so well protected, fell apart, how much more so will Nineveh, whose defenses are vulnerable to any enemy?

I will analyze this indictment against Nineveh's presumption of exceptionalism and shortsightedness in two stages. In the first stage, I consider the example of No-Amon and what the fall of that city should have meant to Nineveh, had Nineveh paid attention to what happened around her. In the second, I examine what the poet says about Nineveh's own defense mechanisms and her inability to understand that she too will fall like No-Amon. The point of this indictment is not that Nineveh did not (in historical fact, though not in the poet's representation) have strong military capabilities, but that no defense can withstand YHWH's opposition.

THE EXAMPLE OF NO-AMON (3:8–10)

Are you better than No-Amon (Thebes)
    who sat by the Nile
with water all around her,
    for whom the sea was an army
    and water a wall,

> Ethiopia was her strength,
>   and Egypt, without limit?
>   Put and Lubim were your helpers.
> Even she went into exile;
>   she went into captivity.
> Even her little babes were dashed
>   at the top of every street;
> and on her nobles, they cast lots,
>   and all her great ones were bound in fetters.
> (Nah 3:8–10)

The comparison between Nineveh and No-Amon in these verses begins with a rhetorical question that implies that Nineveh knew that she was not better than Thebes. The historical reality is that Nineveh *was* militarily better than No-Amon, for it was the Assyrians who destroyed No-Amon in 663 BCE.[7] But, here, the poet exaggerates the strength of No-Amon by imagining it as a city fully protected and benefiting from the help of many nations. The point of this hyperbole here is to suggest that, despite the reality of the fall of No-Amon at the hands of the Assyrians, Nineveh should not have considered itself better militarily than No-Amon. In other words, the poet implies that the victory of Nineveh over Thebes did not depend on Nineveh's military prowess, but on some other force that could overcome any military preparation and defense. Following that line of reasoning, the poet does not even name Assyria as the one who defeated No-Amon. Without extra-biblical knowledge of the fall of Thebes at the hands of the Assyrians in 663 BCE, readers would likely see in the fall of No-Amon the personal intervention of YHWH, who is the main actor in our poem.

As has been pointed by Julia O'Brien, all the verbal forms describing the fall of Thebes are either grammatically passive (Pual) or impersonal ("they cast"), suggesting that the poet does not want to focus on the agent of the destruction.[8] It does not matter to the poet that the Assyrians could have known that they were stronger than the Egyptians whom they had defeated. Since the poem is addressed to a Judahite audience, what he conveys to them is that Nineveh is not impregnable: YHWH defeated

---

7. Kahn, "The Assyrian Invasions of Egypt (673–663 B.C.)," 251–67. No-Amon was the ancient city of Thebes, identified by its Egyptian name, "City of (the god) Amon" (Sweeney, *The Twelve Prophets*, 444). It was the center of Egyptian political life between 711 and 525 BCE, during the Twenty-Fifth Sudanese dynasty. In the seventh century BCE, the city was located on both sides of the Nile.

8. O'Brien, *Nahum*, 63.

nations stronger than her. The focus of the argument is less on historical accuracy. According to the poet, No-Amon is located by the Nile, surrounded by waters, and defended by the sea, natural defenses that were even strengthened by the help of other nations, and yet it fell apart. Even though this description does not fit historical topography of seventh-century BCE Thebes, which was not in fact surrounded by the sea or by waters, the rhetorical strategy here is to use irony and hyperbole to depict Assyria's former enemy as highly protected, before later casting Assyria as weak and without defense. Whether Nahum knew Assyrian topography or not is difficult to prove. What we can say here is that, even though the focus of the comparison between Thebes and Nineveh cannot be seen from the perspective of historical and geographical accuracy, it seems that Nahum was familiar with general Iron Age war strategies and knew of the fall of Thebes in 663 BCE at the hands of the Assyrians and of the nations that would have had political or military alliances with Thebes. Besides that nucleus of information that we can ascertain was available to the writer, the other details seem to have been used to strengthen the point that it was foolish for Nineveh to have believed that she could stand up to YHWH. Nahum does not claim that he gives Judahite audience an accurate description of the geography of Thebes[9] or that of Nineveh. He attempts to show the kind of thinking that is costing Nineveh her destruction.

In 3:10, the poet describes what happened to Thebes: she faced exile and captivity; her little children were dashed against the tops of streets; and her leaders were bound in chains (3:10). The repeated conjunction *gam*, used emphatically, highlights the contrasts between Thebes's former state and the present situation of ruins in which she finds herself. Exile and deportation were common Assyrian ways of treating the people they defeated. Assyrian royal inscriptions revel with details about the captives and the deportees of the Assyrian monarchs. Talking about his victory over the king of Sidon, Esarhaddon (681–669 BCE) boasted about his deportation of Sidonians,

> I uprooted its wall and its foundations and threw them into the sea, and its site I destroyed. Abdi-milkutti, its king, who had fled before my weapons into the midst of the sea, by the command of the god Ashur, my lord, I caught like a fish in the sea (and) cut off his head. His wife, his sons and his daughters, the persons of his

[9]. For a discussion on the topography of Thebes and the book of Nahum, see Huddlestun, "Nahum, Nineveh, and the Nile," 98–104.

palace, gold, silver, property and possessions, precious stones, multicolored linen garments, elephant hides, ivory, ebony and boxwood, everything in his palace treasuries—I carried off in great quantity as spoil. His people, from far and wide, without number, cattle and sheep and asses, I led way to Assyria.[10]

The dashing of little children against street corners, rocks, or walls (along with ripping open pregnant women) seems to have been a common practice in ancient Near Eastern warfare (see 2 Kgs 8:12; Isa 13:16, 18; Hos 10:14; 14:1; Ps 137:9). These brutal acts against children were intended to terrorize the city's population. Similarly, the Lachish reliefs give a visual representation of the Assyrians impaling adults (presumably leaders) at the city gate, in order to quell opposition to Assyrian rule.[11] The poet's verbal depiction of violent acts against all the inhabitants of defeated nations, both combatants and non-combatants, would have reawakened the memories of Nahum's Judahite audience. It affirms that what Nineveh did to Judah is what she does to all the nations. Thebes becomes the mirror through which Judah sees her own history of encounter with Assyrian violence.

The second part of the indictment both shows similarities between Nineveh and Thebes and draws a sharp contrast regarding their military capabilities.

Nineveh too will fall (3:11–18)

> You too (*gam*) will become drunk;
> > you will disappear from people's sight.
> You too (*gam*) will search for a refuge from an enemy.
> All your fortresses are fig trees
> > with ripe fruits:
> if they are shaken,
> > they fall into the mouth of the eater.
> Look, your people,
> > women in your midst!
> To your enemies are the gates of your land wide open;
> > fire consumes your gate bars.

---

10. "Prism Nineveh A," Col. Ii, 65–82, in Cogan, *The Raging Torrent*, 132; see also Slab III in Ussishkin, *The Conquest of Lachish*, 102, where we are shown columns of deportees are seen leaving the city of Lachish.

11. See Ussishkin, *The Conquest of Lachish*, 102 (Slab III).

> Draw for yourself water for the siege;
> > strengthen your fortresses.
>
> Come to the clay,
> > tread the mortar,
> > take hold of the brick mold.
>
> There will fire devour you,
> > the sword will cut you off;
> > it will devour you like locusts.
>
> Be as numerous as locust-swarm;
> > be as numerous as grasshopper.
>
> You have multiplied your traders
> > more than the stars of the sky;
> > the grasshopper sheds its skin and flies away.
>
> Your courtiers are like grasshopper
> > and your officials like hordes of locusts:
>
> they settle on walls
> > on a cold day;
>
> the sun rises and they retreat
> > and it is not known where their place is.
>
> Your shepherds are sleeping,
> > O King of Assyria!
> > Your nobles are lying down;
>
> your people are scattered on the mountains
> > and there is no one to gather them.

The description of Nineveh in these verses is clearly a caricature of the Neo-Assyrian Empire. It does not resemble what we know, both from Assyrian and non-Assyrian sources, of the Neo-Assyrian Empire in the seventh century (see chapter 4). The purpose of this description is to show that Nineveh's thinking is flawed, because she is not even close to Thebes in military preparation, and yet she thinks that she can fare better than Thebes.

The description of Nineveh begins with two parallel cola emphatically asserting that Nineveh's fate will be no different than that of Thebes (3:11). The repetition of the conjunction *gam* shows the connection between this verse and 3:10, where the fate of Thebes is described. In 3:11, however, the poet does not explicitly state what kind of treatment Nineveh will receive: he only mentions symbolic actions of drunkenness, disappearance from people's sight, and (hopeless?) search for a refuge from the enemy (3:11). As Spronk has shown, drunkenness (*škr*) can be used in the Hebrew Bible in reference to people drinking from YHWH's cup of anger (Isa 51:17–23; Jer 25:15–29; Ezek 23:32; Obad 16; Hab

2:16; Lam 4:21).[12] All these texts of course are later than Nahum, and so their use of *škr* could not have determined the meaning given to it in Nahum. However, whether the writers of these texts borrowed that term from Nahum or not, we can see that there was a tradition that considered drunkenness as a metaphor for suffering YHWH's anger. Therefore, we can say that, in 3:11, Nahum is claiming that the destruction of Thebes was due to YHWH's anger, and so Nineveh also is about to experience the same anger.

Within the same colon, the poet also says that Nineveh will be hidden from view (*naʿălāmāh*). Spronk suggests that this term might be referring to the darkness into which YHWH pursues his enemies (1:8b); the Empire will literally disappear from the world stage. However, the word *ʿlm* could also suggest a different kind of hiddenness, namely the erasure of its reputation when YHWH puts an end to its program of global propaganda. As discussed above, royal propaganda was a primary means whereby the Neo-Assyrian Empire, obsessed with its own dominance, projected images of power onto the world screen. Here the poet strikes at the very core of the Assyrian self-esteem. Thus, hiddenness or disappearance can be understood as the opposite of propaganda, as obliteration of the Assyrian self-constructed image and the exposition of its non-identity. The Assyrian empire that went into all the world and gathered and subjected many nations is now on the run, searching for a refuge from the enemy.

Nahum 3:11 can be read not only as a connection between Nineveh's imminent fate and Thebes's fate, but also as an introduction to the exposition of Nineveh's own weakness acerbically described in the next seven verses. The description uses images drawn from several areas of life throughout the ancient Near East, including Judah: military preparation, agriculture (including animal husbandry), and masonry. It gives a mocking analysis of Nineveh's capabilities in order to show her that she should not have thought herself to be any better than the other nations that had been destroyed (by Nineveh herself).

Furthermore, the poet's caricature of the Assyrian empire gives the Judahite audience some kind of consolation and a sense of pride in their own (now ended) military power. When the Assyrians destroyed Lachish for example, the battle was fierce and resistance from inside the city was

---

12. Spronk, *Nahum*, 132.

formidable.¹³ Unlike Judah, who showed some resistance, Nineveh will not even resist; its fortresses are but fig trees whose fruits fall easily to the mouth of eaters as soon as the tree is shaken. Indirectly, the defeat of Judah at the hands of the Assyrians is given a mysterious and theological interpretation. How could an empire so poorly equipped nearly destroy Judah, especially after all the preparations done under King Hezekiah (2 Chr 29–32; 2 Kgs 18; 20)? What is not stated, and yet is implied, is that Nineveh did not defeat Judah because of military power.

In the following verse (3:13), the poet takes the reader into inner Nineveh to see the weakness of the people (military?) of Nineveh, who are compared to women; and then he brings the reader back to the city-gate where the gates are wide open to the enemy and their bars are being burned in fire. In the ancient Near East, comparing an army to women meant to show the weakness and the fear of that army in front the enemy. In a vassal treaty curse, Esarhaddon tells his vassals, "May all the gods who are called by name in this treaty tablet spin you around like a spindle-whorl, may they make you like a woman before your enemy."¹⁴ Biblical OAN also use the image of a woman as a symbol for the weakness and fear of an enemy (Isa 19:16; Jer 50:37; 51:30). By these images, Nah 3:13 shows, in its three parallel cola, how both the gates leading to the city and the army inside the city are not able to protect the city from enemy attacks: the army is fearful and weak, while the city-gates are wide open to the enemy.

In light of the inevitability of the defeat, the poet mocks Nineveh by telling her to prepare for the siege. It has already been said that the fate of Nineveh has been decided (3:11). But in 3:14, YHWH summons Nineveh to draw water for the siege and to strengthen its fortifications. YHWH also tells Nineveh to "Come to the clay, tread the mortar, take hold of the brick mold." These activities are obviously done in preparation for the construction of fortification walls. The point for the poet in this verse is that such measures are futile, because they will not be enough to allow Nineveh to avoid YHWH's vengeance.

The same idea of the futility of Assyrian military preparation continues in 3:15–17. These three verses center around the imagery of the numerous and destructive, and yet unreliable locusts (*yeleq*, '*arbeh*, *gôb*). The imagery is used in three ways. First, in 3:15a, it is used to speak about

13. See Ussishkin, *The Conquest of Lachish*, 80–94.

14. "Vassal Treaty of Esarhaddon" as cited in Christopher B. Hays, *Hidden Riches*, 178.

the destruction of Nineveh, which will resemble destruction brought about by locusts: Nineveh's enemies will be like locusts (*yeleq*). The second meaning of the image speaks about and compares Nineveh to a swarm of insects that attack and destroy others (see Jer 51:14). The connection between these two meanings of the same imagery is important. By using the same image for both Nineveh and her destroyers, the poet seems to intend to establish similarities between Nineveh, those who attack her, and those whom she attacked in the past. In other words, Nineveh herself is not innocent; she is also a destructive locust, and so the punishment that she receives here is the mirror image of what she did to others. She might multiply her people and her officials, but the number of people and officials within her will not make her invincible. We can hear here the echo of the statement in 1:12b that, "though they are at peace, and therefore many, they will pass away."

The third sense of the imagery of the locust is unique to Nahum in the Hebrew Bible. In Nah 3:17, the term for locusts (*gôb gōbāy*) is used to speak about the lack of loyalty and consistency in the Assyrian officials and merchants: they are compared to locusts that stay only as long as the sun has not risen. Those officials are reliable only on cold days; on hot days, they disappear and are nowhere to be found. Here, the poet even overturns metaphors. In the Hebrew Bible, the sun is generally a good thing (see Jer 31:35; Joel 2:10; 3:15; Mal 3:20; Ps 58:9); YHWH is even called the "sun and shield" in Ps 84:11. And the expression "cold day" appears in another instance (Prov 25: 20), where it symbolizes a "bad day." In Nah 3:17, however, the two expressions have been used differently: the rising of the sun is seen as a bad thing for the insects, while a cold day is seen as good thing. Marvin Sweeney has shown that at the background here is the image that YHWH is the sun that destroys wicked Nineveh.[15] The Assyrian merchants and rulers survive only within the conditions where YHWH, the one who brings the sun of righteousness (Mal 3:20), is not present. Indirectly then, the poet also accuses the Assyrian merchants for maintaining their activities within conditions that lack righteousness. Julia O'Brien sees in this reference to the multiplication of merchants an accusation of Assyria's brutal control of international trade (3:4).[16] Without ignoring those indirect accusations against Assyrian evil practices, it is important to note that, here, the main accusation against Nineveh

---

15. Sweeney, *The Twelve Prophets*, 446.
16. O'Brien, *Nahum*, 64.

is about her short-sighted reliance on structures that cannot escape destruction from external forces and that are also untrustworthy, because they give the impression of defending Nineveh; but that impression lasts only as long as conditions are comfortable.

Assyria's delusional self-assertion as an exceptional and invincible nation is more exposed by the imagery of the sleeping shepherds in 3:18. The king of Assyria is addressed for the first time in the poem, and he is addressed only when everything seems to have fallen apart. As far as the book of Nahum is concerned, the king of Assyria—the lion who raged against, attacked, and destroyed his prey—is recognized only when he is sorely wounded. The king is shown how his assistants (shepherds) are sleeping and his people are scattered upon the mountains. The image of sleeping shepherds, incapable of taking care of the flock, highlights the uselessness of the assistants of the king of Assyria. The point here is that it is a mistake for the king of Assyria to think that he is invincible only based on the existence of these shepherds, because they prove unreliable.

YHWH's address to Nineveh in 3:8–18 points to Nineveh's inability to see things clearly, which has led her to believe that she is an exceptional nation, capable of escaping YHWH's vengeance. Indirectly, the message to the Judahite survivors is that the Assyrian destruction of Judah will not be repeated, for Nineveh itself will be paid in her own currency. Nineveh is of course addressed in the poem; but the poet, as we showed in previous chapters, was not interested in convincing the Assyrians to change their thinking or their practices. The exposition of short-sighted Nineveh's belief in her exceptionalism serves more to comfort Judahites in the wake of Assyrian destruction, encouraging them not to accept the Assyrian self-image of invincibility, and to hope that YHWH will restore them.

Violent Crimes

The second kind of crimes of which Nineveh is accused is her actions against other nations. Those actions are described generically as "evil" (*rāʿāh*) that passed over all the nations of the earth (3:19), but that evil takes multiple forms. It takes the forms of invasions (2:1), domination/yoke (1:13), ravages (2:3), lionlike predation (2:12–14), bloodshed (3:1–3), and prostitution and sorcery (3:4).

Domination and invasions

The first time that the poet gives us a hint at the specific crimes of the Assyrian empire is in 1:13, when YHWH promises to remove the yoke from upon Judah.

> And now I will break his yoke from above you,
> And I will burst his chain.

The antecedents of the pronouns used in this verse (and in 1:11–14 in general) are not specified. But, as has been shown by Julia O'Brien, the third masculine singular pronominal suffix on *mṭh* seems to refer to the king of Assyria (the king of Assyria is the only masculine character addressed in the book—3:18), while the second feminine singular pronominal suffix on *mʿl* and *mōsrōt* refers to Judah, who is later identified as the one under a situation of duress (2:1, 3).[17] The term "yoke" is often used as a metaphor for domination or rule over a people (see Isa 10:24; 14:5; Jer 48:17; 27:11, 12); but ruling over a people (imposing one's yoke upon another) is not always seen as a crime in the Hebrew Bible. As we saw it above, when a foreign nation rules over Judah, the situation is complex. The Hebrew Bible claims that their rule over Judah/Israel is a mandate from YHWH; but, at the same time, those nations can also be punished for their excesses. The example of Babylon in the book of Jeremiah is a case in point. From the beginning of the book to chapter 45, Babylon is presented as YHWH's agent, and other nations are encouraged not to rebel against Babylon (see 27:2, 11–12). However, in the rest of the book (46–52, especially 50–51), Babylon is presented as the one who strove against YHWH (50:24) and the "destroying mountain" that "destroys the whole earth" (51:24). Following that pattern (according to which nations that impose yokes on Judah and other nations are both agents of and challengers to YHWH), we can say that, in Nah 1:13, even though YHWH takes some responsibility for the fact that Assyria has imposed its yoke on Judah (1:12), Assyrian domination on Judah is a crime. It will become clear later, when the poet shows us what that domination entails, that Assyrian rule over Judah was marked by violence and predatory spoliation of Judahite goods.

In 2:1, the poet speaks of YHWH stopping "the worthless one" from passing through Judah. Scholars have interpreted this sentence as both a reference to Assyrian invasions in Judah and a statement about the

---

17. O'Brien, *Nahum*, 45–47.

end of Judah's troubles in general.¹⁸ Nahum 2:3 also speaks of ravagers ravaging Judah and cutting off its branches. These instances are general condemnations of Assyrian violence against Judah and other nations. In 2:12–14 and 3:1–3, 4 the poet describes the specific actions committed by Nineveh.

Plundering and terrorizing diplomacy

In 2:12–14, the poet asks a rhetorical question and then names some of the crimes of the Assyrian empire:

> Where is the lion's den
>   and the cave of the young lions,
> where the lion walked, the lioness is there,
>   and the young lions, with no one to disturb?
> The lion tears enough for his cubs
>   and strangles [prey] for his lionesses.
> He has filled his cave with prey
>   and his dens with torn flesh.
> Look, I am against you, says YHWH of hosts.
> And I am about to burn her chariots in smoke;
> and your young lions the sword is about to devour;
> and I am about to cut off your predation from the earth;
> and the voice of your messengers will no longer be heard.

In these three verses, the poet names two major activities that were part of the Assyrian world domination machine: plundering and terrorizing diplomacy (psychological warfare). These three verses are anchored around the imagery of the lion and its predation. The reader is imaginatively taken into the wild forest where the lion is supposed to reign in terror. The repetition of words connected to the root *ṭrp* ("to tear, prey") and the abundance of words for lions (*gûr*, *lābî'*, *kĕpîr*, and *'aryēh*) create in the mind of the reader the experience of a lion's hunting expedition. These images also evoke the celebrated battles (or *mise en scènes* of battles) between the Assyrian monarch and the lion (see chapter 4). However, here, the king of Assyria is the lion and his citizens are lion cubs and lionesses. Nineveh is presented as a lion's den, where all the Assyrian citizens (lionesses and lion's cubs) live and are provided for by the tearing of prey by the lion. The focus of the three verses is on the

---

18. Sweeney, *The Twelve Prophets*, 434.

predatory nature of the lion and on the necessity for YHWH to put an end to such activities. The poet begins 2:12 with a rhetorical question about the whereabouts of the den and the cave of the lion and suggests that they are nowhere to be found. Since the three verses follow the depiction of YHWH's destruction of Nineveh in 2:2–11, they function as the logical conclusion drawn from the fact that YHWH has defeated the king of Assyria, who used to believe himself to be an invincible lion.[19] These images of a predatory lion convey the violent pillage and spoliation of conquered lands by the Assyrians.[20] As we just saw in one of Esarhaddon's inscriptions, where he brags about his spoliation of conquered nations, taking spoils and receiving tributes from the nations that they conquered were some of the features of Assyrian world domination. We saw in chapter 4, in our analysis of Slab IV of the Lachish reliefs, how Assyrian soldiers and Judahite captives leaving the city were carrying booty from Lachish. Also, one of the two inscriptions found on the reliefs tells us about Sennacherib sitting on his throne and receiving spoils from Lachish.[21] Such practices are implied in Nahum's taunt about the disappearance of the lion den in Nah 2:12–14. YHWH then decides to end the terror created by the Assyrian lion both in Judah and in other nations.

After describing Assyrian predatory practices in 2:13–14, in 2:14, YHWH addresses Nineveh directly. Beginning with a challenge formula (*hinĕnî 'ēlayik*), the poet presents the undoing of Nineveh's predatory practices as imminent. Nahum 2:14 has YHWH as the main agent, dismantling the image of the invincible lion that 2:12–13 mockingly depicted. The expression *hinĕnî 'ēlayik* makes the language formulaic, but especially draws the reader's attention to the immediacy of YHWH's presence.[22] That formula is used in other prophetic books within the contexts of YHWH's decision to deal with Israel (Ezek 21:8) or with foreign nations (Jer 21:13; 50:31; 51:25; Ezek 29:10; 35:3; 38:3; 39:1). It expresses YHWH's challenge to the addressee for a duel.[23]

The consequence of YHWH's actions against Nineveh is presented as the cessation of the voice of the messengers of Nineveh—a powerful

---

19. Cassin, "Le Roi et le Lion," 360, 370.
20. Spronk, *Nahum*, 106–7; Maier, *The Book of Nahum*, 278.
21. Ussishkin, *The Conquest of Lachish*, 109.
22. The particle *hinēh* itself functions as an "attention-getter. . . . When it is used in direct discourse, it helps the hearer zero in on a particular person or event" (Berlin, *Poetics and Interpretation*, 91).
23. See Block, *The Book of Ezekiel*, 200–201.

and yet spiteful anticipation of the end of an empire that throve on propaganda and self-aggrandizement. Nineveh's chariots are about to be burned in smoke; her young lions are about to be cut off; Nineveh's own predatory activities are about to be stopped, and the voice of her messengers will no longer be heard.

The expression "voice of your messengers" in 2:14 echoes and contrasts with the mention of the messenger who brings Judah good tidings in 2:1. Grammatically, we see that the "herald of good tidings" who proclaims wholeness in Judah is singular, while the messengers of Nineveh are plural. Also, both the messenger of good tidings who comes to Judah and the messengers of Nineveh have a similar goal: to make their voice heard. However, only the voice of the messenger of good tidings will be heard, while that of the messengers of Nineveh will vanish, just as Nineveh herself and her dignitaries (the den and its lions) are nowhere to be found. This contrast between the two proclamations shows that the arrival of the messenger of *shalom* who comes to Judah will coincide with the silencing of the messengers of Assyria.[24] The implication here is that the presence of the Assyrian messengers creates conditions of no-peace (instability and war), and it is only when YHWH destroys them that wholeness can return to Judah.

Writing about Neo-Assyrian strategies of domination, Peter Dubovský shows that, contrary to what might seem to appear in Assyrian royal inscriptions, the Assyrians did not only use "brute force to achieve their goals." Assyrian messengers (diplomats) were, in their own right, a powerful way for the Assyrian monarch to sow terror and persuade other nations to submit to them. Based on the evidence from Neo-Assyrian letters, it appears

> that the Assyrians employed a whole range of diplomatic, political, economic, religious, and psychological means in order to suppress insurrections, conquer regions, and punish any lack of loyalty. In other words, the Assyrians were well-versed in what we call now psychological warfare. The Assyrians manipulated the masses, offered incentives and promises, used the carrot-and-stick strategy, discredited their adversaries, and presented Assyrian conquests as a mission of liberation couched in religious terminology.[25]

---

24. Cf. O'Brien, *Nahum*, 54–55.

25. Dubovský, "Assyrians under the Walls of Jerusalem and the Confinement of Padi," 120.

Dubovský adds that the Assyrians often had recourse to the army only when diplomacy failed, either to bring the addressees to compliance, to pay tribute, or to dissuade them from rebelling against the Assyrian throne.[26] In the Hebrew Bible, we have an example of Assyrian psychological warfare through diplomacy in Sennacherib's delegation to King Hezekiah (Isa 36:1—37:13; 2 Kgs 18:17—19:13).[27] As has been shown by Peter Machinist, the speech of the Rabshakeh in this scene might reflect Judahite internal discussions about the impact of the Assyrian invasions on Judahite theology, rather than a report of a historical Assyrian diplomatic speech.[28] Nonetheless, it reflects some of the ways Judahite writers perceived Assyrian diplomacy. From the message of the Rabshakeh to Hezekiah, it is clear that the goal of the Assyrian delegation was to terrorize the Judahite king in order to bring him to submission. It is plausible then (though not certain) that, in Nah 2:14, by speaking about the messengers of Nineveh, the poet has the terrorizing Assyrian delegates in mind. Their presence in Judah and in other nations is viewed in Nahum's poem as a way for Nineveh to deprive those nations of peace.

It is noteworthy that, poetically, the cessation of the voice of the messengers of Nineveh is parallel to YHWH's cutting off the predatory activities of Nineveh from the earth. Those two cola are also parallel to the destruction of chariots and the devouring of Assyrian young lions by the sword:

> [And I am about to burn her chariots in smoke;//And your young lions the sword is about to devour;] // [And I am about to cut off your preying from the earth;// And the sound of your messengers will no longer be heard]

The implication of the structure of the verse is that the messages sent through delegates (diplomacy) and actual spoliation of conquered lands were crimes that disrupted shalom and that necessitated YHWH's intervention.

---

26. Dubovský, "Assyrians under the Walls of Jerusalem and the Confinement of Padi," 121.

27. See the delegation of Jephthah to the king of the Ammonites in Judg 11:12ff for an Israelite example of psychological warfare or diplomacy during war time.

28. Machinist, "The Rab Šāqēh at the Wall of Jerusalem," 161.

Bloodshed, deception, sorcery, and debauchery

Assyrian royal inscriptions and palace reliefs give us the image of an empire that used extreme violence against its enemies and celebrated that violence as marker of royal power. Our analysis of the Lachish reliefs in chapter 4 showed an example of such violence on a Judahite town. In Nah 3:1–4, rather than imitating the Assyrian depiction of violence and celebrating it, the poet makes us relive the scenes of Assyrian violence, while at the same time telling us that such actions are criminal: they are bloodshed, deceit, sorcery, and harlotry:

> Ah, city of bloodshed,
>   completely deceitful; full of plunder,
>   [her] predation does not cease.
> Crack of the whips and sound of rattling wheels,
>   and horses galloping and chariots bounding!
> Horseman charging,
>   flash of flashing sword, and the glittering of the spear!
> Piles of slain,
>   heaps of corpses;
> There is no end to slain bodies;
>   they stumble over slain bodies—
> because of the multitude of the harlotries of the prostitute,
>   she who is highly favored, the mistress of sorceries,
> selling nations with her harlotries
>   and families with her sorceries.
> (Nah 3:1–4)

Scholars generally believe that 3:2–3 describes YHWH's attack on Nineveh, while 3:1, 4 describes Nineveh.[29] The reason for these scholars to attribute the actions in 3:2–3 to the army of YHWH is because these two verses seem to rehearse what the poet says in 2:5–11 (describing the attack on Nineveh). However, the structure of Nah 3:1–4 shows that these four verses are giving the reader a description of Nineveh's violence against other nations. In 3:1, we have the exclamation, *hôy*, which often introduces a "woe oracle," that is, a pronouncement that conveys warning about an imminent danger.[30] This exclamation often expresses anticipated mourning over punishment/misfortune against a person or a group of persons. It is generally followed by the description of that "person or

---

29. Sweeney, *The Twelve Prophets*, 442; O'Brien, *Nahum*, 60; Spronk, *Nahum*, 118–19.

30. Sweeney, *The Twelve Prophets*, 442.

a group of persons in regard to what they are doing, their deed being the cause for the foreboding woe-cry."[31] There is nothing between 3:1 and 3:2 that suggests that in 3:2 the poet has switched from the description of the actions of Nineveh to speak about the attack against the city. In 3:4a, the poet uses the causal clause "because of the multitude of the harlotries of the prostitute." This clause explains either what comes before it or what comes after it. In this case, since after 3:4 we have another unit whose introduction is marked by the challenge formula, *hinĕnî 'ēlayik* (3:5), it seems more logical that all of 3:1–4 describes the deeds of Nineveh for which YHWH is attacking her. Thus, in these verses, we have a dirge where the imminent destruction of Nineveh is coupled with a paratactic presentation of Nineveh's violent actions against other nations. The poet certainly does not say that it is Nineveh who performs the actions described in 3:2–3; but, because this is a lyric poem, one would expect such abrupt shifts from evaluative description of Nineveh's actions (3:1) to making the reader actually watch Nineveh act violently.[32]

The four verses use only two finite verbs (*yĕkāšlû* and *yāmîš*); they are made of short verbless clauses or short clauses with nonfinite verbs, giving the event a feeling of immediacy and vividness.[33] The poet makes the reader imagine Assyrian invasions and violence against other nations as if they were unfolding before her.

In 3:1, the poet names bloodshed, deceit, and plunder as three characteristics of Nineveh.[34] In one of his inscriptions, Assyrian King Ashurnasirpal II (885–860 BCE) boasts about the violence that he inflicted against his enemies:

> I flayed all the chief men [in the city of Suru] who had revolted, and I covered the pillar with their skins; some I walled up within the pillar, some I impaled upon the pillar on stakes, and others I bound to stakes round about the pillar. . . . 600 of their [the people in the city of Hulai] warriors I put to the sword; 3,000 captives I burned with fire; I did not leave a single one among

---

31. Gerstenberger, "The Woe-Oracles of the Prophets," 251. See Isa 3:9; 10:5; 29:1; Jer 13:7; 48:46; Ezek 13:3, 18; 16:28; 24:6, 9; Hab 2:12.

32. See Heffelfinger, *I Am Large*, 119–20.

33. O'Brien, *Nahum*, 60.

34. In the Hebrew Bible, the plural *dāmîm* is often used to speak of the blood that has been shed by violence (see Gen 4:10, 11; 2 Sam 3:28; 16:8; 2 Kgs 9:26; Isa 1:15; Hab 2:8, 17).

them alive to serve as hostage.... Their corpses I formed into pillars; their young men and maidens I burned in the fire....

Many captives among them I burned with fire. From some I cut off their hands and fingers, and from others I cut off their noses, their ears, and their fingers (?), of many I put out the eyes.

...

In the midst of the mighty mountain I slaughtered them, with their blood I dyed the mountain red like wool, with the rest of them I darkened the gullies and the precipices of the mountains.[35]

The book of Nahum addresses an audience that experienced similar violence. The poet does not connect the actions through words. Each action is named, then followed immediately by another. The reader has the impression of watching the scene or hearing the poet report the event as it is unfolding. The scene begins with the approach of the Assyrian army and reaches its climax in the vision of the aftermath of the battle, where we are shown a multitude of slain corpses lying on the ground. The reader first hears the crack of the whips and the sound of the rattling of the wheels (3:2a). In this colon, the poet (and his reader) seems to see nothing yet, but he can recognize the kind of sounds he hears. Then, in a quick succession, the sounds are followed by the appearance (visible) of horses and chariots (3:2b). In 3:3, we see the actual battle: horsemen are charging, swords and spears glittering, and the ground is full of corpses. The scene is so confusing that unnamed characters are said to be stumbling over dead bodies. This scene of slain bodies seems to be the culmination of Assyrian crimes.

In 3:4, the poet explains Nineveh's violence as consequences of her harlotry (*zěnûnîm*) and sorcery (*kěšāpîm*). In general, the motif of harlotry is used in prophetic books to speak about the Israel's infidelity toward YHWH (Isa 1:21; Jer 2:20; 3:1, 3, 6, 8; 5:7; Ezek 6:9; 16:15; 20:30; 23:3; Hos 4:15; 5:3; 9:1). Since Assyria had no covenant with YHWH, scholars have shown that, in this instance of the use of harlotry (and sorcery), the poet might be doing two things. First, these two words might have been used to speak about objectionable activities in general (see for example the many harlotries and sorceries of Jezebel in 2 Kgs 9:22).[36] Second, harlotry might be referring here to the deceitful promises of rewards and favors that the Assyrians used to make to the kings of other nations to

---

35. Luckenbill, *Ancient Records of Assyria and Babylon*, 142.
36. See Spronk, *Nahum*, 122.

have them submit to the Assyrian rule (which would make "harlotry" synonym of the term *kaḥaš*, "deceitful," already used in 3:1). According to Walter Maier, the multiple favors and the splendor of the empire itself would have been exposed (just as a prostitute would have exposed herself) in order to attract nations that Nineveh could destroy later.[37] As for sorcery, in the Hebrew Bible, *kšp* is often used in contexts where people lie to others or misguide them by giving them inaccurate information: Pharaoh's sorcerers mislead him (Exod 7:11), Judahites believe using sorcery can avert YHWH's punishment, but they realize that sorcery does not do anything (Isa 47:9, 12), the sorcerers are among the people who deceive the Judahites about the end of the Babylonian domination (Jer 27:9). It seems that Nahum uses this term (as he does with "harlotry") as a synonym for deception (*kḥš*). Just as harlotry attracts other nations to deceive them, sorcery also charms them by offering them a truncated view of the world, which view can lead to the downfall of those nations. If we look back to my previous discussion on the unreliability of Assyrian officials described in 3:17,[38] it will appear that, for Nahum, deceiving is part of what it means to be Assyrian: they deceive one another inside Assyria, and so, as a nation, they bring that behavior into all their relationships with the outside world.

In this section, we have seen that YHWH's indictment against Nineveh addresses both Nineveh's thinking and the actions that embody such thinking. Nineveh has made a deceptive image of herself as an exceptional empire and has also held evil thoughts against YHWH. Through the construction of her own image as a means of propaganda, Nineveh has also come to believe in the image she made of herself as an invincible and indestructible den of lions. Such thinking has led her to commit and celebrate violence against other nations. In response to her thinking and behavior, YHWH inflicts well-deserved violence on Nineveh.

---

37. Maier, *The Book of Nahum*, 302; cf. Spronk, *Nahum*, 122.
38. "Your courtiers are like grasshopper
    and your officials like hordes of locusts:
    they settle on walls
    on a cold day;
    the sun rises and they retreat
    and it is not known where their place is." (Nah 3:17).

The Battle against and the Destruction of Nineveh— Nahum 2:2, 4-11; 3:5-6 (see 1:8-9)

In this second section of the chapter, I will explore how YHWH pays Nineveh for what she did against YHWH and against other nations. I already showed in chapter 5 how in 1:8-9 YHWH is described as destroying those who do not take refuge in him. In the verses that I analyze here, I will see how YHWH attacks and defeats Nineveh. I will present the attack on Nineveh in two stages. In the first stage, I will analyze some verses describing YHWH's threats against the city (2:2, 14; 3:5-7); then in the second, I will analyze verses presenting the attack proper on Nineveh (2:4-11).

Threat and Warning to Nineveh and to the King of Assyria

YHWH threatens Nineveh four times in the book of Nahum (2:2, 14, 3:5-6, 14) and threatens the king of Assyria once (1:14). In all cases, YHWH shows Nineveh that the danger is imminent and there is no way she can escape. The accusations and threats in 2:14 and 3:14 have been discussed; here, I treat the remaining three instances.

Nahum 2:2

> A scatterer (*mēpiṣ*) has come up against you!
>   Guard the rampart,
>   watch the road.
> Strengthen your loins,
>   gather all your strength.

This verse is the first time YHWH addresses Nineveh directly in this poem. The city itself is not named, but the use of the second feminine singular pronominal suffix suggests that it is either Nineveh or Judah. However, since in the poem it is only Nineveh who is warned of an impending danger (2:14; 3:5-7, 14), it is more plausible to consider the addressee to be Nineveh rather than Judah.[39] Based on how the verb *pwṣ* is used in the Hebrew Bible, mainly having YHWH as its subject (Gen 11:8; Deut 4:27; 2 Sam 22:15; Jer 9:15; Ezek 11:16), there is little doubt that "the scatterer"

---

39. Christensen, *Nahum*, 263-64; Maier, *The Book of Nahum*, 221; Spronk, *Nahum*, 83-84.

of this verse is YHWH himself advancing against Nineveh.[40] With one infinitive absolute (*nāṣôr*)[41] and three imperatives (*ḥazzēq, ṣappēh, 'ammēṣ*) the poet commands Nineveh to take precautionary measures in order to survive YHWH's attack against her. The four verbs speak about two kinds of preparation: logistical (guarding the rampart and watching the road) and psychological (strengthening the loins and gathering all strength). As I have already shown above about 3:14 (where Nineveh is also told to prepare for the war), these imperatives are used ironically, because the fate of Nineveh seems to have already been decided.[42] Later in the book, the poet will say that the people of Assyria are scattered on the mountains (3:18), suggesting that the scatterer who came up against Nineveh accomplished his intended task.

Nahum 3:5-6

> Look, I am against you,
>> says YHWH of hosts.
>> And I am about to lift up your skirts upon your face;
> and I am about to show nations your nakedness
>> and kingdoms your ignominy.
> And I am about to throw abominable things against you
>> and treat you with disdain.
> And I am about to set you as a spectacle.

These verses focus on exposing Nineveh for the deceitful city that she is and showing the entire world how despicable her behavior is. The two verses follow the description of Nineveh as prostitute and sorcerer in 3:4. They function as YHWH's way of punishing the city for her harlotry and sorcery. Like 2:14, Nah 3:5 begins with a challenge formula, *hinĕnî 'ēlayik*, which draws the attention of Nineveh (and of the reader) to the impending violence against the city. Because she uses harlotry and sorcery to deceive other nations—that is, by covering her true identity—Nineveh will receive punishments that will expose her worthlessness: she will be stripped naked.

---

40. Roberts, *Nahum, Habakkuk, and Zephaniah*, 64; Christensen, *Nahum*, 262; Spronk, *Nahum*, 83.

41. For the use of the infinitive absolute to express command, see Waltke and O'Connor, *An Introduction to Biblical Hebrew Syntax*, 593-94.

42. Spronk, *Nahum*, 85.

In the Hebrew Bible, punishment by stripping a woman naked can be a euphemism for rape, and the "lifting up of skirts" can be followed by the violation of the exposed woman (see Jer 13:22; Ezek 16: 36).[43] In Nah 3:5, YHWH does not say that Nineveh will be raped by the nations and the kingdoms (they will gaze at her), but, as we will see later, exposing her made her vulnerable to sexual violence by her attackers. Cynthia R. Chapman has studied the aesthetics of sexual violence in the prophets and in Neo-Assyrian art and has shown that exposing the enemy's genitalia was a way for Assyrian combatants to assert their victory over the conquered enemy.[44]

Nahum 3:5b and 3:5c describe two parallel actions: to lift up the skirts upon the face (A) and to show nations and kingdoms Nineveh's nakedness and ignominy (B). Colon A states an action that, in itself, violates the privacy of Nineveh. Colon B however adds that the purpose of YHWH's lifting up her skirts is so that nations and kingdoms may see her nakedness and ignominy.

The intensity of the punishment is heightened from A to B. Stripping the prostitute of her skirts already makes her vulnerable to the gaze of others. But YHWH does not simply strip her; he also invites nations and kingdoms to see her nakedness and ignominy. Colon B also presents two parallel semi-cola, each representing one idea: nakedness and ignominy. In colon Ba, YHWH exposes the nakedness of Nineveh. In colon Bb, the poet shows that by uncovering her nakedness, what YHWH wants to show is actually her ignominy.

It is important to note that the nakedness and worthlessness are exposed to nations and kingdoms. In Nah 3:4, we saw that Nineveh deceived and sold nations and families with her harlotries and sorceries. The pair nations/families is not repeated in 3:5; but the pair nations/kingdoms seems to carry the same idea of groups of people as nations/families. The main idea of the verse is that, through YHWH's actions, the same people whom Nineveh deceived will now see her for the ignominious city that she is.

The skirts in that sense can be a metaphor for both Nineveh's actual defense mechanisms against the enemy and her self-image that would have made others fear her. Thus, once YHWH exposes Nineveh for who

---

43. O'Brien, *Nahum*, 62; O'Connor, "Reclaiming Jeremiah's Violence," 45.
44. Chapman, "Sculpted Warriors," 10–12.

she is, any enemy will have the courage to invade her, because the deceptive image that she made of herself has been lifted up.

After stripping Nineveh naked and exposing her ignominy (3:5), YHWH throws abominable things against her, treats her with disdain, and places her as a spectacle (3:6). The word *šqṣ* is often used to speak about idols, especially the idols of foreign nations (Deut 29:17; 1 Kgs 11:5, 7; 2 Kgs 23:13, 24; Isa 66:3; Jer 4:1; 7:30; 13:27; Ezek 5:11; Hos 9:10; Zech 9:7). Scholars generally consider this word to mean "anything despicable" that YHWH can throw against Nineveh.[45] Throwing "abominable things" against Nineveh is in parallel relationship with *nibbaltēyk* (in the intensive piel), "treating disdainfully." Both actions have to do with YHWH reserving a debasing treatment to Nineveh in order to disfigure her. Nahum 3:6 ends with the promise to make Nineveh a spectacle (*rō'î*). By the time we reach this end of 3:6, we realize that all of YHWH's actions have been leading to this exposition of the "city of bloodshed" and the (implicit) invitation to passersby to come and gaze at the naked and disfigured city.

Nahum 1:14

> And YHWH has commanded against you:
>   Your name will no longer be perpetuated;
> From the house of your gods I will cut off
>   the carved image and the cast image.
> I will make your grave, for you are ignominious.

Unlike the other threats and warnings discussed above (addressed to the city of Nineveh), this verse is addressed to the king of Assyria himself (second masculine singular). The threats speak about the end of the family line, the death of the king himself, and the end of his religious practices. As was shown in chapter 3, in ancient Near Eastern city-lament tradition, the destruction of a city was often preceded by the abandonment of that city by the patron god.[46] Here, in Nahum, the gods of the king of Assyria are no gods, but carved and cast images. Unlike in city laments proper, where the deity leaves the city, here, it is YHWH (the only God recognized by the poet), who *cuts off* those images from their temples. However, within the tradition where the absence of the deity

---

45. Maier, *The Book of Nahum*, 109; Christensen, *Nahum*, 344.
46. See Dobbs-Allsopp, *Weep, O Daughter of Zion*, 45.

meant destruction for the city, this gesture symbolizes the fall of the city at the hand of the one who cuts the images, YHWH.

Attack on Nineveh—Nahum 2:4–11

The attack of YHWH (or YHWH's army) on Nineveh is presented as a succession of intertwined scenes of war. We hear about the description of the weapons of the attacking army (2:4), then we hear about the approach of the attacking army (2:5), the attempts of the defending army to protect the city (2:6), and the entry of the attacking army into the city (2:7). Then the poet presents the battle scene through a series of exclamations that give the reader the impression of finding herself within the battle scene and listening to the poet comment on the unfolding battle (2:8–11).

> The shields of his mighty ones (*gibbōrim*) are in red;
>   the warriors (*'anšēy-ḥail*) are [dressed in] purple.
> The chariots are in flashing iron
>   on the day they are prepared;
>   and the cypress trees are made to quiver.
> On the streets chariots race madly!
>   They rush wildly in the squares!
> Their appearance is like torches!
>   They run fast like lightnings!
> He remembers his nobles;
>   they stumble in their walk!
> They rush to the wall!
>   The mantelet is set!
> The gates of the rivers are opened!
>   The palace is dissolved!
> And he is put down! She is uncovered! She is taken up!
>   And her maidens are moaning
> like the voice of doves,
>   drumming upon their breasts!
> (Now Nineveh used to be like a pool of water in her days).
>   But they are fleeing!
> "Stop! Stop!"
>   But no one turns back!
> "Plunder the silver!
>   Plunder the gold!
> There is no end to treasure,
>   from the abundance of desirable vessels"

> Devastation! Desolation! Destruction!
>   Hearts melt! Knees tremble!
> Anguish in all loins!
>   The faces of all are in grief!

We saw above that the scatterer mentioned in 2:2 refers either to YHWH himself and/or to his army. The poet places the "mighty ones" (*gibbōrim*) in parallel relationship with "warriors" (*'anšēy-ḥail*). As has been shown by Spronk, *gbwr* can sometimes be used to refer to YHWH's heavenly army (see Ps 103:20), while *'anšēy-ḥail* always refers to the regular human army.[47] Even though these two expressions are used elsewhere in parallelism with each other to speak of human beings (see Isa 5:22; Jer 48:14), in this context where YHWH himself is involved in the battle, it is plausible to read the pair *gibbōrim/'anšēy-ḥail* intertextually with Ps 103:20 and see it as a reference to an army composed of both of heavenly and human forces.[48]

Before the attack proper, the poet describes the weapons of the attacking army: red shields, dreadful clothes, and fiery chariots. Various explanations have been given about the colors of the weapons (red and crimson). Some scholars (like Julia O'Brien) have suggested that the red on the shields of the warriors can be explained by showing that the battle against Nineveh is not the first and only one YHWH has fought; the weapons are reddened by blood from previous battles (see Isa 63:1–6).[49] Others have suggested that red and purple dyes were used to make weapons more terrifying to the enemy.[50]

The description of weapons in Nah 2:4 adds also the expression, "and the cypress trees are made to quiver," which has caused scholars interpretative difficulties. The main question has centered on the purpose of cypress trees in the context of this verse dealing with weapons of war. Some interpreters (including the BHS) have suggested amending the text to read *brwš* (cypress) as *prš* (horseman). The term *prš* is used in 3:3, so it is possible to see here a reference to horsemen. Others retain the received text. Walter Maier argues that the term *brwš* refers to spears made of

---

47. Dobbs-Allsopp, *Weep, O Daughter of Zion*, 89.

48. Note also the similarity between the chariots of fiery iron in this verse and the image of chariots of fire in the incident of Elisha and the Syrians in 2 Kgs 6:17. The army that surrounds Elisha is an army sent by YHWH (in answer to Elisha's prayer).

49. O'Brien, *Nahum*, 52; cf. Roberts, *Nahum, Habakkuk, Zephaniah*, 65.

50. Sweeney, *The Twelve Prophets*, 438.

cypress trees.[51] Similarly, Sweeney sees in this term a reference to poles on which chariots were harnessed.[52] Julia O'Brien makes the attractive suggestion that the shaking of cypress trees is caused by the coming of the Divine Warrior, at whose presence the world shakes (see 1:5–6).[53] Just as mountains, hills, and forests shake at the approach of YHWH, so do the cypress trees at the beginning of YHWH's battle against Nineveh.

After describing the weapons of YHWH's army, the poet shows the advance of the army into the city (2:5).[54] The actions of the army are described in parallelisms. In 2:5a, the chariots are described as racing madly through the streets and rushing through the squares. The pair *ḥwṣ/rḥbwt* is used in the book of Jeremiah to speak about all the areas of the city (Jer 5:1; see Song 3:2). Even though Jeremiah is a later book, it is possible that the use of this expression in Jeremiah has some similarities with the way it is used in Nahum. Thus, in this verse, the poet seems to present the army of YHWH as having invaded and occupied the entire city. Nahum 3:5b has two semi-cola, where semi-colon B describes actions that are the intensification of those described in semi-colon A. First, in semi-colon A, we are told about the appearance of the chariots: they look like torches. Both "appearing" and "torches" give the reader a feeling of immobility. Torches burn and are scary, but they can be held by human beings (see Judg 7:16). In semi-colon B, however, the chariots do not simply appear; they rush, and their speed is like that of the lightning. The image of the lightning here evokes motifs of the YHWH's theophany (see Exod 19:16; Ps 77:18), but also gives the reader a sensation of inevitable danger that is rapidly approaching the doomed city.

Chapter 2, verse 6 moves the focus of the depiction from the attacking army to the Assyrians' desperate attempts to defend the city. Two activities are described in the verse: the summons of the officers by the Assyrian king and the advance of those officers to the wall to defend it. Some scholars have argued that 2:6 cannot be interpreted as describing the activities of the defending Assyrian army. The main reason for that argument has been that in the previous verse all the third masculine singular pronominal suffixes refer to the "scatterer" (see 2:2) who leads the attacking army. J. M. P. Smith, for example, suggests that we consider *yzkr*

51. Maier, *The Book of Nahum*, 238–39.
52. Sweeney, *The Twelve Prophets*, 438.
53. O'Brien, *Nahum*, 52.
54. Scholars have often suggested that the activities described in 3:5 take place outside the city, in the open fields, since the army is still outside the city.

as referring to the summoning of the attacking officers by the scatterer. However, he faces difficulties, since the same officers who are summoned "stumble in their walk." Finding it unlikely that the poet would have described such a powerful army as stumbling in its advance, Smith proposes amending the verb *kšl* to *mšl*.[55] He also translates *bohălikātām* as "in their companies," considering *hălîkāh* as a reference to a "company of soldiers"—a meaning Smith himself admits is unattested in the Hebrew Bible.[56] After the emendation and the adoption of that unusual sense for *hălîkāh*, 2:6a reads as "He summons his nobles; they take command of their companies." The BHS too, assuming that 2:6 continues the description of the attacking army, suggests that we add *lō'* before *ykšlw*, meaning that the attacking army does *not* stumble in its advance. Walter Maier maintains the MT, but suggests that the attacking soldiers are so numerous that they stumble over one another.[57] Marvin Sweeney sees here a reference to the urgency of the soldiers as they carry heavy weapons.[58]

Klaas Spronk shows that the term *'addîrāyw* (2:6) is the same term that is used in 3:18 to speak about the assistants to the king of Assyria; it is therefore more plausible that here the poet intends to speak about those same officials.[59] Julia O'Brien follows Spronk in reading this verse as a reference to the defending army.[60] I concur with this reading. However, neither Spronk nor O'Brien adequately explains the abrupt shift in reference, from the attackers (2:5) to the defenders (2:6), nor do they consider the lack of a specified subject for verb *yzkr*. But this is a striking instance of the paratactic style of biblical lyric poetry (see 3:1–4). The poet juxtaposes two different events in the form of a diptych, giving the reader simultaneous access to both the advance of YHWH's army and the unsuccessful defense of the Assyrians. The reader's interest is primarily drawn to the lavish picture of the attackers that begins in 2:4–5 and continues with the effects of the attack in 2:7–11. However, the sudden shift of subject and scene in 2:6 forces the reader to consider (however briefly) the other side of the duel. The reader witnesses the Assyrians' attempts at

---

55. Smith, *A Critical and Exegetical Commentary*, 330.
56. Smith, *A Critical and Exegetical Commentary*, 317.
57. Maier, *The Book of Nahum*, 246.
58. Sweeney, *The Twelve Prophets*, 438.
59. Spronk, *Nahum*, 93.
60. O'Brien, *Nahum*, 52.

defense, and sees also that they are nothing compared to the power of the attacking army, and will only last for a brief time.

Nahum 2:7 returns to the attackers and the devastating effects of their invasion. The gates of the rivers are opened and the palace is dissolved. Some scholars have read this verse as a literal reference to flooding used by the invading army to destroy Nineveh. Some have even affirmed that this verse makes clear historical reference to the invasion of Babylonians and their destruction of Nineveh by flood.[61] However, water was often used as a metaphor for destruction in the ancient Near East, especially in city laments.[62] The collapse of the palace also echoes the dissolution of hills at the approach of YHWH in 1:5 (both verses using the verb *mwg*, "to melt"). The thrust of 2:7 then is that Nineveh is being attacked by YHWH—the one at whose approach everything melts—and her defense mechanisms have proved unsuccessful. The collapse of the palace, the city's primary symbol of royal power, marks the end of Assyrian hegemony in the world.[63]

In 2:8–11, the poet not only describes war but also lets the reader vividly experience the heat of battle. He shifts between his own voice and quotations of unidentified voices, so as to give the reader the impression of watching the war unfold and of hearing its confusion. Nahum 2:8 is made of the poet's own paratactically connected exclamations. The verse has three cola of decreasing length, the longest colon (2:8a) depicting the most appalling scene. Nahum 2:8a is made of three verbs: *huṣṣab*, *gultāh*, and *hōʿălātāh*. The first verb has been translated in various ways. Some scholars have taken it as the proper name of an Assyrian queen called *Huzzab*.[64] Unfortunately for that position, the name "Huzzab" has not been attested anywhere else. Other scholars have viewed the passage as a reference to the Assyrian goddess, Ishtar.[65]

---

61. This verse was discussed in chapter 4, and we showed there that Nah 2:7 does not refer to a historical event.

62. See for example the description of the destruction of Ur in the Lament over Ur,
The destructive storm makes the land tremble and quake;
Like the storm of the flood it destroys the cities.
The land-annihilating storm set up (its) decrees in the cities;
The all-destroying storm came doing evil. (LU, 198–201).

63. Spronk, *Nahum*, 96.

64. Maier, *The Book of Nahum*, 236.

65. Smith, *Critical and Exegetical Commentary*, 321; Dobbs-Allsopp, *Weep, O Daughter of Zion*, 129–30.

The decision for these two groups of scholars to attribute the feminine gender to *ḥṣb* is influenced by the gender of the two verbs that follow it. So, they translate v. 8a as "And Huzzab is stripped; she is brought up." The assumption underlying that translation and all the suggestions that follow it is that the poet is trying to write a full sentence. However, based on the existence of abrupt interjections, especially in 2:9 and 2:10, it seems that here too the poet is making exclamations so as to create a vivid scene in which he seems to be calling out each action once it takes place. I then follow Klaas Spronk's translation of *huṣṣab* as the hophal perfect third person masculine singular of *nṣb*, "he is put down." Spronk suggests that in this colon the poet is depicting a scene at the Assyrian royal court, where the attacking army has tied the king down, while his queen is being uncovered (*gultāh*) and mounted/raped (*hōʽălātāh*).[66] Spronk's own translation, though guiding us toward a good direction, is not without problems. First, identifying the one who is put down as the king and the exposed woman as the queen is a bit far-fetched. It is more plausible that the poet envisions a typical battle scene, where a nameless Assyrian is "put (tied) down" and an ordinary woman is stripped. Second, even though *glh* certainly denotes humiliating exposure and danger of sexual violence, rape is not specified here. The Hebrew is more oblique in its reference to the sexualized violence it implies: "She is taken up"—perhaps raped, taken prisoner, publicly exposed in her nakedness.

In 2:8bc, the poet describes maidens moaning and drumming on their breasts. They may be servants of the woman who is being stripped naked. It is not clear whether these maidens have also suffered physical violence, or they are moaning because of the violence being inflicted against their mistress. Spronk shows that by saying that the maidens moan like doves, the poet intends to show that they are close to death (see Isa 8:19; 38:14; 59:10–11).[67] He also points out that "beating breasts" conveys the sense of mourning that accompanied the war (Isa 32:12).[68]

The description of the unfolding battle is interrupted in 2:9a, where the poet makes a parenthetical comment about Nineveh's past glories. This is the first time the city is mentioned by name in the poem. The image chosen to describe the falling city in its former days is that of a pool of water; its population and its treasures are now draining away. Nahum

---

66. Spronk, *Nahum*, 96–97.
67. Spronk, *Nahum*, 98.
68. Spronk, *Nahum*, 98.

acknowledges that Nineveh was populous. But this population, like its leaders, is unreliable. It cannot stand duress (see 3:17).

In 2:9b, an unidentified voice urges others not to flee from the city, but the exhortation goes unheeded. At the same time, the invaders shout to one another to take spoils: gold, silver, and all the desirable vessels (2:10). The absence of the poet's narrative voice heightens the drama. The reader/hearer lives now in the very heat of the battle. Nineveh plundered other nations (2:12–14); now, she is getting the taste of her own medicine, and the reader is allowed to see it.

The two parallel cola of 2:11 give a summary of the battle. Colon 2:11a is entirely made of hapax logomena: *bûqāh, mĕbûqāh, mĕbûlāqāh.* The striking alliteration and assonance increase the sense of confusion and destruction.[69] There is an intensifying effect; each of the three synonymous terms for destruction is one syllable longer than the previous one.[70] The more the reader dwells upon the scene, the more she realizes how complete the destruction of the city is. In the second colon of 2:11, the poet focuses on the pains of surviving human beings: hearts melt, knees tremble, all the loins are "in anguish," and the faces of all become sad. The Hebrew Bible uses the expression "melting of hearts" to speak about the loss of courage in a situation of war or danger (see Josh 2:11; 5:1; Isa 13:7; 19:1; Ezek 21:12; Ps 22:15). Knees are understood as the element of the body that allows one to stand firm; their shaking means the person is in fear (see Isa 35:3; Job 4:4; Dan 5:6). The description of loins being "in anguish" expresses fear and pain (see Isa 21:3). The last expression of the verse, "*ûpnēy kullām qibṣû pā'rûr,*" has caused some difficulty in translation. The word *pā'rûr* seems to derive from the root *p'r*, which speaks of beauty. When *pā'rûr* is used with *qbṣ*, both here in Nahum and in Joel 2:6, it seems to describe a situation of suffering or sadness. If we take *pā'rûr* to be related to beauty, "gathering the beauty of the face" might be the visual description of a face overwhelmed by grief.

Noteworthy is that the poet alternates between the description of inner experiences of the survivors and the bodily expression of those experiences. The melting of hearts/minds is expressed through the shaking of knees; the anguish in the loins is expressed through the facial expression of anguish. The poet knows the language and experience of war, and how it damages both minds and bodies. In addition, because this poem

---

69. Spronk, *Nahum*, 102.
70. I take this observation from Maier, *The Book of Nahum*, 272.

is addressed to an audience that is afflicted by Assyrian violence (and because YHWH's violence against Nineveh is a measure-for-measure payback), it is plausible that Nahum's audience too can remember their experiences by hearing or viewing the sufferings of the empire that destroyed their cities and dismantled their minds and bodies. By the same token, Nahum's depiction of YHWH's destruction of Nineveh can speak powerfully to contemporary contexts where war and violence have brought destruction and physical and mental wounds.

Conclusion

These two chapters have explored the rhetoric of the book of Nahum and they have allowed us to view the kind of world that Nahum intends to depict for his afflicted audience. The powerful description of YHWH and the depiction of war are interwoven so as to awaken in the reader the memory of war. However, that evocation of the memory of war takes place within a context where YHWH is powerfully enacting justice and restoring those who have been afflicted. YHWH is shown battling Nineveh—the archenemy of Judah—but that battle is presented as a means toward the restoration of Judah. How a contemporary afflicted community can appropriate the message of the book of Nahum will be the focus of the next chapter.

7

Reflections on the Way to Appropriation of Nahum in the DRC

Context, Form, and Reconciliation

Introduction

It has been shown in the preceding chapters that the book of Nahum poetically presents us a world of violence and destruction, where YHWH is affirmed as the dominant power, effecting justice and restoring those who have been afflicted by violence. Following my understanding of appropriation as a way for contemporary readers to own the world projected by the text, this chapter begins a reflection on the way the book of Nahum can be appropriated within the Congolese context marked by massive violence. The task of owning the text, of course, requires that each reader or each community of readers engage the text and appropriate it. This chapter is not a report on how Congolese readers understand the book of Nahum. Rather, it is my own account, in which I combine personal experience, the stories of the subjects I interviewed, and *my* reading of the book of Nahum, to propose what this book might mean for a Congolese audience and how it can be useful to all seeking healing and reconciliation after wars and conflicts.

The DRC experiences the paradox that some scholars have pointed out about areas where the majority of the population identifies as Christian, and yet those same Christians live in deep divisions with one another or kill one another. Ugandan scholar Emmanuel Katongole speaks of "Christianity without consequence," when writing about the tragedy of the 1994 genocide in Rwanda. At the time of the genocide, Rwanda was more than 85 percent Christian, and yet most of those Christians engaged in killing one another. Katongole comments:

> Maybe the deepest tragedy of the Rwandan genocide is that Christianity didn't seem to make any difference. Rwandans performed a *script that had shaped them more deeply than the biblical story had*. Behind the silences of genocide, Hutus and Tutsis alike were shaped by a story that held their imaginations captive.[1]

In the DRC as in Rwanda and many areas of the world, Christians have not allowed their Christian identity to challenge their other allegiances (e.g., tribalism). Christians more easily follow the demands of their tribes than the challenge of the gospel. According to CIA World Factbook, more than 80 percent of Congolese identify as Christians; most actively participate in the life of congregations.[2] Despite this fact, the country is deeply divided by various civil wars.

There have been some political efforts to address the question of violence in the DRC, but they have been of little help in dealing with violence and its aftermath. One of the first efforts was the signing of an agreement between all the former enemies of the second Congolese war in Pretoria (December 17, 2002). Despite the official end of the wars in 2003 following that accord, violence has continued to plague communities in the DRC. The Pretoria agreement called for the establishment of a Truth and Reconciliation Commission (TRC) that was going to "establish truth about atrocities committed during the wars; to promote peace, justice, reparations, and reconciliation; and to consolidate national unit."[3] However, that commission was not able to do much beyond establishing its own by-laws and legal status. From the start, it seemed illusory to have a TRC in a country where the same perpetrators of violence were still in charge of the institutions of the country. The commission had no power or resources to call former combatants to admit the atrocities that they

---

1. Katongole and Wilson-Hartgrove, *Mirror to the Church*, 84–85. Emphasis added.
2. CIA World Factbook (https://www.cia.gov/library/publications/the-world-factbook/geos/cg.html). Accessed on August 10, 2017.
3. Commission Congolaise Vérité et Réconciliation, *Règlement d'Ordre Intérieur*, Chapter II, Article 7. (http://www.leganet.cd/Legislation/DroitPenal/ReglementInt.CVR.htm). Accessed on August 16, 2017.

had committed, nor could it investigate such crimes. Political leaders and their international partners then focused all their efforts on what they believed could be achieved: a political compromise in which each party would take its share of power and national resources. Even after the 2006 and 2011 elections, the endless compromises and collusions among politicians have continued. Meanwhile, violence plagues many regions of the country, mistrust among communities and individuals is growing, and the effects of war have left many incapable of flourishing as fully alive individuals.

Some relief to this situation has come from international and national NGOs, churches, and civil society. In the absence of the political will to reunite the country and heal the wounds of war, those entities have endeavored to work with local communities to help them recover part of their dignity and live flourishing lives.

This book intends to participate in the work already being done by churches and religious communities in the formation of Christians for reconciliation. In this chapter, I specifically intend to provide those churches committed to reconciliation with a model of appropriating a biblical text for the sake of healing and reconciliation. I would like to demonstrate how the images in the book of Nahum can open up paths toward reconciliation within the context of violence in the DRC. I show that the two themes around which the book of Nahum is anchored—divine presence and memories of war—can help Congolese Christians face their past of individual and communal wounds, and (hopefully) imagine new possibilities for reconciled communities where trust, justice, love, belonging, and respect for human dignity are upheld as ineluctable elements of communal flourishing.

It is important to make it clear that claiming that Nahum can help communities heal from the wounds of war is not the same as saying that Nahum envisions such healed communities. What the book can do for the traumatized reader is to offer her the language to vent her rage, a venue where she can take her anger and wounds and bring in the presence of God.

I begin by showing that the image of a powerful (though violent) and vengeful God is both comforting and threatening to a traumatized audience. It can respond to the need for justice among survivors of war, and it can show Congolese churches and religious communities that the work of healing and reconciliation among communities needs to be explicitly framed as a *theological* task, rather than one that is purely humanitarian.

However, it might also lead Christians to believe that if God does not take vengeance on the perpetrator of violence, it is up to God's believers to fulfill that task of exacting vengeance on the violent. Next, I show that the scenes depicted by Nahum can evoke in the Congolese survivors of war their own experiences with violence. That evocation can allow the survivors to deal with their past, but it can also worsen the effects of war on the reader. In the end, I will show that because Nahum evokes memories of war and does not specify what the community should do with such memories, each community should look at how Israel responded to the memories evoked by Nahum and find ways of integrating those memories into their own lives.

YHWH's Attributes in Nahum and the Need for Justice and Restoration in the DRC

Most of the subjects I interviewed in eastern DRC lamented the lack of security in their communities. Militias, rebel groups, and even single individuals could come to the villages and terrorize the members of those villages without any opposition from law enforcement. Those violent actions are never punished or investigated. As a result, some members of the community decide to take matters into their own hands and seek vengeance on the perpetrators of violence. The remaining majority simply loses hope in survival or in the return of peace. The description of YHWH in the book of Nahum can speak into the concerns of those survivors of violence and give them comfort. In the following paragraphs, I analyze some images of YHWH and show how they can speak to the community of survivors.

YHWH as Guarantor of Hope against the Terror of the Perpetrators

I showed in chapter 5 how the image of YHWH contrasts with the images of kings who make themselves into gods or usurp YHWH's prerogatives. Because YHWH is the unchallenged ruler of the world, all other rulers are temporary. This image of YHWH speaks into the situation of violence in the DRC, where warlords and perpetrators of atrocities assume all power and demoralize populations. In that cauldron of violence and desolation, the perpetrators make their victims believe that they are the sole arbiters of life and death, just as seventh-century BCE Assyrians, through their violence and propaganda, spread the belief that there was no authority above Assyria. Nahum's affirmation of YHWH's uniqueness as divine Governor of world affairs delegitimizes such pretentions and thus gives victims hope for an end to oppression and violence. If YHWH is the God who will not tolerate being challenged by any world ruler, then the perpetrators of violence will themselves be destroyed.

However, that does not mean the believer will necessarily see clear signs of that salvific destruction. With the ongoing spread of violence in many areas of the DRC, it is still difficult to imagine an end to atrocities and suffering. In such conditions, hope in God's liberation from atrocity might sound utopic. Mathilde Muhindo, one of my interviewees in Bukavu, stated that the population in Bukavu lives in a "whirlwind of violence," which sums up the feeling of most people living in that region. This situation calls for a prophetic voice and ministry in the sense identified by Ellen F. Davis: "Prophetic ministry entails making God real, present, and *necessary* in situations that seem to deny that God exists, that God has any power in our lives, that God's will for us is not death but life."[4]

When read within the DRC context, Nahum can encourage hope by naming YHWH as the Avenger on the oppressor and by showing that YHWH is the only enduring Source of security to victims. It is notable that no human deliverer is mentioned in Nahum. In the books of Exodus and Isaiah, for example, we are told that in order to free the Israelites from bondage and oppression, God chooses to use human agents. In Exodus, Moses is chosen to lead the people of Israel from Egypt to the land of Canaan (Exod 3:7). In Isaiah, God chooses Cyrus to bring the Israelites from Babylon to Judea (Isa 45:1). In Nahum, it is *YHWH himself* who will end Judah's affliction by destroying Assyria. With its exclusively theocentric focus, the book of Nahum discourages its readers from placing too much confidence in human rulers or deliverers. In chapter 2, I recounted the story about the way the inhabitants of Kaniola, Walungu, Ninja, and Mulamba in eastern DRC held General FM in high esteem because they considered him to have been their savior from atrocities. FM certainly brought some relief to the victims of those communities. However, FM himself was not invincible; his own disappearance after

---

4. Davis, *Biblical Prophecy*, 145.

only a short period of activity underscores the ephemerality of merely human leadership.

YHWH's Wrath and Vengeance and the Question of Justice in the DRC

It was shown above that YHWH becomes angry and exacts vengeance on his enemies to preserve his uniqueness as God and to bring consolation and comfort to the afflicted. The image of a wrathful and vengeful God, however, seems shocking to many readers of the Bible. Eric Zenger catalogues various Christian responses to the Hebrew Bible image of God as wrathful. He shows how those Christians abhor what they consider to be an unchristian image of God because they find this God reactionary, prone to vengeance, and in contradiction with the image of the "gentle God of the New Testament," incarnate in Jesus Christ and preaching love and forgiveness.[5] They then suggest that we either omit some of those texts or preserve only verses that do not depict YHWH as violent.[6]

The depiction of God as vengeful and wrathful can certainly be dangerous for some readers, not because it does not fit "New Testament criteria,"—for the New Testament also depicts God as violent (see Matt 21:12–17; 25:45–46; Luke 3:9, 17; Rev 2:22–23)—but because, as shown by Anathea Portier-Young, by ascribing anger and violence to God, the text might inscribe "the same violence in social structures, identities, ideations, and reifications."[7] Leaders who believe themselves to have received the mandate to enforce God's instructions can consider perpetrating violence against perceived enemies of God as a form of *imitatio Dei*. The story of Phineas in the book of Numbers (Num 25), the request of James and John to call down fire against the Samaritans who did not welcome Jesus (Luke 9:52–55), the medieval Crusades, the Inquisitions, and the spread of Jihadism in today's world are some illustrations of humans taking matters into their own hands by punishing those who do not conform to God's laws in their eyes.

However, while it is important to acknowledge those dangers, I admit that there are instances in life when the only image of God that makes sense is that of a God who can use all his power (and anger!) to pay back

---

5. Zenger, *A God of Vengeance?* 13–22.
6. Zenger, *A God of Vengeance?* viii, 13–22.
7. Portier-Young, "Drinking the Cup of Horror," 399.

the perpetrator of violence for what they have done to a victim. I build on the scholars who have shown that, when the Bible ascribes wrath and vengeance to God, it intends to underscore God's personal involvement in human affairs and his disposition to right the wrongs when they occur. Abraham J. Heschel wrote that God's anger and vengeance bear witness to the fact that what happens to human beings matters to God. God's anger is not an uncontrolled outburst of emotions, but rather his righteous reaction to the evils that destroy human beings.[8] Heschel adds that anger and vengeance are not permanent attributes of God. They are contingent and important only in situations of evil and violence, where describing God as unmoved might suggest divine indifference and willingness to let injustice and evil continue.[9]

Further, as has been shown by Eric Zenger, ascribing vengeance to YHWH can suggest to the victims of violence that *they do not have to take matters into their own hands because YHWH himself will intervene.* Thus, while showing that God is provoked when anyone commits violence against other humans, texts that ascribe vengeance to God also call for an end to the cycle of violence among humans.[10]

The survivors whom I interviewed in eastern DRC lamented not only the violence that is widespread in their communities, but also the fact that the perpetrators of violence have never been held accountable for their offenses. At both local and national levels, there seems to be no interest in putting an end to violence, let alone in bringing the perpetrators of violence to justice.[11] In this context, where human justice is nonexistent, the image of God as presented by the book of Nahum can function as the affirmation that, even though present conditions suggest that violence, injustice, and death will go on, YHWH—the vengeful God—will at last bring the culprit to justice (and even destroy it). Portier-Young's thoughts about the appropriation of Nahum in contemporary societies is particularly fitting for the Congolese context:

8. Heschel, *The Prophets*, 4, 6, 62.
9. Heschel, *The Prophets*, 64.
10. Zenger, *A God of Vengeance?* 22–23, 28.
11. The irony about justice in the DRC today is that the current president of the senate, Alix Tambwe Mwamba, is himself one of the former warlords who was integrated into the national government without ever being judged for the atrocities he authorized while he was member of RCD (*Rassemblement Congolais pour la Démocratie*), one of the most violent rebel groups operating in eastern DRC between 1998 and 2003.

> [If] we listen to Nahum's cry of pain, we can hear and affirm in this book the desire for justice, the desire for God to act in this life, in this stretch of time, to reverse the conditions of oppression, to make straight the crooked, to dismantle the oppressing empires, to make the killers stop killing, and to restore life and honor those who have been shamed and forced to live a living death.[12]

My insistence on the appropriateness of the image of a vengeful God for the Congolese context might suggest that I favor retributive justice as a way of dealing with violence, while at the same time arguing for the importance of reconciliation in situations of conflict and violence. Practitioners of reconciliation have warned against emphasizing retribution, because retribution can undermine unity and forgiveness. Reflecting on the process of reconciliation in post-apartheid South Africa, South African Anglican Bishop and former President of South African TRC, Desmond Tutu, writes,

> Retributive justice . . . is not the only form of justice, . . . there is another kind of justice, restorative justice, which was characteristic of traditional African jurisprudence. Here the central concern is not retribution or punishment but, in the spirit of ubuntu, the healing of breaches, the redressing of imbalances, the restoration of broken relationships. . . . [R]estorative justice is being served when efforts are being made to work for healing, for forgiveness and for reconciliation.[13]

South African TRC favored reconciliation, but it did not simply accord amnesty to all the perpetrators of violence. Its committee on amnesty examined each case and granted amnesty only to those who made full confession of their deeds.[14] The hearings conducted by the Commission show that there was concern for holding each perpetrator of violence accountable for his actions. In other words, even though South African TRC did not focus on punishing the perpetrators of violence, naming the authors of violence and requiring them to confess their actions publicly was a way of serving the demands of justice.

It is important to note the difference between the context of post-apartheid South Africa and today's Congolese context. When South

---

12. Portier-Young, "Drinking the Cup of Horror," 406.

13. Tutu, *No Future without Forgiveness*, 51–52.

14. *Promotion of National Unity and Reconciliation Act of 1995*, chapter 2, section 3a.

Africa established its TRC, the country had already begun the process of establishing democracy. The government was no longer in the hands of a racist minority, but was now shared by all South Africans and was led by a black man, Nelson Mandela, as president. For the victims of violence during apartheid, this new situation offered hope and created the conditions in which it could have made sense to work together for reconciliation. In the DRC, such conditions are nonexistent. Even though reconciliation within communities is the goal of the Christians' engagement with Scripture, the path toward reconciliation needs to include the assurance that violence will stop. It is necessary to show that order and security can be established in the DRC. Therefore, by showing that YHWH will dismantle the structures that sponsor and carry out violence and atrocities, the book of Nahum proves promising for assuring Congolese Christians that God will restore order amid current chaos.

Nahum's War Scenes and the Evocation of War Memories in Congolese Readers

In this section, following insights from trauma studies—viz. that traumatic events resist being named and integrated into the survivor's consciousness—I show that the images Nahum uses to evoke memories of war in Judah can evoke such memories in Congolese readers. In trauma research, one of the methods that therapists use to recover feared or fragmented memories is "Prolonged Exposure Therapy" (PET). This form of therapy is based on the evidence that exposing a traumatized person to images resembling the event that caused her trauma can help the survivor to confront the trauma-related thoughts and memories and thus, can help her to reconnect with her past.[15] The event that is meant to revive traumatic memories is often placed in front of the survivor in such a way as to evoke the traumatic memories, while also showing the survivor that what she sees is not taking place in her body. The advantage of this method is that the experience the survivor fears to bring to mind can be relived from a distance, as it were, within the controlled context of therapy.

However, it should be noted that reliving a similar event and retelling the story can retraumatize the survivor. To prevent retraumatization,

---

15. Rothbaum, Foa, and Hembree, *Reclaiming Your Life from Traumatic Experience*, 5.

Judith Herman advises therapists to approach this stage of the recovery process with caution, acknowledging the need to negotiate between the dangers of intrusion and constriction: "Avoiding the traumatic memories leads to stagnation in the recovery process, while approaching them too precipitately leads to a fruitless and damaging reliving of the trauma."[16]

Nonetheless, PET can offer immense benefits within the context of collective trauma, where groups try to reclaim their past in order to integrate it in a fruitful way. Exposure to images of war can give the community the language to name their past and can also bring to the center of community life events that might have been repressed from collective memory (and yet continue to exert their power on the lives of individuals). The book of Nahum is particularly suitable for such use in reconnecting with one's own past, because it is written in lyric poetry, and one of the functions of lyric poetry is, as was said in chapter 3, to present a world that can help the reader contemplate her own memories and that can lead her to finding similarities between her experience and what the poem describes.[17]

I build on that axiom about lyric poetry to explore ways in which the scenes described in the book of Nahum can evoke in Congolese survivors memories of their own experiences during the wars. Those memories can be both personal and collective.[18] In the following paragraphs, I select some scenes depicted by Nahum that can evoke in Congolese audiences those memories, both personal and collective.

Invasions and Omnipresent Violence

The book of Nahum speaks about invasions of Judah by the Assyrians (2:1, 3) and about invasions of Nineveh by enemies (2:4–7; 3:12–13). The scenes of violent invasions described in Nahum would resonate with many DRC villages that suffered from invasions at the hands of various rebel groups and militias. If in Nahum it is the gates, the palaces and the whole of Nineveh that are burned (2:7; 3:15), in the Congolese villages, it is houses, farms, and even human beings that vanish into smoke. These attacks on the villages destroy physical objects and human lives and undermine the very identity of those villages.

16. Herman, *Trauma and Recovery*, 176.
17. Johnson, *The Idea of Lyric*, 74.
18. I wrote about the interaction between collective and personal memories in chapter three. Cf. Johnson, "Unremembered," 75; Ricoeur, *La Mémoire*, 99.

The Stripping of Women and Sexual violence

Another aspect of the book of Nahum that can speak to Congolese communities is the depiction of sexual violence. In Nah 3:5, YHWH threatens that he is going to strip Nineveh and expose her nakedness. We are also told in Nah 2:8 about a woman who is stripped during the war. I demonstrated earlier that the stripping of those women might suggest that YHWH is shaming them or that he is exposing them to the possibility of being raped. Within the context of war in the DRC, rape is so rampant that there would be no doubt that the stripped women of Nahum will bring to memory the experiences of the many sexually assaulted women of eastern DRC. The tied man who watches the stripping of women and the moaning of helpless slave girls (Nah 2:8) can bring to Congolese memories the multiple scenes of public rapes that have demoralized many villages. We saw in chapter 2 how some men were tied and obliged to watch the rape of their wives and daughters (or daughters-in law).

Plundering and Kidnapping

I already commented on how the Assyrians amassed the wealth of all the nations and how they too were threatened with similar plundering (2:10, 12–14). I also showed how Nahum and the Lachish Reliefs depict deportation as common practice in wartime (3:10; see Salb IV of the Lachish Reliefs). During wartime in the DRC, taking civilians captive and forcing them to carry booty and items stolen from villages is a common practice among both government and rebel soldiers. In addition, many Congolese civilians are held captive in forests as sex slaves and for the sake of instilling fear in villages. The images of Assyrian deportations can also evoke in Congolese memories the current phenomenon of population exoduses from villages to cities, because villages have become centers of violence. The consequence is that most of the elite—i.e., the educated people with some means, who are therefore capable of migrating—leave the villages and thus deprive them of valuable human resources.

The scenes selected here are representative of ways the tableaux presented by the book of Nahum can evoke among Congolese readers the memories of wars and violence. However, it is the whole book of Nahum with its ability to recreate the experience of war—more than those individual scenes—that can evoke in the reader her own experience with war and violence. Just as the book could return Judahites to familiar landscapes of destruction, so it can take Congolese survivors back to the forests, bushes, or rivers where they suffered at the hands of the perpetrators of violence.

Going beyond the Text: War Memories, Lament, and the Search for Reconciliation

I said above that reawakening traumatic memories can be dangerous to the survivor. They can overwhelm her to the point of retraumatizing her. Evoking memories of war, therefore, cannot become an end in itself. It is important for the survivor and the traumatized community to organize and own those memories and integrate them into their common life. In other words, the surviving community needs to go through the processes of interpreting and building a new identity through those memories. Trauma and memory researchers find that the best way for a survivor community to deal with traumatic memories is to organize them in narrative form and give them a shape that defines their new identity. For psychologist Jonathan Shay,

> Severe trauma explodes the cohesion of consciousness. When a survivor creates fully realized narrative that brings together the shattered knowledge of what happened, the emotions that were aroused by the meanings of the events, and the bodily sensations that the physical events created, the survivor pieces back together the fragmentation of consciousness that trauma has caused.[19]

The book of Nahum does not show the reader a way of organizing the memories it evokes. Contrary to the notion that the book presents an anti-Assyrian ideology,[20] it only impresses images on the readers and leaves them with the task of interpretation. We are not told whether to join in celebrating the fall of Nineveh or not. We do not know whether we should hate Nineveh or Thebes, or feel compassion for their destruction. I showed that, as a lyric poem, the book evokes memories and does not encourage its readers to take any specific action. Each reader will react to this book based on her conditions of life. Some fortunate readers can have the ability to imagine the world beyond revenge. But as for the readers still living in the "whirlwind of violence"—as do most survivors

---

19. Shay, *Achilles in Vietnam*, 188.
20. O'Brien, *Nahum*, 124–25.

of violence in the DRC—Nahum is probably the best place to be. It will be premature to suggest an easy solution to traumatized readers before they have expressed their anger and have invited God to avenge them. This is not to discredit all the other efforts for forgiveness and reconciliation. It is a way of making it clear that not all the readers of Scripture are ready for gentle messages. Texts that are often considered "cups of horror"[21] are sometimes the only meaningful ones for some audiences. Thus, inviting Congolese survivors of violence to use the unpalatable message of Nahum as a means to help them stay for a moment in their vengeful sentiments is a necessary path toward reconciliation. Two decades ago, Ellen F. Davis used Qoheleth's observation that "There is a time to embrace, and a time to refrain from embracing" (Qoh 3:5) to urge Bible readers not to rush through the imprecatory psalms or prematurely switch from imprecation to intercession for the enemy. For Davis, to get from cursing to intercession on behalf of the enemy is "the prerogative of the one praying. Not everyone can take that step, and no one should take it prematurely."[22] If anything then, reading Nahum can help the wounded Congolese acknowledge the danger of rushing to the embrace of the enemy while their hearts are still hard with anger and undealt-with feelings of revenge. Rather, with honesty—through the poetry of vengeance and rage—they can voice their rage and desire for vengeance in the presence of God.

Conclusion

Discernment about what Congolese post-conflict communities should look like and what each community can do will require conversations and communal studies among members of those communities. I have attempted in this study to show that the book of Nahum is a viable resource for communities that seek healing after war and violence. Having offered some tools about how to read Nahum in such a context, I hope these tools will serve community leaders, pastors, and caregivers working in Congolese and other communities affected by war.

---

21. Phrase used by Portier-Young, "Drinking the Cup of Horror."
22. Davis, *Getting Involved with God*, 27.

Bibliography

Achtemeier, Elizabeth. *Nahum–Malachi*. Interpretation. Atlanta: John Knox, 1986.
Alexander, Jeffrey C. *Trauma: A Social Theory*. Cambridge: Polity, 2012.
Alter, Robert. *The Art of Biblical Poetry*. Rev. ed. New York: Basic, 2011.
Amnesty International. "Sudan, Darfur: Rape as a Weapon of War: Sexual Violence and Its Consequences." 2004.
Assis, Elie. "Chiasmus in Biblical Narrative: Rhetoric of Characterization." *Prooftexts* 22.3 (2002) 273–304.
Atikson, Paul. *For Ethnography*. Los Angeles: Sage, 2015.
Attinger, Pascal *La Lamentation sur Nippur*. 2010, 2015; http://www.iaw.unibe.ch/e39448/e99428/e122665/e122821/pane122850/e122917/2_2_4.pdf.
Barnett, R. D. *Sculptures from the North Palace of Ashurbanipal at Nineveh (668–627 B.C.)*. The Trustees of the British Museum. London: British Museum Publications, 1976.
Becking, Bob. "Is God Good for His People? Critical Remarks on a Recently Proposed Emendation of Nahum 1,7." *Zeitschrift für die Alttestamentliche Wissenschaft* 117 (2005) 621–23.
Ben Zvi, Ehud. "Twelve Prophetic Books or 'the Twelve': A Few Preliminary Considerations." In *Forming Prophetic Literature: Essays on Isaiah and the Twelve in Honor of John D. W. Watts*, edited by James W. Watts and Paul R. House, 125–56. Sheffield, UK: Sheffield Academic Press, 1996.
Benedict XVI. *Africae Munus: On the Church in Africa in the Service of Reconciliation, Justice and Peace*. Vatican, 2011.
———. Post-Synodal Apostolic Constitution, *Verbum Domini: On the Word of God in the Life and Mission of the Church*. Vatican City, 2010.
Berlin, Adele. *Poetics and Interpretation of Biblical Narrative*. Sheffield, UK: Almond, 1983.
———. "Review of *Weep, O Daughter of Zion: A Study of the City-Lament Genre in the Hebrew Bible* by F. W. Dobbs-Allsopp." *Journal of the American Oriental Society* 115.2 (1995) 319.
Berry, Wendell. *What Are People for? Essays*. Berkeley: Counterpoint, 1988.
Betz, Hans Dieter. *The Sermon on the Mount: A Commentary on the Sermon on the Mount, Including the Sermon on the Plain (Matthew 5:3—7:27 and Luke 6:20–49)*. Hermeneia. Minneapolis, MN: Fortress, 1995.
Block, Daniel I. *The Book of Ezekiel, Chapters 1–24*. New International Commentary on the Old Testament. Grand Rapids: Eerdmans, 1997.

Brown, William P. *Seeing the Psalms: A Theology of Metaphor*. Louisville: Westminster John Knox, 2002.

Brueggemann, Walter. *To Build, to Plant: Jeremiah 26–52*. International Theological Commentary. Grand Rapids: Eerdmans, 1991.

Card, Claudia. "Rape as a Weapon of War." *Hypatia* 11.4 (1996) 5–18.

Carr, David M. *Holy Resilience: The Bible's Traumatic Origins*. New Haven, CT: Yale University Press, 2014.

Cassin, Elena. "Le Roi et le Lion." *Revue de l'Histoire des Religions* 198.4 (1981) 355–401.

Caruth, Cathy. *Unclaimed Experience: Trauma, Narrative, and History*. Baltimore: Johns Hopkins University Press, 1996.

Chapman, Cynthia R. "Sculpted Warriors: Sexuality and the Sacred in the Depiction of Warfare in the Assyrian Palace Reliefs and in Ezekiel 23:14–17." In *Aesthetics of Violence in the Prophets*, edited by Chris Franke and Julia M. O'Brien, 1–17. Library of Hebrew Bible/Old Testament Studies 517. London: T. & T. Clark, 2010.

Childs, Brevard S. *Isaiah and the Assyrian Crisis*. London: SCM, 1967.

———. *Myth and Reality in the Old Testament*. Studies in Biblical Theology 27. 1957. Reprint, Eugene, OR: Wipf & Stock, 2009.

Christensen, Duane L. *Nahum: A New Translation with Introduction and Commentary*. The Anchor Yale Bible. New Haven, CT: Yale University Press, 2009.

Cleland, James T. "Exposition on Nahum." *The Interpreter's Bible*, Vol. 6, 951–69. Nashville: Abingdon, 2001.

Cogan, Mordechai. *The Raging Torrent: Historical Inscriptions from Assyria and Babylonia Relating to Ancient Israel*. Jerusalem: Carta, 2008.

Collins, Peter, and Gallinat, Anselma. "The Ethnographic Self as Resource: An Introduction." In *The Ethnographic Self as Resource: Writing Memory and Experience into Ethnography*, edited by Peter Collins and Anselma Gallinat, 1–24. New York: Berghahn, 2010.

Commission Congolaise Vérité et Réconciliation. *Règlement d'Ordre Intérieur*. Kinshasa, 2003.

Cooper, Jerrold S. *The Curse of Agade*. Baltimore: John Hopkins University Press, 1983.

Cross, Frank Moore. *Canaanite Myth and Hebrew Epic: Essays in the History of the Religion of Israel*. Cambridge: Harvard University Press, 1973.

Culler, Jonathan. *Literary Theory: A Very Short Introduction*. Very Short Introductions. Oxford: Oxford University Press, 1997.

Davis, Ellen F. "'And Pharaoh Will Change His Mind . . .' (Ezekiel 32:31): Dismantling Mythical Discourse." In *Theological Exegesis: Essays in Honor of Brevard S. Childs*, edited by Christopher Seitz and Kathryn Greene-McGreight, 224–39. Grand Rapids: Eerdmans, 1998.

———. *Biblical Prophecy: Perspectives for Christian Theology, Discipleship, and Ministry*. Louisville, KY: Westminster John Knox, 2014.

———. *Getting Involved with God: Rediscovering the Old Testament*. Lanham, MD: Rowman & Littlefield, 2001.

———. *Reading Israel's Scriptures*. New York: Oxford University Press, 2019.

———. "Teaching the Bible Confessionally in the Church." In *The Art of Reading Scripture*, edited by Ellen F. Davis and Richard B. Hays, 9–26. Grand Rapids: Eerdmans, 2003.

Davis, Ellen F., and Richard B. Hays. "Beyond Criticism: Learning to Read the Bible Again." *The Christian Century* 121.8 (2004) 23–27.

de Hulster, Izaak J. *Iconographic Exegesis and Third Isaiah.* Tübingen: Mohr Siebeck, 2009.

de Hulster Izaak J., and Joel M. LeMon. "Introduction: The Interpretive Nexus of Image and Text." In *Image, Text, Exegesis: Iconographic Interpretation and the Hebrew Bible,* edited by Izaak J. de Hulster and Joel M. LeMon, xix–xxiv. London: Bloomsbury, 2014.

Diabang, Angèle, director. *Congo: The Doctor Who Saves Women.* Documentary film. New York: Icarus Films, 2015.

Dobbs-Allsopp, F. W. "Darwinism, Genre Theory, and City Laments." *Journal of the American Oriental Society* 120.4 (2000) 625–30.

———. *Lamentations.* Interpretation. Louisville, KY: John Knox, 2002.

———. *On Biblical Poetry.* Oxford Scholarship Online, 2015. DOI:10.1093/acprof:oso/9780199766901.001.0001/.

———. *Weep, O Daughter of Zion: A Study of the City-Lament Genre in the Hebrew Bible.* BibOr 44. Rome: Editrice Pontificio Istituto Biblico, 1993.

Draper, Jonathan A. "African Contextual Hermeneutics: Readers, Reading Communities, and Their Options between Text and Context." *Religion & Theology* 22 (2015) 3–22.

———. "'For the Kingdom Is Inside You and It Is Outside of You': Contextual Exegesis in South Africa." In *Text and Interpretation: New Approaches in the Criticism of the New Testament,* edited by P. J. Hartin and J. H. Petzer, 235–57. Leiden: Brill, 1991.

———. "Old Scores and New Notes: Where and What Is Contextual Exegesis in the New South Africa." In *Towards an Agenda for Contextual Theology,* edited by M. Speckman, 148–68. Pietermaritzburg: Cluster, 2001.

———. "Reading the Bible as Conversation: A Theory and Methodology for Contextual Interpretation of the Bible in Africa." *Grace and Truth* 19.2 (2002) 12–24.

Dubovský, Peter. "Assyrians under the Walls of Jerusalem and the Confinement of Padi." *Journal of Near Eastern studies* 75.1 (2016) 109–26.

Eph'al, Israel. *The City Besieged: Siege and Its Manifestation in the Ancient Near East.* Culture and History of the Ancient Near East. Leiden: Brill, 2009.

Evans, Paul S. *The Invasion of Sennacherib in the Book of Kings: A Source-Critical and Rhetorical Study of 2 Kings 18–19.* Leiden: Brill, 2009.

Floyd, Michael H. "The מַשָּׂא (Maśśā') as a Type of Prophetic Book." *Journal of Biblical Literature* 121.3 (2002) 401–22.

———. *Minor Prophets,* Part 2. The Forms of the Old Testament Literature. Grand Rapids: Eerdmans, 2000.

Fretheim, Terence E. "'I Was Only a Little Angry': Divine Violence in the Prophets." In *What Kind of God? Collected Essays of Terence E. Fretheim,* edited by Michael J. Chan and Brent A. Strawn, 172–84. Siphrut 14. Winona Lake, IN: Eisenbrauns, 2015.

Gallinat, Anselma. "Playing the Native Card: The Anthropologist as Informant in Eastern Germany." In *The Ethnographic Self as Resource: Writing Memory and Experience into Ethnography,* edited by Peter Collins and Anselma Gallinat, 25–44. New York: Berghahn, 2010.

Gerstenberger, Erhard. "The Woe-Oracles of the Prophets." *Journal of Biblical Literature* 81.3 (1962) 249–63.

Ginkel, Rob van. "Writing Culture from Within: Reflections on Endogenous Ethnography." *Etnofoor* 7.1 (1994) 5–23.

Goldingay, John. "How I have Drifted through Life." In *I (Still) Believe: Leading Bible Scholars Share Their Stories of Faith and Scholarship*, edited by John Byron and Joel N. Lohr, 93–104. Grand Rapids: Zondervan, 2015.

Graffy, Adrian *A Prophet Confronts His People: The Disputation Speech in the Prophets*. Rome: Biblical Institute Press, 1984.

Green, M. W. "The Uruk Lament." *Journal of the American Oriental Society* 104.2 (1984) 253–79.

Grenholm, Cristina, and Daniel Patte. "Receptions, Critical Interpretations, and Scriptural Criticism." In *Reading Israel in Romans: Legitimacy and Plausibility of Divergent Interpretations*, edited by Cristina Grenholm and Daniel Patte, 1–54. Harrisburg, PA: Trinity, 2000.

Halbwachs, Maurice. *La Mémoire Collective*. Bibliothèque de Sociologie Contemporaine. Paris : Presses Universitaires de France, 1950.

———. *Les Cadres Sociaux de la Mémoire*. Paris: Presses Universitaires de France, 1952.

Haldar, Alfred. *Studies in the Book of Nahum*. Uppsala: Lundequistska, 1947.

Haupt, Paul. "The Book of Nahum." *Journal of Biblical Literature* 26.1 (1907) 1–53.

Hauser, Alan J. "Judges 5: Parataxis in Hebrew Poetry." *Journal of Biblical Literature* 99 (1980) 23–41.

Hays, Christopher B. *Hidden Riches: A Sourcebook for the Comparative Study of the Hebrew Bible and Ancient Near East*. Louisville: Westminster John Knox, 2014.

Hayes, John H. "The Usage of Oracles against Foreign Nations in Ancient Israel." *Journal of Biblical Literature* 87.1 (1969) 81–92.

Heffelfinger, Katie M. *I Am Large, I Contain Multitudes: Lyric and Conflict in Second Isaiah*. Boston: Brill, 2011.

Herman, Judith. *Trauma and Recovery: The Aftermath of Violence—from Domestic Abuse to Political Terror*. New York: Basic, 1992.

Heschel, Abraham J. *The Prophets. Two Volumes in One*. Vol. II; Peabody, MA: Hendrickson, 1962.

Hetata, Sherif. "The Self and Autobiography." *Publications of the Modern Language Association of America* 118.1 (2003) 123–25.

Hooker, David Anderson. *The Little Book of Transformative Community Conferencing: A Hopeful, Practical Approach to Dialogue*. The Little Books of Justice and Peacebuilding. New York: Good Books, 2016. Kindle Edition.

Huddlestun, John R. "Nahum, Nineveh, and the Nile: The Description of Thebes in Nahum 3:8–9." *Journal of Near Eastern Studies* 62.2 (2003) 97–110.

Huehnergard, John. "Asseverative *la and Hypothetical *lu/law in Semitic." *Journal of the American Oriental Society* 103.3 (1983) 569–93.

Humbert, Paul. "Essai d'analyse de Nahoum 1,2–2,3." *Zeitschrift für die Alttestamentliche Wissenschaft* 44 (1926) 266–80.

Johnson, Laurie. "Unremembered: Memorial, Sentimentality, Dislocation." In *Trauma and Public Memory*, edited by John Goodall and Christopher Lee, 70–84. London: Palgrave Macmillan, 2015.

Johnson, W. R. *The Idea of Lyric: Lyric Modes in Ancient and Modern Poetry*. Berkeley: University of California Press, 1982.

Jones, Barry A. "The Book of the Twelve as a Witness to Ancient Biblical Interpretation." In *Reading and Hearing the Book of the Twelve*, edited by James D. Nogalski and Marvin A. Sweeney, 65–87. SBLSymS 15. Atlanta: Society of Biblical Literature, 2000.

Kahn, Daniel. "The Assyrian Invasions of Egypt (673–663 B.C.) and the Final Expulsion of the Kushites." *Studien zur Altägyptischen Kultur*, Bd. 34 (2006) 251–68.

Katongole, Emmanuel, and Jonathan Wilson-Hartgrove. *Mirror to the Church: Resurrecting Faith after Genocide in Rwanda*. Grand Rapids: Zondervan, 2009.

Keel, Othmar. *The Symbolism of the Biblical World: Ancient Near Eastern Iconography and the Book of Psalms*. Translated by Timothy J. Hallett. New York: Seabury, 1978

Kelly, Joseph Ryan. "Joel, Jonah, and the Yhwh Creed: Determining the Trajectory of the Literary Influence." *Journal of Biblical Literature* 132.4 (2013) 805–26.

Kramer, Samuel N. *Lamentation over the Destruction of Ur*. Chicago: University of Chicago Press, 1940.

Lanner, Laurel. *"Who Will Lament Her?" The Feminine and The Fantastic in the Book of Nahum*. London: T. & T. Clark, 2006.

Layard, Austen H. *Discoveries among the Ruins of Nineveh and Babylon, with Travels in Armenia, Kurdistan, and the Desert; Being the Result of a Second Expedition Undertaken for the Trustees of the British Museum*. New York: Harper and Brothers, 1856.

Levenson, Jon D. *Creation and the Persistence of Evil: The Jewish Drama of Divine Omnipotence*. Princeton, NJ: Princeton University Press, 1994. Kindle Edition.

———. "Textual and Semantic Notes on Nah. I 7–8." *Vetus Testamentum* 25.4 (1975) 792–95.

Lichtenstein, Murray H. "Biblical Poetry." In *Back to the Sources: Reading the Classic Jewish Texts*, edited by Barry W. Holtz, 105–27. New York: Touchstone, 1984.

Longinus. *On the Sublime*. Translated into English by H. L. Havell. New York: Macmillan, 1890.

Lowth, Robert. *Lectures on the Sacred Poetry of the Hebrews*. 1753. ET 1787. Kindle Edition.

Luckenbill, Daniel D. *Ancient Records of Assyria and Babylon*, I. Chicago: University of Chicago Press, 1927.

———. *The Annals of Sennacherib*, Vol. 2. Chicago: University of Chicago Press, 1924.

Machinist, Peter. "The Fall of Assyria in Comparative Ancient Perspective." In *Assyria 1995: Proceedings of the 10th Anniversary Symposium of the Neo-Assyrian Text Corpus Project, Helsinki, September 1–11, 1995*, edited by S. Parpola and R. M. Whiting, 179–96. Helsinki: The Neo-Assyrian Text Corpus Project, 1997.

———. "The Rab Šāqēh at the Wall of Jerusalem: Israelite Identity in the Face of Assyrian 'Other.'" *Hebrew Studies* 41 (2000) 151–68.

Magessa, Laurenti. "From Privatized to Popular Biblical Hermeneutics in Africa." In *The Bible in African Christianity: Essays in Biblical Theology*, edited by H. W. Kinoti and J. M. Waligoo, 25–39. Nairobi: Acton, 1997.

Maier, Walter A. *The Book of Nahum*. Thornapple Commentaries. Grand Rapids: Baker, 1959.

Marion, Jean-Luc. *God without Being: Hors-Texte*. 2nd ed. Religion and Postmodernism. Chicago: University of Chicago Press, 2012.

Mihelic, Joseph L. "The Influence of Form Criticism on the Study of the Old Testament." *Journal of Bible and Religion* 19.3 (1951) 120–29.

Miller, J. Maxwell, and John H. Hayes. *A History of Ancient Israel and Judah*. Philadelphia: Westminster, 1986.

Moschella, Mary Clark. *Ethnography as a Pastoral Practice: An Introduction* Cleveland, OH: Pilgrim, 2008.

Moshavi, Adina. "What Can I Say? Implications and Communicative Functions of Rhetorical 'WH' Questions in Classical Biblical Hebrew Prose." *Vetus Testamentum* 64.1 (2014) 93–108.

Mukangendo, Marie Consolée. "Caring for Children Born of Rape in Rwanda." In *Born of War: Protecting Children of Sexual Violence Survivors in Conflict Zones*, edited by R. Charli Carpenter, 40–52. Bloomfield, CT: Kumarian, 2007.

Namujimbo, Déo. *Je reviens de l'Enfer: Reportage de Guerre à l'est de la RD Congo (août–septembre 1998)*. Paris: L'Harmattan, 2014.

Nogalski, James D. "Joel as 'Literary Anchor' for the Book of the Twelve." In *Reading and Hearing the Book of the Twelve*, edited by James D. Nogalski and Marvin A. Sweeney, 91–109. SBLSymS 15. Atlanta: Society of Biblical Literature, 2000.

Nogalski, James D., and Marvin A. Sweeney, eds. *Reading and Hearing the Book of the Twelve*. Atlanta: Society of Biblical Literature, 2000.

Nzuzi, Justin. *La Pastorale Justice et Paix dans l'Archidiocèse de Bukavu: 25 ans de Combat pour la promotion de la Dignité Humaine*. Bukavu: Editions de l'Archevêché, 2013.

O'Brien, Julia M. *Nahum. Readings: A New Biblical Commentary*. London: Sheffield Academic Press, 2002.

———. *Nahum, Habakkuk, Zephaniah, Haggai, Zechariah, Malachi*. Abingdon Old Testament Commentary. Nashville: Abingdon, 2004.

O'Connor, Kathleen. "Reclaiming Jeremiah's Violence." In *Aesthetics of Violence in the Prophets*, edited by Chris Franke and Julia M. O'Brien, 37–49. Library of Hebrew Bible/Old testament Studies 517. London: T. & T. Clark, 2010.

Onyumbe, Jacob. *Kevin the Wild Boy: The Diaries of a Survivor*. Baltimore, MD: PublishAmerica, 2010.

Petersen, David L. "A Book of the Twelve?" In *Reading and Hearing the Book of the Twelve*, edited by James D. Nogalski and Marvin A. Sweeney, 3–10. SBLSymS 15. Atlanta: Society of Biblical Literature, 2000.

Portier-Young, Anathea. "Drinking the Cup of Horror and Gnawing on Its Shards: Biblical Theology though Violence, Not around It." In *Beyond Biblical Theologies*, edited by Heinrich Assel, Stefan Beyerle, and Christfried Böttrich, 387–408. Tübingen: Mohr Siebeck, 2012.

Prunier, Gerard. *Africa's World War: Congo, the Rwandan Genocide, and the Making of a Continental Catastrophe*. Oxford: Oxford University Press, 2009.

Reddit, Paul L. "The Production and Reading of the Book of the Twelve." In *Reading and Hearing the Book of the Twelve*, edited by James D. Nogalski and Marvin A. Sweeney, 11–33. SBLSymS 15. Atlanta: Society of Biblical Literature, 2000.

Ricoeur, Paul. *Hermeneutics and the Human Sciences*. Translated and edited by John B. Thompson. Cambridge: Cambridge University Press, 1981.

———. *Interpretation Theory: Discourse and the Surplus of Meaning*. Fort Worth, TX: Texas Christian University Press, 1976.

———. *La Mémoire, l'Histoire, l'Oubli*. Paris: Seuil, 2000.

Roberts, J. J. M. *Nahum, Habakkuk, and Zephaniah: A Commentary*. The Old Testament Library. Louisville, KY: Westminster/John Knox, 1991.

Robertson, O. Palmer. *The Books of Nahum, Habakkuk, and Zephaniah*. New International Commentary on the Old Testament. Grand Rapids: Eerdmans, 1990.

Rosenbaum, Jonathan. "Hezekiah's Reform and the Deuteronomistic Tradition." *The Harvard Theological Review* 72.1/2 (1979) 23–44.

Rosenthal, M. L., and Sally M. Gall. *The Modern Poetic Sequence: The Genius of Modern Poetry.* New York: Oxford University Press, 1983.

Rothbaum, B., E. Foa, and E. Hembree. *Reclaiming Your Life from Traumatic Experience: A Prolonged Exposure Treatment Program: Workbook.* Treatments that Work. Oxford: Oxford University Press, 2007.

Russel, John M. *Sennacherib's Palace without Rival at Nineveh.* Chicago: University of Chicago Press, 1991.

Sasson, Jack M. *Jonah.* Anchor Bible 24 b. Garden City, NY: Doubleday, 1990.

Scott, James C. *Domination and the Arts of Resistance: The Hidden Transcripts.* New Haven, CT: Yale University Press, 1990.

Second Vatican Ecumenical Council. *Dei Verbum: Dogmatic Constitution on Divine Revelation.* Vatican City, 1965.

Seculus, Diodorus. *Complete Works of Diodorus Siculus.* Delphi Classics. Delphi Ancient Classics Book 32. No loc, no date. Kindle Edition.

Shay, Jonathan. *Achilles in Vietnam: Combat Trauma and the Undoing of Character.* New York: Scribner, 1994.

Smith, George Adam. *The Book of The Twelve Prophets Commonly Called Minor.* Vol. 2. The Expositor's Bible. New York: Armstrong and Son, 1898.

Smith, J. M. P. *A Critical and Exegetical Commentary on Micah, Zephaniah, Nahum, Habakkuk, Obadiah and Joel.* International Critical Commentary. Edinburgh: T. & T. Clark, 1911.

Smith-Spark, Laura "How Did Rape Become a Weapon of War?" http://news.bbc.co.uk/2/hi/4078677.stm, 2004/12/08.

South African Promotion of National Unity and Reconciliation Act of 1995. https://www.gov.za/documents/promotion-national-unity-and-reconciliation-act#/.

Spronk, Klaas. *Nahum.* Historical Commentary on the Old Testament. Kampen, Netherlands: Kok Pharos, 1997.

Stearns, Jason K. *Dancing in the Glory of Monsters: The Collapse of the Congo and the Great War of Africa.* New York: Public Affairs, 2011.

Strawn, Brent. *What Is Stronger Than a Lion? Leonine Image and Metaphor in the Hebrew Bible and the Ancient Near East?* Orbis Biblicus et Orientalis 212. Fribourg: Academic Press, 2005.

Sweeney, Marvin A. "The Latter Prophets and Prophecy." In *The Cambridge Companion to the Hebrew Bible/Old Testament,* edited by Stephen B. Chapman and Marvin A. Sweeney, 233–52. New York: Cambridge University Press, 2016.

———. "Sequence and Interpretation in the Book of the Twelve." In *Reading and Hearing the Book of the Twelve,* edited by James D. Nogalski and Marvin A. Sweeney, 49–64. SBLSymS 15. Atlanta: Society of Biblical Literature, 2000.

———. *The Twelve Prophets.* Berit Olam, vol. 2. Collegeville, MN: Liturgical, 2000.

The Kairos Document. Johannesburg, 1985.

Tufnell, Olga. *Lachish III (Tell ed-Duweir): The Iron Age.* London: Oxford University Press, 1953.

Turner, Thomas. *Congo Wars: Conflict and Reality.* London: Zed, 2007.

Tutu, Desmond Mpilo. *No Future without Forgiveness.* New York: Doubleday, 1999.

Uehlinger, Christoph. "Clio in a World of Pictures—Another Look at the Lachish Reliefs from Sennacherib's Southwest Pala at Nineveh." In *"Like a Bird in a Cage": The Invasion of Sennacherib in 701 BCE,* edited by Lester L. Grabbe, 221–305. London: Sheffield Academic Press, 2003.

Ussishkin, David. *The Conquest of Lachish by Sennacherib*. Tel Aviv: Tel Aviv University Institute of Archaeology, 1982.

———. "Lachish." In *The New Interpreter's Dictionary of the Bible*, I-Ma, Vol. 3, edited by Katharine Doob Sakenfeld, 555–62. Nashville: Abingdon, 2008.

———. "The 'Lachish Reliefs' and the City of Lachish." *Israel Exploration Journal* 30.3/4 (1980) 174–95.

———. "Sennacherib's Campaign to Philistia and Judah: Ekron, Lachish and Jerusalem." In *Essays on Ancient Israel in Its Near Eastern Context; A Tribute to Nadav Na'aman*, edited by Y. Amit et al., 339–57. Winona Lake, IN: Eisenbrauns, 2006.

van Oyen, Geert. «'A Bon Lecteur, Salut!' La Lecture du Nouveau Testament Comme Dialogue entre Lecteurs.» In *Le Lecteur. Sixième Colloque International du RRENA, Université Catholique de Louvain. 24-26 Mai 2012*, edited by Régis Burnet, Didier Luciani and Geert van Oyen. Leuven: Peeters, 2015.

Walsh, Carey. "Iconic Presence: A Marion Reading of Biblical Theophanies." *The Heythrop Journal* LVI (2015) 87–98.

Waltke, Bruce K., and Michael O'Connor. *An Introduction to Biblical Hebrew Syntax*. Winona Lake, IN: Eisenbrauns, 1990.

Watanambe, Chikako E. *Animal Symbolism in Mesopotamia*. Wiener Offene Orientalistik Band I. Wien: Institut für Orientalistik der Universität Wien, 2002.

Watters, Ethan. *Crazy Like Us: The Globalization of the American Psyche*. New York: Free Press, 2010.

Weigl, Michael. "Current Research on the Book of Nahum: Exegetical Methodologies in Turmoil?" *Currents in Research* 9 (2001) 81–130.

Weissert, E. "Royal Hunt and Royal Triumph in the Prism Fragment of Ashurbanipal (82–5–22,3)." In *Assyria 1995: Proceedings of the 10th Anniversary Symposium of the Neo-Assyrian Text Corpus Project, Helsinki, September 1–11, 1995*, edited by S. Parpola and R. M. Whiting, 339–58. Helsinki: The Neo-Assyrian Text Corpus Project, 1997.

Wessels, Wilhelm J. "Nahum, an Uneasy Expression of Yahweh's Power!" *Old Testament Essays* 11.3 (1998) 615–28.

West, Gerald O. "Biblical Hermeneutics in Africa." *African Theology on the Way: Current Conversations*, edited by Diane B. Stinton, 21–31. SPCK International Study Guide 46. London: SPCK, 2010.

———. "Contextual Bible Reading: A South African Case Study." *Analecta Bruxellensia* 11 (2006) 131–48.

———. "Interpreting 'the Exile' in African Biblical Scholarship: An Ideo-theological Dilemma in Post-Colonial South Africa." In *Exile and Suffering: A Selection of Papers Read at the 50th Anniversary Meeting of the Old Testament Society of South Africa, OTWSA/OTSSA Pretoria 2007*, edited by Bob Becking and Dirk Human, 247–67. Leiden: Brill, 2009.

———. "The Vocation of an African Biblical Scholar on the Margins of Biblical Scholarship." *Old Testament Essays* 19.1 (2006) 307–36.

Zenger, Eric. *A God of Vengeance? Understanding the Psalms of Divine Wrath*. Translated by Linda M. Maloney. Louisville, KY: Westminster John Knox, 1996.

Scripture Index

OLD TESTAMENT

Genesis
1	123
1:2	123
4:10	152 n34
4:15	110
11:8	155

Exodus
3:7	171
7:11	154
15:9	134
15:15	85
19:16	161
19:16–21	124
20:3–6	111
21:20	110
21:24	33, 56, 111
33:19	112
33:22	34, 127, 111
34,33	111
34:6–7	78, 111, 113
34:14–15	111
34:6, 14	111, 112

Leviticus
26:25	110

Numbers
14:18	78
25	172

Deuteronomy
4:24	111
4:27	155
5:6–10	111
6:15	111
19:21	56
29:17	158
32:7	127
32:16, 21	111
32:41	110

Joshua
2:9, 24	85
2:9–11	119, 120
2:11	165
10:31–32	94n49
24:19	111, 111n10

Judges
5:4–5	124
7:16	161
11:12ff	150n27
18:16–17	120n21

1 Samuel
2:2	127
3:7	120n21

1 Samuel (continued)

14:16	85
23:22–23	120n21

2 Samuel

3:28	152n34
16:8	119n21
19:27–28	119n21
22:15	155

1 Kings

11:15	158

2 Kings

5:3	120n21
6:17	160n48
8:12	140
9:17	110
9:22	153
9:26	152n34
14:19	95
17:1–6	93n45
17:6–23	117
17:13–23	103
18–19	102
18	102, 143
18:3–6	103
18:13	94
18:14	94
18:17—19:13	150
18:19	102
18:22	102
18:25	62, 117, 118n25
18:28–35	136
18:28–36	55
18:30	102
18:32c–35	87, 102
19	102
19:3–4	136
19:4	55
19:6	103
19:14–19	136
19:22–37	136
19:36	54
20	102, 143
23:13, 24	159

Isaiah

1:15	152n34
1:21	153
1:24	110
3	67
3:9	152n31
5:22	160
6:1	76
8:19	164
9:4	66
10	63
10:5	66, 118, 152n31
10:5–11	55, 56
10:5–10	118n17
10:5–6	102
10:5–8	118
10:8–11, 13–14	134n1
10:12–13	118
10:24	146
13–23	160n1
13:1–23	55
13:16, 18	140
13:7	165
14	62
14:05	146
14:13	75
14:31	85
14:7–8	74, 75
14:9–11	75
15–16	63
18	55
19:1	124, 165
19:7	67
19:16	143
21:1–10	62
21:3	165
24:1	67
28:22	67
29:1	152n31
32:12	164
35:3	165
36	94
36:2	94
36:4	102
36:1—37:13	150
36:10	118
36:18	102

36:19-20	102	46-51	106n1
36,37	102	46:8	134n1
37:3-4	136	48:11	146
37:14-19	136	48:14	160
37:23-38	136	48:46	152n31
37:37	54	49:2	62
38:14	164	49:4	134n1
45:1	171	49:23	85
47:9,12	154	49:85	104
51:17-23	141	50:8	62
52:2	67	50:24	146
52:7	78	50:31	148
53:7	66	50:37	143
59:10-44	164	50:41-46	57
61:1-2	117	50-51	146
63:1-6	160	51:14	144
66:3	158	51:2	67
		51:24	146
		51:25	148
		51:30	143
		51:56	104

Jeremiah

2:20	67, 153
3:1, 3, 6, 8	153
4:1	158
4:23-26	76
5:1	161
5:5	67
5:7	153
6:22-24	57
7:30	158
8:18-23	65
9:16-18	65
10:1-6	124
13:7	152n31
13:22	157
13:27	158
15:19	76
19:7	67
21:13	148
25:14	118
25:15-29	141
27:11, 12, 45	146
27:2	67
27:2, 11, 12	146
29:9	154
31:35	144
38:6	76
45-51	55
46-52	146

Ezekiel

5:11	158
6:9	153
13:3, 18	152n31
16:15	153
16:28	152n31
16:36	157
20:30	153
21:12	165
21:15	85
21:8	148
23:03	153
23:32	141
24:6, 9	152n31
25-31	55
26:2	134n1
27:3	134n1
28:2	56
28:3	134n1
29:3, 13	134n1
29:10	148
32:2	134n1
35:3	148
38:3	148
39:1	148

Hosea

1:5	104
4:15	153
5:3	153
9:1	153
9:10	159
10:14	140
14:1	140

Joel

2:1–11	113
2:6	165
2:10	144
2:12–13	112
2:13	78
3:15	144

Amos

1	62
1–2	55
1:2	124
1:13–15	56
9:15, 13	85

Obadiah

16	141
15–16	64n63
18	62

Jonah

1:2–3	120
1:3	119n21
4:1–5	120
4:2	78, 114

Micah

1:13	94n48
3:6–7	118
7:18–20	113

Nahum

1	53
1:1	60, 54, 62, 81, 105, 114
1:2	72, 87, 109, 110, 111, 114, 117, 119, 121, 128, 130, 131
1:2–3	61, 108, 109, 110, 114
1:2–8	60
1:3	62, 72, 78, 86, 111, 117, 119, 121, 128
1:3–5	124, 126
1:3–6	72, 108, 109, 121, 122, 124, 130
1:4	72, 125
1:5	63, 72, 85, 109, 125, 126, 163
1:5–6	161
1:6	63, 73, 104, 126, 127
1:6, 9	76
1:7	50, 108, 130
1:7–8	108, 129
1:7–11	128
1:7–8, 9–11, 12–13	109
1:8	62, 108, 142
1:8, 9	63
1:8–9	155
1:9	53, 55
1:9–11	131
1:10	104
1:10–14	74
1:11	54, 105, 134, 135, 136, 137
1:11–1:14	146
1:12	49, 54, 62, 66, 108, 115, 116, 117, 132, 135, 144, 146
1:12–13	76, 108
1:12–14	54, 128
1:12—3:19	105
1:13	49, 54, 62, 66, 67, 72, 115, 116, 117, 132, 145, 146
1:14	61, 63, 64, 158
2:1	50, 54, 61, 62, 65, 72, 73, 78, 108,

	115, 117, 135, 136, 145, 146, 176
2:1, 3	146
2:1–3	60
2:2	62n59, 72, 155, 160, 161
2:2–11	148
2:3	50, 61, 62, 64, 67, 76, 109, 115, 116, 128, 132, 145, 147
2:4	104, 160
2:4–5	69, 162
2:4–11	155, 159, 176
2:4–14	109
2:4—3:19	108
2:5	161, 162
2:5, 7	63
2:5–11	151
2:6	64, 65, 104, 161, 162
2:7	85, 163, 176
2:7–9	69, 83
2:7–11	162
2:8	60, 61, 63, 65, 68, 72, 114, 164, 177
2:8, 11	60
2:8–11	163
2:9	60, 61, 62, 64, 85, 164
2:9–10	74
2:10	164, 165
2:10, 12–14	177
2:10, 14	63
2:11	60, 68, 69, 165
2:12	127, 148
2:12–13	73
2:12–14	145, 147, 148, 165
2:13–14	148
2:14	106, 149, 150, 155, 156
2–3	63
3	54, 108, 176
3:1	55, 152, 154
3:1–3	145, 147
3:1–4	61, 151, 152, 162
3:2	73, 153, 152
3:2–3	151
3:3	60, 64, 153, 160
3:4	55, 144, 145, 152, 156, 157
3:4–6	109
3:5	60, 83, 106, 152, 156, 157, 158, 161, 177
3:5–6	63, 155, 156
3:5–7	136
3:6	158
3:7	60, 62, 63, 65, 69, 72, 116, 135
3:7, 8–9, 19	127
3:7, 18	114
3:8	55, 126, 135
3:8–10	57, 86, 138
3:8–11	64, 109, 128
3:8–18	134, 137, 145
3:10	64, 139, 141
3:11	57, 72, 141, 142, 143
3:11–18	130, 140
3:12–13	61, 176
3:12–18	137
3:13	143
3:13, 16–18	65
3:13, 15	104
3:13, 17	63
3:14	143, 155, 156
3:15	143, 176
3:15–17	143
3:17	144, 154, 164
3:18	61, 62, 146, 156, 162
3:18, 19	76
3:19	60, 63, 65, 69, 72, 134, 137, 145

Habakkuk

1:1	72n81
2:8, 17	152n34
2:12	152n31
2:16	141–142
3:3–4	124
3:14	62n59

Zephaniah

2	62

Zechariah

9:7	158
13:7	62n59

Malachi

3:20	144

PSALMS

2	55
18:32	127
18:9–14	124
22:15	165
25:18	67
37:15	104
44:1–23	54
44:18–23	56
46:7	85
46:9	104
47	53
58:9	144
60:1–2	66
60:8–10	66
65:11	85
68:4	124
68:7–8	124
74:13–14	124
75:4	85
76:3	104
77:16–19	124
77:18	161
77:20	124
83	55
86:1	68
88:1, 7	66
88:7–9	54
89:9–10	124
90:15	66
93	53
99	53
102:24	66
103:20	160
104	124
104:7	124
107:26	85
137	56
137:7–9	56
137:8–9	55, 82
137:9	140
149:6–9	55

Proverbs

25:20	144

Job

2:3	61
2:10	144
2:12–13	112
2:13	78
4:4	165
7:12–14	54
30:11	66
30:22	85
38:1	124

The Song of Songs

3:2	161

Lamentations

1:2, 16	65
1:4; 2:6–7	65
1:9, 11, 12, 18, 20	67
1:9, 11, 12; 2:20–22; 4:6; 5:1, 20, 22	61
1:12	52
2:20	67
2:5, 2:7–8, 2:21	63
3:33	66
3:59, 60	67
3:64–66	56
4:21	142
5:11	66

Daniel

5:6	165

2 Chronicles

11:5–12	94
29–32	109, 143
30:12	103
32:2	94
32:9	94
32:21	54

Sirach

49:10	79

NEW TESTAMENT

Matthew

5:20–7:28	8,9
5:23–26	8,9
21:12–17	172
25:45–46	172

Luke

3:19,17	172
9:52–55	172

Revelation

2:22–23	172

Name/Subject Index

Abduction, 40, 41, 42
Abomination, xviii
Achtemeier, Elizabeth, 107, 107n6, 107n7
Afflict, 66, 115
Affliction, 54, 55, 62, 65, 67, 72, 76, 78–79, 105, 108–9, 114–16, 133, 136, 171
Alexander, Jeffrey C., 20, 20n64, 20n65, 20n66
Amnesty International, 35, 35n19
Apartheid, 4–6, 174–75
Appropriate (to)/appropriation, x–xi, xxi, 4, 7–8, 10, 22–23, 28, 54, 109, 166–67, 169, 173
Archaeology (Archaeological), xi, 58n38, 82, 84, 97, 101, 104
Army/Armies, 11, 31, 44, 59, 62, 62n59, 63–64, 69, 74, 83, 88, 98–99, 102, 127, 137, 143, 150, 151, 153, 159–60, 160n48, 161, 161n54, 162–64
Art, x–xi, 76–77, 82, 87–90, 109, 157
Ashurbanipal, x, 82, 89–91, 91n33, 91n34, 91n35, 91n36, 91n37, 92n39, 92n42
Assis, Elie, 119, 119n20, 120, 121n22
Atikson, Paul, 15n52
Attack/attacking, xx, 43, 63, 84, 85, 92, 94n48, 96, 99, 100, 103, 105, 108, 109, 134, 144, 151, 152, 155, 156, 159, 160, 162, 163, 164

Attinger, Pascal, 63n61
Autobiography, 14, 14n48, 15, 19
Avenger (YHWH as), ix, 117, 171

Ba'al (god), 110, 123, 123n25, 124, 125,
Babylon, 56, 57, 74–75, 101n96, 117, 146, 153n35, 171
Banyamulenge, 29, 29n10
Barnett, R.D., 91n33, 91n34, 91n35, 91n36, 91n37, 91n38, 92n39, 92n42
Bas-relief, x, xx, 29, 82–83, 87, 91, 94, 97, 101, 104
Battering ram, 84, 99–100
Beast (s), x, 63, 90–91, 93
Beating, 40, 42, 65, 68, 164
Becking, Bob, 130n38
Ben Zvi, Ehud, 79n101
Benedict XVI, 1, 1n2, 1n3, 2n4, 12n45
Berlin, Adele, 58n38, 69, 69n73, 148n22
Berry, Wendell, 77, 77n96
Betz, Hans Dieter, 8–9, 9n32
Block, Daniel, 148n23
Bloodshed, 145, 151–52, 158
Blow-for-blow, ix
British Museum, x, 91, 91n38, 98,
Brown, William P., 88n20
Brueggemann, Walter, 56, 56n31, 56n33, 57, 57n34, 57n36
Byron, John and Lohr, Joel, 14, 14n49

NAME/SUBJECT INDEX   197

Card, Claudia, 35n19, 38n24
Carr, David, 19n61
Caruth, Cathy, 20, 20n67, 46, 46n31, 47n32, 102n98
Cassin, Elena, 89n24, 89n25, 90n28, 90n31, 90n32, 93n43, 148n19
Chaos, ix, xx, 38, 47, 74, 90, 93, 105, 175
Chapman, Cynthia, 157, 157n44
Chariot(s), 63, 74, 92, 94n48, 100, 101, 124, 147, 149-53, 159, 160, 160n48, 161
Chiasm (chiasmus), 110, 119, 119n20, 120-21, 121n22
Childs, Brevard S., 94n46, 123n26, 123n27, 124, 124n28
Christensen, Duane, 155n39, 156n40, 158n45
City lament(s), xviii, xix, 49, 52-53, 58, 58n37, 58n38, 59-65, 82, 109, 158, 163
Cleland, James, xviin1
Cloud, 72, 109, 121-22, 123n35, 124-25
Cogan, Mordechai, 84n8, 93n44, 94n47, 101n97, 140n10
Collective Memory, x, xviii-xx, 26-29, 81-82, 176
Collective trauma, 20, 82, 176
Collins, Peter and Gallinat, Anselma, 18n60
Comfort(ing), ix, xviii, xx, 79-80, 105, 108-10, 115-17, 132, 145, 169-70, 172
Comforter(s), x, 69, 106, 127
Commission Congolaise Vérité et Réconciliation, 168n3
Conflict(s), ix, xix, 25, 35-36, 47, 167, 174, 179
Confront, xviii, 4, 11, 20, 175
Contextual biblical interpretation, xix, 2, 7, 13
Cooper, Jerrold S., 58, 63n60
Covenant loyalty (ḥesed), 78, 111n11, 112-14
Crime, 35, 134, 146
Cross, Frank Moore, 123n25

Culler, Jonathan, 70, 70n76, 71n77
Curse of Agade, 58, 58n39, 60, 63n60

Davis, Ellen F., 76, 76n89-90, 171, 171n4, 179, 179n22, 12n43-45, 23n79, 55, 55n30, 56n32
de Hulster Izaak J., and Joel M. LeMon, 87n18
Deception, 134, 137, 151, 154
Defeat/defeated, 93, 101, 123n25, 126, 136, 138-40, 143, 148
Dei Verbum, 12n42, 12n45,
Desolation, xvii, 32, 36, 44, 69, 71, 160, 170
Deuteronomistic History, 103
Devastation, ix, xvii, 69, 86, 116, 137, 160
Diplomacy, 147, 150, 150n27
Distantiation, 6-10, 21-22, 24
Dobbs-Allsopp, F. W, 51n7, 58, 58n37, 58n38, 58n39, 59n40-48, 60, 60n49-50, 62n52-54, 62n57-58, 63, 63n62, 65n64-65, 67, 67n68, 73, 73n82-83, 158n46, 160n48, 163n65
Domination, 6, 35, 37, 55, 72, 82, 87, 92n40, 93, 116, 136, 145-49, 154,
Draper, Jonathan A., xix, 1n1, 3-11, 4n11-13, 6n20-22, 7n23, 7n26-30, 8n31, 9n33-35, 10n39-40, 11n41, 13, 13n47, 21-22, 22n71-72, 22n75, 23, 23n78, 25, 48, 48n33
Dubovský, Peter, 149-50, 149n25, 150n26

Empire, ix-x, xx, 82-93, 126, 133, 141-54, 166
Enemies and protégés, 128
Enemy (YHWH's), 109-34
Primeval (era/time, battle), 123-24, 123n23
Esarhaddon, 90n31, 139, 143, 143n14
Ethnographic, xviii, xix, 14-18, 18n60

Ethnography, xi, 15–19, 15n51–53,
Evans, Paul S., 94n46
Evil thoughts, 135–37, 154
Evocation, xx, 52, 82, 105, 166, 170, 175
Evoke, xi, xviii, xix, 11, 23, 49–50, 63–67, 70, 76, 83, 86, 105, 125, 133–34, 147, 161, 170, 175–78
Excavation/Excavate, x, 82, 84, 96, 101, 104
Execution (summary), 40, 41, 47, 56, 77
Explanation, 6, 8, 22–24, 69, 82, 91, 115
Extravagance of Lyric, 70, 71

FDLR, 30, 36, 38, 40, 44, 45, 45n30
Flood, 62, 70, 83–85, 129, 163, 163n62
Floyd, Michael H., 53, 53n20, 53n23, 54, 54n25, 136, 136n4–5
Fretheim, Terence E., 118, 118n117

Gall, Sally M., 69, 70n74–75
Gallinat, Anselma, 18n59–60
Genocide, 29–31, 168
Genre, xix, 48–54, 58n38, 81, 105
Gerstenberger, Erhard, 152n31
Ginkel, Rob van, 15n54, 16n55–56, 17n57–58
Gold, 74, 140, 159, 165
Goldingay, John, 14, 14n50
Graffy, Adrian, 53, 53n24
Graphic, xvii, 83
Great Empire, ix
Great King, x, 73, 90, 93, 102
Green, M. W, 62
Grenholm, Cristina, 7, 7n24, 25

Halbwachs, Maurice, 27, 27n2–4
Haldar, Alfred, 53n18
Haupt, Paul, 53n17
Hauser, Alan J., 68, 68n70
Hayes, John H., 66, 66n66–67, 103n99
Hays, Christopher B., 143

Hays, Richard, 12n44–45, 23n7–9
Healing, x–xii, xvii, 2, 11, 13, 18, 24, 33, 44, 48, 107, 167, 169, 174, 179
Heaps of corpses, xvii, xviii, 42, 151
Heffelfinger, Katie M., 50n4–5, 68n71, 70n75, 152n32
Hembree, E., 175n15
Herman, Judith L., 19, 19n62–63, 26n1, 42, 42n27–28, 176, 176n16
Hermeneutics, xix, 1–13, 3n8–9, 4n11, 6n19, 10n39–40, 11n41, 13n47, 22n72, 22n75, 24n82, 25
Heschel, Abraham J., 173, 173n8–9
Hetata, Sherif, 14, 14n48
Hezekiah, 93–95, 102, 103, 103n99, 143, 150
Historical report/reference, xviii, 52, 85, 136, 163
Hooker, David Anderson, 21, 21n69
Horse(s), 74, 89, 92, 151, 153
Huddlestun, John R., 139n9
Huehnergard, John, 130n38
Humbert, Paul, 53n16
Huzzab, 163–164

Icon, x, 82, 83, 87, 88, 108, 124, 125
Iconic, 124, 124n30, 125
Iconography, x, xviii, 89
Iconographic, 82, 83, 88, 88n21
Ideology/ideological, 3, 88, 89, 103, 107, 178
Ideo-theological orientation, 3, 4, 9, 10
Imagination, x, 12, 13, 23, 24, 77, 137
Imaginative (imaginatively), x, 50, 91, 133, 147
Impact, xvii, xix, 5, 14, 19, 20, 31, 35, 45–47, 55, 94, 101, 103, 130, 136, 150
Indictment, 134, 137, 140, 154
Interview, 15, 16, 18, 21, 26, 31, 32, 47
Intractable Situation, 69–70

NAME/SUBJECT INDEX   199

Invasion, xviii, 57, 62n59, 82, 86, 87, 93, 94n46–47, 95, 103, 105, 115, 117, 163

Jealous (Jealousy), 110–11, 111n11, 121
Johnson, Laurie, 28, 28n7–8, 176n18
Johnson, W. R., 49n1, 50, 50n6, 70n76, 73n82, 74n86, 76, 77n93
Jones, Barry A., 79n101
Jurisprudence (African), 174
Justice, 1, 6, 10, 31n14, 32, 40, 41n26, 44n29, 56, 57, 61, 82, 107, 108, 113, 114, 118n17, 121, 134, 166–74, 173n11
Justice (Restorative), 174

Kahn, Dan'el, 138n7
Kairos Document (The), 4, 5, 5n14–18
Kaniola, 16, 33, 35–46, 171
Katongole, Emmanuel, 168, 168n1
Keel, Othmar, 82n3
Kelly, Joseph Ryan, 78n97
Kidnap, 177
King Ahab, 93
Kramer, Samuel N., 60n51, 62n55
Kurkh Monolith, 93

Lachish, x. xviii, xx, xxi, 82–104, 127, 134, 140, 140n10–11, 142–43, 148, 148n21, 151, 177
Lanner, Laurel, 86n13, 118n17
Layard, Austen H., 94, 97, 98, 98n78, 101n96
Levenson, Jon D., 125, 126n31, 129, 129n36–37
Liberation (hermeneutics), 3–10, 27
Lichtenstein, Murray H., 68n71, 77, 77n94–95, 122n24, 135, 135n2
Lion hunt, x, xviii, 82, 89, 90, 91, 93
Lion's den, 73, 127n34, 147
Literary form, 55, 73
Locust(s), 141, 143, 144, 154n38

Longinus, 71, 71n79, 72n80, 75n88, 76n91
Lowth, Robert, 71, 71n78, 74n87
Luckenbill, Daniel D., 89n23, 153n35
Lyric, ix, xviii, xix, 23, 49–52, 49n1, 50n6, 67–73, 70n76, 73n82, 74n86, 75, 77n93, 80, 109, 122, 152, 162, 176, 176n17, 178

Machinist, Peter, 52n15, 83–86, 84n9, 85n10, 103, 103n100–102, 150, 150n28
Magessa, Laurenti, 3n9
Maier, Walter A., 69n72, 86, 86n12, 86n14–15, 130n40, 135n3, 136n6, 148n20, 154, 154n37, 155n39, 158n45, 160, 161n51, 162, 162n57, 165n70
Mai-mai, 36, 36n22, 44, 45
Majestic, 64, 71, 72, 105, 121
Mandela (Nelson), 175
Marion, Jean-Luc, 124, 124n29
Massacre, 40, 41, 92
Meaning (of biblical texts), 5, 7, 10, 11, 23–27, 51, 67
Mesopotamian, 58, 58n37, 58n38, 61, 62, 84, 90n30
Metanoia, 24
Metaphor, 85, 88, 142, 146, 157, 163
Methodology, x 2, 3, 7, 13, 14
Mihelic, Joseph L., 50n3
Miller, J. Maxwell, 103n99
Mise en scène, 92, 147
Mobutu, 29–31
Mock (mocking), 113, 136, 142, 148
Moment of the text, 22
Moschella, Mary Clark, 15n51, 15n53
Moshavi, Adina, 76n92, 127, 127n33
Mukangendo, Marie Consolée, 39, 40, 40n25
Myth, 122–25, 123n25, 124n28

Naked (nakedness), 38, 45, 67, 100, 156–58, 164, 177

Namujimbo, Déo, 29n9
Nemedu Throne, 101
Neo-Assyrian, xvii, 29, 81, 83, 88, 89, 96, 100
NGO, 33–35, 39, 47, 169
Nogalski, James D., 79n98, 79n100
North Palace (of Ashurbanipal), 82, 89–92, 91n33–37
Nzuzi, Justin, 41n26, 44, 44n29

O'Brien, Julia M., 51, 51n8–11, 52, 52n12–14, 55, 62n59, 73, 73n84, 81n2, 85n11, 87n17, 106, 106n2–3, 107, 107n4–5, 108, 108n9, 112n12, 128, 128n35, 130n38, 131, 131n43, 136n4–5, 138, 138n8, 144, 144n16, 146, 146n17, 149n24, 151, 152n33, 157n43, 160, 160n49, 161, 162, 162n60, 178n20
O'Connor, Kathleen, 157n43
O'Connor, Michael, 119n19, 129n37, 130n38–39, 156n41
OAN, xviii, xix, 49, 55–58, 62, 66, 82, 86, 143
Oppression, 4, 6, 17, 55, 66, 171, 174
Overwhelm, ix, 19, 21, 64, 134, 165, 178

Palace without Rival, 82n4, 94–98
Parallelism (parallel), 106, 119, 132, 141, 143, 150, 157, 158, 160, 165
Paratactic (parataxis), 50, 67, 68, 68n70, 69, 109, 152, 162
Patte, Daniel, 7, 7n24–25
Peace, 9, 32, 40, 78, 115, 125, 144, 149, 150, 168, 170
Perpetrator, xixn5, 17, 19, 30, 42, 44, 45, 116, 132, 168, 170, 171, 173, 174, 178
Petersen, David L., 79, 79n102–103
Phonological proximity, 127
Piles of slain, xvii, xviii, 64, 151
Plotting evil, 134–35

Plunder/plundering, 36, 43, 63, 74, 118, 134, 147, 151, 152, 159, 165, 177
Poetic analysis, xviii
Poetics, xix, 49, 67, 69n73, 125, 148n22
Poetry, ix, x, xi, xvii, xix, xx, 23, 49, 50, 51, 51n7, 52, 67, 68, 68n70–71, 70n76, 71, 71n78, 73n82–83, 75, 76n91, 77, 77n94–95, 78, 80, 86, 105, 122, 122n24, 135n2, 162, 176, 179
Portier-Young, Anathea, xviii, xviiin4, 172, 172n7, 173, 174n12, 179n21
Powerful, xi, 6, 12, 31n14, 36, 51, 54, 91, 108, 125, 128, 130, 148, 149, 162, 166, 169
Predator, 90, 146, 148–50
Presumption of Exceptionalism, 137, 145
Proclamation, x, 57, 67, 90
Prolonged Exposure Therapy (PET), 175
Propaganda, x, 53, 82, 87–90, 142, 149, 154, 171
Prophetic, ix, x, xviii, 4, 53, 54n25, 55, 58, 72, 72n81, 74, 76, 79, 79n101, 83, 112, 113, 148, 153, 171
Prunier, Gerard, 29n9
Psychological consequence, 82
Psychological warfare, 147–50, 150n27

Qarqar (Battle of), 93

Rage, ix, 55, 92, 169, 179
Rape, 25, 33–47, 52, 57, 164, 177
Reconciliation, xii, xviii, xix, xxi, 1–5, 8, 11, 12, 12n46, 13, 18, 24, 25, 33, 44, 167–69, 174, 174n14, 178, 179
Recovery, 19, 19n62–63, 26n1, 42n27–28, 176, 176n16
Reddit, Paul L., 79n99

NAME/SUBJECT INDEX   201

Resistance (literature of), 38, 55, 92n40
Retribution, 115, 174
Rhetorical, 57, 76, 86, 87, 126, 127, 133, 134, 138, 139, 147, 148
Ricoeur, Paul, 6, 22, 22n73–74, 23, 23n76–77, 24n80–82, 27, 28, 28n5–6, 28n8
Roberts, J. J. M., 69n72, 130n41, 156n40, 160n49
Robertson, O. Palmer, 136n6
Room C (Ashurbanipal's palace), 91, 91n38
Room XXXVI (Sennacherib's palace), 97–98
Rosenbaum, Jonathan, 103n99
Rosenthal, M. L., 69, 70n74–75
Rothbaum, B., 175n15
Russel, John M., 82n4

Sasson, Jack M., 58n39
Scott, James C., 92, 92n40
Scripture, xvii, xviii, xix, 2, 23, 24, 175, 179
Sculpture, 91, 91n33–37, 92n39, 92n42
Seculus, Diodorus, 83
Sennacherib, x, 54, 82, 83, 89, 89n23, 90n31, 93–103, 136, 148
Shalmaneser (III and V), 93
Shatter (shattering), 63, 72, 104, 122, 127, 178
Shay, Jonathan, 178, 178n19
Sheol, 74–75
Short-sight (shortsightedness), 135, 137, 145
Siege ramp, 96, 99, 99n85, 100, 104, 127
Siege (warfare), x, xx, 84, 94, 97–99, 141, 143
Silver, 74, 140, 159, 165
Slab, 92, 99–101, 140n10, 148
Smith, George Adam, 106n1, 114n14, 136n5
Smith, J. M. P., xviin2, 106, 106n1, 114, 114n14, 121, 121n23,
129n36, 161, 162, 162n55–56, 163n65
Smith-Spark, Laura, 35n20
Sorcery, 145, 151, 153, 154, 156
Spronk, Klaas, 49n2, 68n69, 69n72, 74n85, 130n38, 141, 142, 142n12, 148n20, 151n29, 153n36, 154n37, 155n39, 156n40, 156n42, 160, 162, 162n59, 163n63, 164, 164n66–68, 165n69
Stearns, Jason K., 29n9, 32n12
Strawn, Brent, 89n26, 90n27, 90n29
Sublime, 70, 71, 71n79, 72n80, 74, 75n88, 76n91, 80
Survive, 38, 144, 156
Survivor(s), x, xi, xiv, xviii, xixn5, 2, 11, 18, 20, 26, 29, 31–47, 82, 83, 103, 104, 133, 145, 165, 169, 170, 173, 175, 176, 178, 179
Sweeney, Marvin A., 52n15, 53, 53n19, 53n22, 79n98, 81n1, 83n5, 86n16, 114n13, 115n15, 136n5, 138n7, 144, 144n15, 147n18, 151n29–30, 160n50, 161, 161n52, 162, 162n58

Tarshish, 114, 119–20
Terror, 19, 37, 38, 147–49, 170
Terrorizing/terrorize, 36, 140, 147, 150, 170
Theophany (storm), 109, 121–27, 161
Treasure, 74, 164
Tripolar biblical hermeneutics, xix, 1–13
Truth and Reconciliation Commission (TRC), 168
Tufnell, Olga, 96, 96n61, 96n64–65, 97, 97n69–70
Turner, Thomas, 29n9–10, 30n13
Tutu, Desmond Mpilo, 174, 174n13
Twelve (Book of), 79, 106, 112, 114n14

Uehlinger, Christoph, 87n19, 88, 97n73, 99n81, 101
Unclaimed experience, 20, 20n67, 46n31, 47n32, 102n98
Unspeakable, x, xii, 26
Ussishkin, David, 94–101, 127, 140, 143, 148

van Oyen, Geert, 21, 21n70
Vassal, 143
Vengeful, ix, xvii, 109, 110, 130, 133, 169, 172–74, 179
Vivid (vividness), xvii, xviii, xx, 50, 52, 58n39, 60, 71, 74, 75, 82, 83, 87, 88, 109, 133, 164

Walsh, Carey, 124, 124n30
Waltke, Bruce K., 119n19, 129n37, 130n38–39, 156n41
Warning about imminent danger (war), 151, 155
Watanambe, Chikako E., 90n30
Watters, Ethan, 21n68

Weeping, 59, 65, 112
Weigl, Michael, 86n12
Weissert, E., 92n41, 93n43
Wessels, Wilhelm J., 53n21, 55, 55n26–28
West, Gerald O., xix, 2n5, 3–5, 9–13, 25
Whirlwind, 31, 32, 72, 76, 109, 121, 122–25, 171, 178
Wilson-Hartgrove, Jonathan, 168
Wound (-ed), 1, 11, 13, 20, 24, 25, 28, 33, 42, 46, 47, 72, 145, 166, 169, 179
Wrath (of YHWH), 110, 122, 172–173
Wrathful, xvii, 172

Yamm, 123, 125
Yoke, 49, 62, 66, 86, 115–17, 126, 145, 146

Zenger, Eric, 172, 172n5–6, 173, 173n10